GODIVA'S RIDE

Women of Letters
Sandra M. Gilbert and Susan Gubar
General Editors

GODIVA'S RIDE

WOMEN OF LETTERS
IN ENGLAND,
1830-1880
❧ ❧ ❧

Dorothy Mermin

INDIANA UNIVERSITY PRESS
Bloomington and Indianapolis

The paper used in this publication meets the minimum requirements of American
National Standard for Information Sciences—Permanence of Paper for Printed
Library Materials, ANSI Z39.48-1984.

Manufactured in the United States of America

Library of Congress Cataloging-in-Publication Data

Mermin, Dorothy, date.
    Godiva's ride : women of letters in England, 1830-1880 / Dorothy
Mermin.
        p.   cm. — (Women of letters)
    Includes bibliographical references and index.
    ISBN 0-253-33749-6. — ISBN 0-253-20824-6 (paper)
    1. English literature—Women authors—History and criticism.
2. English literature—19th century—History and criticism.
3. Women and literature—England—History—19th century.   4. Women
authors, English—19th century—Biography.   5. Authorship—Sex
differences.   I. Title.   II. Series: Women of letters (Bloomington,
Ind.)
PR115.M47   1993
820.9'9287'09034—dc20   92-45186

1   2   3   4   5   97   96   95   94   93

For my mother, Charlotte Milman,
and in memory of Howard Milman, my father

Orlando now performed in spirit . . . a deep obeisance to the spirit of her age [the nineteenth century]. . . . She had just managed, by some dexterous deference to the spirit of the age, by putting on a ring and finding a man on a moor, by loving nature and being no satirist, cynic, or psychologist . . . to pass its examination successfully. And she heaved a deep sigh of relief, as, indeed, well she might, for the transaction between a writer and the spirit of the age is one of infinite delicacy, and upon a nice arrangement between the two the whole fortune of his works depends. Orlando had so ordered it that she was in an extremely happy position; she need neither fight her age, nor submit to it; she was of it, yet remained herself. Now, therefore, she could write, and write she did. She wrote. She wrote. She wrote.

Virginia Woolf, *Orlando: A Biography*

Contents

Foreword by Sandra M. Gilbert
and Susan Gubar
ix
Acknowledgments
xi
Introduction
xiii

Part One

1. Beginning to Write
3
2. Travel, Trials, Fame
20

Part Two

3. Entering the Literary Market
43
4. Poetry
60
5. The Range of Prose Fiction
81

Part Three

6. The Female Sage
95
7. Religion
107
8. Science
127

Conclusion
141

Contents

Notes
147
Bibliography
163
Index
175

Foreword

"On the Field of Letters"

> Then Lady Reason . . . said, "Get up, daughter! Without waiting any longer, let us go to the Field of Letters. There the City of Ladies will be founded on a flat and fertile plain, where all fruits and freshwater rivers are found and where the earth abounds in all good things. Take the pick of your understanding and dig and clear out a great ditch wherever you see the marks of my ruler, and I will help you carry away the earth on my own shoulders."
>
> I immediately stood up to obey her commands and . . . I felt stronger and lighter than before. She went ahead, and I followed behind, and after we had arrived at this field I began to excavate and dig, following her marks with the pick of cross-examination.

So wrote Christine de Pizan at the beginning of the fifteenth century in *The Book of the City of Ladies*, the first feminist utopia. She was imagining a "strongly constructed and well founded" community which would be inhabited by "ladies of fame and women worthy of praise," and one of her speakers prophesied, "as a true sybil, that this City . . . will never be destroyed, nor will it ever fall, but will remain prosperous forever, regardless of all its jealous enemies. Although it will be stormed by numerous assaults, it will never be taken or conquered."

Founded on the "Field of Letters," the female literary tradition *is*, at least metaphorically speaking, the City of which Christine dreamed. Yet despite the optimism of this Renaissance woman's vision, most of its walls and towers disappeared from view for centuries. Even when its individual inhabitants gained recognition as "ladies of fame and women worthy of praise," the avenues they strolled and the cafes where they conversed were largely forgotten. Louise Labé, Aphra Behn, Jane Austen, Charlotte Brontë, George Eliot, Emily Dickinson, Gertrude Stein, Virginia Woolf—all these figures were duly recorded in literary histories, but their membership in a "strongly constructed and well founded" community—a *female* literary community—went, until recently, unremarked. Only in the last two decades, in fact, have feminist critics established thematic and stylistic links between women from very different places and periods. Moreover, only in recent years have scholars begun "to excavate and dig" in a general effort to recover the lives and works of forgotten or neglected "women worthy of praise." Mary Wroth, Mary Astell, Charlotte Smith, Kate Chopin, Charlotte Perkins Gilman, Mary Elizabeth Coleridge, H.D., Zora Neale Hurston—all these figures had been relegated to the margins of literary history despite the fact that they too deserved places on the "fertile plain" where Christine's utopia was founded.

Our "Women of Letters" series is designed to introduce general as well as academic readers to the historical situations and aesthetic achievements of many of the citizens of Christine's City. The national, chronological, racial, ethnic, economic, and social circumstances of these women vary widely: the contours of the female literary community are complex, its highways and by-ways labyrinthine and often unfamiliar. Thus each volume in this series will pay close attention to what is in effect a single neighborhood. At the same time, precisely because the subject matter is complex, no volume in the series is intended as an encyclopedic guide to women writers in a particular place or period. Rather, each book will have a distinctive argument of its own, framed independently by its author; we should stress that we have not provided blueprints or even construction codes to the surveyors of our City, all of whom have used their own methodologies and developed their own critical perspectives. We do, however, expect that every volume will explore the individual situations of literary women in their specific cultural contexts.

Finally, we should emphasize that we see this series as part of an ongoing project in which a range of feminist critics, scholars, essayists, novelists, and poets have increasingly participated in recent years, one that seeks to understand the strictures and structures that may have affected (or will affect) the lives and works of, in Christine's words, "ladies from the past as well as from the present and future." Such a project can by its nature come to no definitive conclusion, offer no single last word, because the City of Ladies, along with our vision of the Field of Letters, is growing and changing all the time. Furthermore, the heightened awareness on the part of current feminist theorists that such a City has always existed, and that it is ever evolving, has itself transformed our general sense of history, putting in question received modes of periodization, traditional genre hierarchies, and what once seemed to be universal evaluative criteria. Yet, diverse as may be the solutions posed by different thinkers to theoretical problems presented by contemporary literary study, we hope that in their various ways the volumes in this series will confirm Christine's faith that the City she helped found might be a "refuge" as well as a "defense and guard" against enemies and that it would be "so resplendant that you may see yourselves mirrored in it."

Composed c. 1405, Christine's utopia went unpublished and virtually untranslated for more than five centuries, a fact that gives special urgency to the admonitions with which she concluded her text. Indeed, her advice should still be taken to heart by those who study the field of women's letters: ". . . my dear ladies," Christine counseled, "do not misuse this new inheritance" but instead "increase and multiply our City." And as she herself knew, such a resettlement of the old grounds can best be accomplished by following "the marks" of Reason with "the pick of cross-examination."

Sandra M. Gilbert and Susan Gubar

Acknowledgments

Brief passages of this book were first published in "Heroic Sisterhood in *Goblin Market*," *Victorian Poetry* 21 (1983) : 107-18; "The Damsel, the Knight, and the Victorian Woman Poet," *Critical Inquiry* 13 (1986) : 64-80; and the Introduction to Dolores Rosenblum, *Christina Rossetti: The Poetry of Endurance* (Carbondale: Southern Illinois University Press, 1986). I am grateful to The Pierpont Morgan Library, New York, for permission to publish passages from Charlotte Brontë's manuscripts.

Page or line references to novels and poems are given parenthetically, without footnotes. Editions used are listed in the bibliography of primary texts.

Introduction

In 1826 *A Lady's Diary* (later called *Diary of an Ennuyée*) was published anonymously in London and aroused considerable sympathy for its author, who was ostensibly dead. It records a young woman's tour of France and Italy and her reflections on scenery and cities, society and history, literature and art, her melancholy and her failing health, and other topics that catch her attention along the way. Interspersed poems suggest that her misery springs from an unhappy love affair. In an introductory paragraph an unidentified male editor explains that the diarist has recently died; that the diary is "a real picture of natural and feminine feeling"; that some pages of the manuscript have been torn out; and that he found the poems in another manuscript left by the diarist and inserted them in the diary himself.[1] The book is presented, that is, as a collection of impromptu effusions that were not intended for publication, making no pretense to completeness, logical coherence, or generic consistency: the kind of writing that was expected of women during most of the nineteenth century and often, indeed, afterward. The responsibility for organizing these inchoate materials into a published book is ascribed to a man.

In fact the author of the whole elaborate production was a young woman named Anna Jameson who had traveled the *Ennuyée*'s route not to nurse a broken heart but in the capacity of a governess, and the book inaugurated her long and exceptionally energetic career as one of the foremost women of letters in early Victorian England. But it inaugurated it by disclaiming any such intention.

> Now if my poor little Diary should ever be seen! I tremble but to think of it! — what egotism and vanity, what discontent, — repining, — caprice — should I be accused of! . . . Such strange vicissitudes of temper — such opposite extremes of thinking and feeling, written down at the moment, without noticing the intervening links of circumstances and impressions which led to them, would appear like distraction, if they should meet the eye of any indifferent person — but I think I have taken sufficient precautions against the possibility of such an exposure, and the only eyes which will ever glance over this blotted page, when the hand that writes it is cold, will read, not to *criticize*, but to *sympathise*. (137-38)

The diarist's denigration of herself and her work (her "poor little" book), her helpless submission to the ebb and flow of contradictory emotions, her denial of any intention to organize or publish what she writes, her timid appeal to pity rather than judgment, and above all her terror of displaying vanity and of "exposure" to hostile eyes, typify the flutters of incompetence and self-doubt with which during most of the nineteenth century women were expected to begin a literary career.

In the first entry the diarist disavows ambition, and in the second she notes ambition's consequences.

> I do not pity Joan of Arc: that heroic woman only paid the price which all must pay for celebrity in some shape or other; the sword or the faggot, the scaffold or the field, public hatred or private heart-break; what matter? . . . could Charles . . . with all the knights, and nobles of France, look on while their champion, and a woman, was devoted to chains and death without one effort to save her? (15)

Perhaps the single most important gender difference among writers in the period from 1830 to 1880 was that almost all women, but almost no men, assumed that celebrity exacts such a price. Women characteristically thought of ambition — including literary ambition — in terms of a figure who, like Joan of Arc as Jameson describes her, is both a heroic actor and a victim waiting for a rescue that does not come. And they were likely to imagine the realization of ambition as self-exposure, with a crowd of men ("all the knights, and nobles of France") looking on. Dreams of glory turned into dreams of martyrdom.

Such attitudes colored the imaginations of even the strongest, most confident women. But they did not necessarily inhibit writing. On the contrary, they provided psychological materials to work with, frameworks on which to construct plots, and a way to turn fears about writing to the service of writing itself. In *Diary of an Ennuyée* women's assumed unfitness for a literary career is imitated in the fictional form, thematized in the text, and wittily belied by the artistry that mimics innocence: the fabrication for the purpose of publication of what is supposed to be the most artless and private, and therefore most feminine, of literary forms. The fiction with which the book presents itself enacts the paradoxical situation of literary women at the intersection of the two spheres, public and private, into which Victorian ideology divided the world and which Victorian culture tried with extraordinary intensity to keep apart. Women belonged only in the private sphere, where they were expected to be modestly unself-conscious and shun the gaze of men, while printed books were public and courted admiration. Any venture into public life by a woman risked being greeted as a highly sexualized self-exposure: the morals of women who went on the stage were notoriously suspect, and "public woman" (in French, "*fille publique*") is an old term, still in use in the nineteenth century, for a prostitute.[2] These highly charged associations may have deterred some women from writing, but they gave an energizing undercurrent of excitement to the work of many others.

The social and psychological pressures that *Diary of an Ennuyée* so elegantly manipulates had existed in England at least since the Renaissance, and had combined with other circumstances to exclude women from most areas of literature, especially those with high visibility and prestige. Women wrote and published, but only rarely and briefly were any of them considered on a level with men. Until just a few years ago (and perhaps even today), a typical survey course or short history of British literature before 1800 was unlikely to include more than a very brief mention of any female author. Nineteenth-century works by women, however, not only commanded large audiences but also entered the canon of high culture, in their century and our own; and almost all the works that did so were written between 1830 and 1880. Women's impact during these years was greatest in prose fiction, moderate in poetry, and not negligible although least impressive in nonfictional prose.

This efflorescence of women's writing had, of course, many causes. Extension of education combined with increased efficiency in the production and distribution of reading matter enormously enlarged the market for novels, stories, poems, and educational and edifying materials, providing opportunities for publication at many levels. Prose fiction, which dominated the literary market and in which women achieved their most stunning success, was a relatively recent and unprestigious form that had established no exclusively male tradition and for which the audience was assumed to be mostly female. The field was left unusually clear for newcomers, moreover, by the death of the most widely read and admired novelist, Sir Walter Scott, in 1832, as well as by the early deaths of the younger generation of Romantic poets: Keats in 1821, Shelley in 1822, Byron in 1824. In the 1830s and '40s their places were still open and there was room for a crowd of new talents to aspire and be noticed. And the traditional restriction of men's formal education to Latin, Greek, and mathematics meant that many intellectual disciplines, such as Anna Jameson's eventual specialty, art history, had not yet erected educational or institutional barriers that would keep women out.

The relegation of middle-class women to the home made these opportunities all the more attractive to those who were restless or ambitious or needed to earn money. For middle-class women during much of this period, writing was the only respectable outlet for ambition. It was also the only respectable way for them to earn a living aside from being a governess or paid companion (precarious occupations which paid very badly and carried painfully marginal status), or, if they had some money to start with, keeping a school. Anna Jameson escaped from being a governess by getting married, and escaped from marriage to an independence achieved by her pen. Writing could be done in one's home at negligible expense. It could be attempted in secret, safe from discouragement or ridicule, and acknowledged only when success was assured.

There were reasons beyond the widening market, too, why women might hope to succeed. Their expectations were usually modest: for a woman to publish at all was sufficiently rare to be counted success. And since they were almost always reviewed and evaluated in relation to other women, competition was minimal, especially before Elizabeth Barrett Browning, Charlotte Brontë, and George Eliot had made their reputations and raised the standard of comparison. Nor did they suffer from the sense of belatedness, of living in unpoetic, unheroic times and being unable to rise to the level of their great predecessors, that oppressed men of high aspiration; the female tradition was recent and relatively undistinguished, and the genre in which most women made their mark, prose fiction, had no glorious past to intimidate aspirants.

The authors who most often inspired eager girls were Scott and Byron. Scott's richness of characterization and story filled their imaginations, while Byron's verse narratives enthralled them and his defiance of respectability stimulated their rebelliousness against constraints of gender. Many women who eventually made careers writing prose tried poetry first, and Byron suggested imaginative and stylistic possibilities more open and flexible, less embedded in an exclusively male literary tradition, than had been available before. *Diary of an Ennuyée* tells its story partly through interspersed lyrics and openly imitates Byron in its conscientious travelogue, self-dramatizing swings of feeling, and satirical disdain for polite society.

For women who found Byron too shocking and Scott too worldly, religious belief (or, in some celebrated instances, disbelief) could provide not only subject matter but also a justification for writing. To the most painful and intractable problems of the age, moreover—the vast scale of human misery incident to an industrializing society, the threat to religion and to moral and social values apparently posed by new intellectual currents—the only truly helpful responses possible, it seemed to many people, were sympathy and love: qualities believed to be quintessentially feminine and communicable through literature, and therefore doubly in the domain of literary women. Many careers were fueled by sympathy for victims of poverty and oppression, and this fellow-feeling often sprang from resentment of the injustices girls suffered because of their gender.

In such contexts the virtues that were thought to preclude women's participation in public affairs—the piety, selflessness, and unlimited capacity for love that defined true femininity—could be used instead to justify it. Ambition turned into altruism, and the eroticism and vulnerability that went with self-exposure became signs of chastity and modes of power. As young girls Anna Jameson and Elizabeth Barrett daydreamed of being knights in armor riding off to do brave deeds of rescue, but when they grew up they found an appropriately gendered model for emulation in Lady Godiva, who legend had it rode through the streets of Coventry not only unarmed but naked, so that her husband would remit his taxes on the poor. For Jameson and Barrett Browning, as for Harriet Martineau, Godiva's courage was an inspiration to speak out boldly on behalf of the disempowered. "If I were Queen of England," Jameson wrote at mid-century, "I would have [Lady Godiva] painted in Fresco in my council chamber"; and in fact a few years later Queen Victoria gave Prince Albert a statuette of Godiva (nude, on horseback) for his birthday.[3]

Lady Godiva's powerlessness is her power, her nakedness her shield: Peeping Tom, as Victorians told the story, was struck blind for looking at her. She represents to the highest degree, and in a singularly enabling form, the multifarious contradictions that encompassed women writers in early and mid-Victorian England. Literature was coming to seem essentially feminine: like women, it was valued for embodying unself-conscious sincerity, eliciting emotional response, nourishing and embellishing private life, and providing a higher and finer world than that of business and public affairs. But the location of literature on the border between private and public—where personal matters are presented to the general view—meant that for a man to become a writer was to make a partial retreat into the private sphere, while for a woman it meant emerging into the public one. Godiva rides into town for a political purpose; but the political issue is worked out in terms of matrimonial relations, and her privacy remains inviolate because no one is allowed to see her. Her story miraculously unites display and modesty, courage and safety, political engagement and family life.

The feminization of literature and the opening of the world of letters to feminine intrusion were accompanied by counterforces of resistance, however, that turned the paradoxes of women's situation against them. Their writing was usually treated as a separate category and devalued as such by reviewers. They were derided for feminine weakness on the one hand and scolded for displaying unwomanly force on the other, dismissed for ignorance of life or sneered at for knowing too much. Weakness was considered their peculiar strength, but neither strength nor weakness, it often seemed, was valued in their works. Christianity provided them with subject matter, justification, and authority for many kinds of writing, but almost always at the price of accepting their inferiority to men and restricting their imaginative and intellectual scope. Those who found a kind of liberation in battling religious orthodoxy generally paid for it with familial conflict and cultural marginalization. And although the developing sciences helped to undermine patriarchal religious authority, the ingrained misogyny of Victorian biological and social science was as oppressive in its way as that of theology.

Victoria herself was a queen of paradox. She detested childbearing, found infants disgusting, and thought women unfit for public responsibility, but she was revered (and sometimes reviled) for her prolific maternity and as queen and then empress of the most powerful empire the world had ever known. Despite their own accomplishments, similarly, many women of letters doubted that the sexes had equal abilities or should have equal rights. They enshrined domesticity, especially motherhood, even when their work was made possible by relative freedom from domestic responsibilities. Their works and lives provided essential evidence for feminist claims about women's abilities, but their support of the feminist movement was often qualified and limited. Mary Somerville, a scientist who received many honors in England and abroad and vigorously supported higher education for women, mused sadly at the end of a very impressive career that women do not attain to "genius": "that spark from heaven is not granted to the sex."[4] In fiction, women gave female characters significantly less freedom—for education, or travel, or extramarital domestic felicity—and scope for achievement and intellectual development than they experienced themselves; the worlds they imagined were more restricted by ideology and custom than the lives they actually led. And yet the social and psychological dangers of writing, the anomalousness of the positions they forged for themselves, and the effort of staking out new ground gave an impulsion of energy and excitement to their works that their immediate successors, coming in safer and easier times, could not recapture.

In this study I describe and attempt to explain the brilliant outburst of writing by women in the period from 1830 to 1880. I begin with the early years of Elizabeth Barrett Browning, Charlotte Brontë, and George Eliot, and try to show how their imaginative lives took form: the family constellations that shaped their sense of themselves, their daydreams and ambitions, their education and how they obtained it, their difficulties in appropriating literary patterns designed from a male point of view, and the fears and doubts about imagination and self-exposure they had to overcome in order to write. I trace these and related concerns through the lives and works of other poets and novelists, attempting to show something of the range and variety, and also the limitations, of women's writing. The last part of the book considers nonfictional prose, defining women's position in the intellectual community of letters and some of the effects on them of Victorian upheavals in religion and science. I conclude with a brief consideration of Eliot's *Daniel Deronda*, the last work by any of the great Victorian women writers, which brings many of the major issues that concerned them to a somewhat ambiguous conclusion.

The project of this book has been made immeasurably easier, and more dauntingly difficult, by the fact that much of the pioneering work of feminist literary criticism and cultural history has taken this rich and fruitful period for its field of exploration.[5] Unlike its predecessors, this book treats poetry, fiction, and nonfictional prose in an attempt to map the cultural arena as a whole. Since it deals primarily with high culture and its environs, however, it excludes women of the lower classes (class having been a sturdier barrier than gender), and pays little attention to kinds of writing (hymns, conduct books, political pamphlets, most periodical literature) that were defined as outside the world of high culture. It focuses on writers who have entered the canon or, like Margaret Oliphant, seem now, perhaps, as if they might do so; and on others such as Adelaide Procter, Jean Ingelow, Charlotte Yonge, Mary Braddon, and Ouida, who loomed significantly in the literary landscape of their time. And it includes notable women who wrote about religion, science, and other intellectual matters, such as Anna Jameson, Harriet Martineau, Mary Somerville, Frances Power Cobbe, and Annie Besant.

These are the female counterparts of the men of letters who have been taken to represent the literary history of the period, and this study is therefore in some respects a history that parallels and interlocks with traditional pre-feminist ones. In addition, however, I try to define some of the distinctive qualities of women's writing and the various forces that enabled or hindered its development. And I offer some tentative explanations for its flowering at the beginning of the period and also for its relative decline at the end, when many of the social, psychological, and educational barriers that appeared impregnable in the 1830s seemed to be falling at last.

Most women objected to being penned in a separate category and judged by standards morally stricter and artistically more lax than those applied to men. Elizabeth Barrett Browning summed it up in words addressed to her poet-heroine, Aurora Leigh:

> You never can be satisfied with praise
> Which men give women when they judge a book
> Not as mere work but as mere woman's work,
> Expressing the comparative respect
> Which means the absolute scorn. "Oh, excellent,
> What grace, what facile turns, what fluent sweeps,
> What delicate discernment . . . almost thought!
> The book does honor to the sex, we hold.
> Among our female authors we make room
> For this fair writer, and congratulate
> The country that produces in these times
> Such women, competent to . . . spell."
>   (*Aurora Leigh* 2: 232-43)

It might perhaps seem, therefore, that a book such as this denies its own subjects' desires and achievements. To some extent this may be so. But in fact — as the passage from *Aurora Leigh* attests despite itself — they all thought of themselves in gendered terms. Their works everywhere bear the marks of conscious confrontation with a literature made by men, and they knew that their successes and failures would be adduced as evidence in the ongoing argument about the capacities and incapacities of their sex that runs through almost every aspect of Victorian intellectual life. Most of them judged themselves, too, in relation more to each other than to their male counterparts, and they looked to each other for examples, approval, and support. Their pervasive and inescapable consciousness of gender is what, finally, they all have in common; it weaves their disparate works into a disorderly but essentially coherent tapestry, and it provides the unifying threads in the pattern of this book.

🍎 🍎 🍎 *Part One*

1. Beginning to Write

❧ ❧ ❧

The first of the great Victorian women writers to achieve popular success were Elizabeth Barrett Browning and Charlotte Brontë. They were born just a decade apart, Barrett Browning in 1806, Brontë in 1816. Their formative years spanned the transition from Romanticism to Victorianism, and their works and lives were potent forces in the shaping of Victorian literary culture. They were legends in their own time, figures of pathos and romance and also of rebellion and power. And an unusually large collection of documents from early childhood and adolescence survive to show how their shaping imaginations developed in response to domestic circumstances, literary influences, and the social and literary constraints of gender. Writers usually come before us with the lineaments of their imaginative worlds already determined, needing only to be pruned, polished, and elaborated; but in the juvenilia and recorded memories of Elizabeth Barrett and the Brontës we see these worlds in the making.

The circumstances of their childhoods seem quite different. Growing up in a luxurious country house in the lushly beautiful Malvern Hills, Elizabeth Barrett was the much loved, much admired, much indulged eldest child in a rich, healthy, happy family, and the first two decades of her life were almost untouched by sorrow. In poignant contrast, the Brontës' austere home in the rectory next to the church and graveyard on a bleak, wind-swept Yorkshire hillside was shadowed by the early death of the children's mother, and before her tenth year was over Charlotte had spent many months at a school (the infamous "Lowood" of *Jane Eyre*) where she was miserable and her two older sisters contracted the fever from which they died. And while the four surviving Brontë children were all devoted to writing or painting, or both, Elizabeth Barrett had only one close companion among her numerous siblings, and he was not an artist.

Yet in many essentials the two families were similar. Large, isolated households amply provided with books and periodicals and with few other distractions gave fertile ground for concentrated intellectual and imaginative work and play. In both, strong, dominating fathers fostered their gifted daughters' talents and encouraged their precocious intellectual development, although they followed the practice of the time in giving vastly greater freedom and educational opportunity to their sons. Mothers and aunts, on the other hand, inculcated feminine submissiveness by example or precept and provided no useful models for ambitious girls. Charlotte's mother bore six children in seven years and died when Charlotte (the third child) was five; she was replaced in the household by her sister, who taught the little girls the role and responsibilities—sewing and housekeeping, mostly—of women, and favored Branwell, the fourth child and only boy. The oldest of the girls, Maria, was by all accounts a paragon of precocious intelligence and virtue, but the portrait of her as Helen Burns in *Jane Eyre* delineates her as a model of resignation and self-effacement. Elizabeth Barrett's mother had a lively mind, high intelligence, vigorous common sense, and warm appreciation of her daughter's extraordinary talents, but she could not stand against her husband's domestic tyranny: "A sweet, gentle nature," her daughter said, "One of those women who never can resist. . . . Too womanly she was—it was her only fault."[1] When she died, after having borne twelve children, her sister made protracted visits during which she tried to make her brilliant niece behave like a proper young lady; but Elizabeth was twenty-two by then and could resist intrusive aunts.

But in both families the pattern of male domination and female weakness was shaken in the children's own generation. Elizabeth Barrett and Charlotte Brontë each had a younger brother who served as literary partner or confidant and who, although in every way less talented, was given a better education and greater scope for ambition. This manifestly inequitable treatment fed the resentment against both the favored brother and their own femaleness that smoldered through Barrett's and Brontë's childhoods and fueled some of their greatest works. At the same time their evident creative and intellectual superiority to their brothers, reinforced by the advantage of age, disinclined them to credit the prevailing doctrine of women's inferiority, bred self-confidence, and helped fire the ferocious independence of their exemplary heroines, Jane Eyre and Aurora Leigh.

For both Barrett and Brontë, however, the passage to adulthood was clouded and difficult. From the age of fifteen Elizabeth Barrett was prey to debilitating illnesses, while Charlotte Brontë at school training to be a teacher or during her brief stint as a governess suffered agonies of homesickness, loneliness, and longing for a sphere of activity adequate to her genius. As young women, both were painfully shy (although Elizabeth Barrett had been a self-assertive, confident child), and they regarded most of their small circles of acquaintances with impatient disdain. They knew no young men whose abilities matched their own and seemed increasingly unlikely to find a safe haven in marriage.

Even when they had become famous authors they stayed mostly in their fathers' houses, subject to paternal condescension and authority and nervously aloof from the literary world that was eager to make much of them. The fathers who had empowered them as children bitterly resisted their growth into womanhood, as if a daughter's ambitions were encouraged only with the proviso that she remain a child. Mr. Barrett expected absolute obedience from all his children, female and male alike, and would allow none of them to marry: his famous and financially independent daughter eloped at the age of forty-one and was never forgiven. Brontë in her mid-thirties "submitted" to her father's rule "with a quiet docility that half amused, half astonished" Elizabeth Gaskell,[2] and although after a long resistance he acceded to her marriage, he petulantly absented himself from the wedding in the church next door. With marriage, however, the two writers' paths poignantly diverged: Brontë married a man she did not love who had no respect for literature, and she died soon afterward in childbirth, whereas Elizabeth Barrett's elopement with Robert Browning led to fifteen happy years of marriage and her greatest works.

Their position in their families mirrored and reinforced girls' inevitable perceptions of women's place in literature. Not for nothing have fathers rather than mothers been called the authors of their children's being. While Barrett and Brontë read some women authors when they were young — not Jane Austen, though, whom we now consider their greatest female precursor but whom they found unpoetical and cold, nor George Sand, who later inspired them both[3] — the literary tradition they first sought to enter was obdurately and entirely male. In the literature they read, women existed only as men saw or desired them. Where were they to find a place for themselves? As child-authors of pre-sexual plots they could evade the issue; but once the fact of gender was acknowledged, contradiction was inescapable: girls had to think of themselves both as (traditionally male) author and as (traditionally female) object of desire. In life, it took Brontë and Barrett a very long time to work their way out of the child's position and resolve the apparent contradictions between femininity and authority, and it is not clear that Brontë ever did achieve resolution. In literature, however, there was room to maneuver.

They began in epic vein. As children they were preoccupied with heroes, politics, and war. Pope's translation of the *Iliad* enthralled Elizabeth Barrett, who by the age of eight had read histories of England, Rome, and Greece. The young Brontës followed the politics of the post-Napoleonic era and the first Reform Bill with fanatical partisanship, and eagerly read the political-historical novels and poetry of Sir Walter Scott. Elizabeth Barrett's first printed composition (she was fourteen, and her proud father arranged for the printing) was "The Battle of Marathon," a small Homeric epic about ancient Greece. The Brontës' imaginative worlds first took shape from a set of toy soldiers given by their father to Branwell, who allowed his three sisters to share them. The "plays" growing out of their play with the soldiers — stories of invented worlds that they elaborated until they were well into their twenties — reflected their political enthusiasm. Initially Charlotte's soldier was the Duke of Wellington and Branwell's was Bonaparte. The dramatis personae shifted as play succeeded play, from "Young Men" to "Our Fellows" to "The Islanders" (each child claimed an island and installed rulers), and embraced other public figures, including writers (Emily chose Scott) — but no women. Similarly, all the interesting characters in "The Battle of Marathon" are men. The exceptions in Elizabeth Barrett's epic are goddesses, their counterparts in the Brontë plays being the Brontë children themselves, who as genii, fairies, or queens and king were the presiding deities of their imagined world: partaking of the qualities of both human characters and their authors, identical with neither, but something in between. For where could a girl place herself, with whom could she identify, in these wholly masculine worlds?[4]

Narratives containing only men in a sense obviated issues of gender. But in the nineteenth century it was almost impossible to write long or well in the epic mode, and in any event the problem of gender became both more acute and more interesting when the heroic world of childhood was disrupted by the foreshadowings of puberty and the advent of Byron. Byron was by far the most famous and influential poet of his time. The imaginations of children and adolescents susceptible to literature—including those, and they were many, who were forbidden to read his works—as well as of sober adults were fired by his poetry and the drama of his scandalous life and heroic death. His poetry was the definitive presentation of some quintessentially Romantic attitudes: enthusiasm for solitude and natural grandeur, hatred of social falsity and shams, an intense, world-weary melancholy invigorated by dark irony. His narrative verse celebrated mysterious sins and sorrows and various kinds of doomed but fascinating love, generally in exotic places. He was beautiful, aristocratic, eccentric, proud, and extremely attractive to women, and his adventures amatory and otherwise made a continuing feast for gossip.

Byron's death in 1824, at the age of thirty-six, had a stunning impact on such diverse people as fourteen-year-old Alfred Tennyson, who rushed into the churchyard and carved on a rock the words "Byron is dead," and Thomas Carlyle, who disapproved of almost everything Byron stood for but felt nonetheless a "blank" in his heart at the passing of "the noblest spirit in Europe."[5] Elizabeth Barrett's first published poem was a lament for his death. The Brontës would have read about him in *Blackwood's*, which purveyed while deploring them the various sensational accusations against him, and by 1833 they had access to his complete works.[6]

Byron's poems, like their author, were considered exceedingly dangerous and carried the excitement of the forbidden. He was his own hero, and reading his works was a Byronic experience. Fanny Kemble, born to a famous theatrical family and herself to become a famous actress and successful writer, chanced upon a volume of Byron when she was at boarding school in Paris, read two lines, "quivering with excitement," and took the book to bed.

> I confided to the companion whose bed was next to mine that I had a volume of Lord Byron under my pillow. The emphatic whispered warnings of terror and dismay with which she received this information, her horror at the wickedness of the book (of which she knew nothing), her dread of the result of detection for me, and her entreaties, enforced with tears, that I would not keep the terrible volume where it was, at length, combined with my own nervous excitement about it [led her to hide it elsewhere and then return it to its owner]. And so I then read no more of that wonderful poetry, which, in my after days of familiar acquaintance with it, always affected me like an evil potion taken into my blood.[7]

For teenaged girls (and some boys) Byron was a high-culture equivalent of to-day's rock stars. Not even the most strictly bred were immune. Lady Georgiana Fullerton, daughter of the ambassador to France, granddaughter of a duke and a marquis, who afterward became a novelist and an eminent Catholic convert, was as susceptible at fourteen as Fanny Kemble.

> My mother had known him and his wife very well, and had the worst possible opinion of him. But somehow his poetry, his picture at the beginning of the vol-ume, and the idea of his having been a wild, strange, and even bad man, took hold of my fancy, and I actually *fell in love* with him.
>
> He had been dead some years, but it really was like being in love. I would have given up any pleasure for the sake of reading the least bit of his poetry, and kept constantly thinking of him. If his name was mentioned I coloured, and my heart beat. . . . This strange infatuation lasted nearly a year.[8]

This erotic stimulus was not only felt by girls as transgressive against familial and social authority; it was embedded in a political context of the sort that formed the basis of Elizabeth Barrett's and the Brontës' imaginative worlds. The key concepts were tyranny and freedom. Despiser of tyrants, champion of oppressed nationalities, Byron supported the Greek struggle against Turkish domination (the contemporary version of the events Elizabeth Barrett cele-brated in "The Battle of Marathon") and in 1824 he died, young and beautiful, in Greece, a martyr in the cause of freedom.

Elizabeth Barrett's and the Brontës' enthusiasm for glamorous heroes and exotic places flared into passionate life at the impulsion of Byron and his ar-dent, world-wandering, idealistic, and mordantly cynical heroes. In 1834 Charlotte and Branwell created the imaginary land of Angria, the chronicling of which completed Charlotte's literary apprenticeship. Its hero was the Duke of Wellington's son Arthur Wellesley, who had appeared in the earliest plays and now evolved into the quintessentially Byronic Arthur Augustus Adrian, duke of Zamorna and emperor of Angria. The inhabitants of Gondal, Emily and Anne Brontë's counterpart to Angria, appear to have been as Byronic as the Angrians. Elizabeth Barrett's Byron was more political and less erotic than the figures the Brontës created in his image, perhaps because she came upon him as a child (whereas Charlotte Brontë was in her late teens when the impact of his poetry fell upon her); but she daydreamed of running off to be Byron's page, or falling in love with him, or becoming in transparent emulation the poet-liberator of Greece.

Byron fed girls' daydreams both of becoming famous authors—ordinarily a rather pacific and homebound, not to say sedentary, occupation—and of hav-ing thrilling adventures in exotic places. He exemplified escape from domestic morality: brooding, self-centered, vain, deliberately flouting social convention, he rebelled against patriarchal authority in religion, politics, and sexual con-duct, and also—and for girls who wanted to write, at least as important—in literature. His lively, loosely written narrative verse undid the solemn authority of the high Miltonic style, undermined the neoclassical tradition, laughed at his Romantic elders, and was moreover easily imitated. In the 1820s and '30s Letitia Landon and Caroline Norton made poetic careers mostly with quasi-Byronic narratives. He was a model on many levels — stylistic, political, moral, erotic — for the rebellion implicit in the fact of female ambition.

But while Byron's example fed girls' restlessness, their desire for scope and freedom, it also brought them up sharply against the barriers of gender. They could emulate him as writer, rebel, or adventurer, but their relation to the Byronic myth was complicated by the fact that he was a very sexy figure who mocked his high-minded intellectual wife and celebrated women in his amatory narratives only for their sexual allure and responsiveness to men. Love, according to a famous passage in *Don Juan*, is "woman's whole existence" (I: 1546). For girls who wanted to be writers he was a potential self, but also an ideal lover with conventional and repressive ideas about women.[9] And even as a potential self, his gender could not be ignored. Brontë and Barrett as girls conceived of romance — the romantic — as travel: setting forth into the world. The usual model for this was the knight who rides about rescuing damsels; damsels sometimes ride forth too, seeking a champion, but they usually remain in one place and wait to be rescued. Anna Jameson in her childhood daydreams was "always a princess-heroine in the disguise of a knight, a sort of Clorinda or Britomart, going about to redress the wrongs of the poor, fight giants, and kill dragons."[10] But well-bred girls could not expect to pursue adventure any more than they could participate in knightly combat, and so when Elizabeth Barrett imagined herself joining Byron she imagined herself doing so dressed as a boy.

In a transparently autobiographical essay about a ten-year-old girl called Beth, probably written when she was in her late twenties, Elizabeth Barrett delineates the paradox Byron evoked. Beth imagines herself as a conventional heroine, the object of male desire: she looks in the mirror, wants to be beautiful, and intends to fall in love when she is fifteen because "that was the age when all the princesses in the fairy tales were fallen in love with."[11] "Her lover was to be a poet . . . and Beth was inclined to believe that he wd be Ld Byron." The fairytales, however, do not allow for her un-princess-like ambition.

> But Beth was a poet herself — & there was the reigning thought — No woman was ever before such a poet as she wd be. As Homer was among men, so wd she be among women — she wd be the feminine of Homer. . . . When she grew up she wd wear men's clothes, & live in a Greek island, the sea melting into turquoises all around it. . . . Or she wd live in a cave on Parnassus mount, and feed upon cresses & Helicon water. (361)

Similarly, when Anna Jameson was not fighting giants, she was "founding a society in some far-off solitude or desolate island . . . , where there were to be no tears, no tasks, and no laws — except those which I made myself — no caged birds nor tormented kittens."[12] Beth's Greek island is the setting of Byronic romance; but her dreams of being a poet preclude dreams of love: she will "wear men's clothes."

A quiet, desexualized paradise does not, however, satisfy Beth's ambition.

> Beth was also a warrior. When she was fifteen [the age at which in another fantasy she intended to fall in love] she wd arm herself in complete steel [. . .] & ride on a steed, along the banks of the Danube, every where by her chanted songs, . . . for she was to sing her own poetry all the way she went . . . attracting to her side many warriors—so that by the time she reached Stambol, Beth wd be the chief of a battalion & she wd destroy the Turkish empire, & deliver "Greece the glorious." (361)

But while armor might cover her body, it could not conceal the fact of gender.

> Poor Beth had one great misfortune. She was born a woman. Now she despised nearly all the women in the world [. . .] She could not abide their littlenesses called delicacies, their pretty headaches, & soft mincing voices, their nerves & affectations.[. . .] Beth thanked her gods that she was not & never wd be feminine. (361)

She prides herself on her strength, which she defines as unfeminine and experiences as motion that escapes social, cultural, or gendered context.

> Beth could run rapidly & leap high,—and though her hands were miserably little to be sure, she had very strong wrists. [. . .] [S]he cd climb too pretty well up trees [. . .] And best of all, though she cared for bows & arrows, & squirts & popguns—best of all, did she like riding . . . galloping till the trees raced past her & the clouds were shot over her head like horizontal arrows from a giant's bow— galloping till she felt the still air gathered against her face & chest like a wind— leaping over ditches—feeling the live creature beneath her, swerve and bound with its own force like a ball in its course, running races till the goal in sight vanished in the rapidity of reaching it. (361-62)

In contrast to her fantasies of purposeful travel to a literary-political goal (Greece), her actual pleasure is of motion so swift and joyous that the goal vanishes. Her imagination creates a living universe of mythic dimensions and sensuous satisfaction that exists only while she rides. The essence of her prepubertal romanticism is solitary motion.[13]

The same essential elements appear in Charlotte Brontë's accounts, written in 1835 when she was a restless, homesick teacher at Roe Head School, of visionary moments in which Angrian scenes arise before her. One such vision contains, like Beth's, a Byronic object of both emulation and desire, a landscape throbbing with life, and a horse. Brontë being in her late teens, however, rather than a prepubescent child like Beth, the erotic element is stronger.

> Never shall I, Charlotte Brontë, forget what a voice of wild and wailing music
> now came thrillingly to my mind's—almost to my body's—ear; nor how dis-
> tinctly I, sitting in the school-room at Roe-Head, saw the Duke of Zamorna lean-
> ing against that obelisk, with the mute marble Victory above him, the fern waving
> at his feet, his black horse turned loose grazing among the heather, the moonlight
> so mild and so exquisitely tranquil, sleeping upon that vast and vacant road, and
> the African sky quivering and shaking with stars expanded above all. I was quite
> gone. I had really utterly forgot where I was and all the gloom and cheerlessness
> of my situation. I felt myself breathing quick and short as I beheld the Duke lifting
> up his sable crest . . . and knew that music . . . was exciting him and quickening
> his ever-rapid pulse.[14]

Conflating identification and erotic response—Zamorna's quickened pulse,
her own quickened breathing—she simultaneously desires *with* Zamorna and
desires *him*. The impossible doubleness is doubled when, even as she recalls
losing herself in the dream, she asserts and reasserts the identity and social
context—"I, Charlotte Brontë, . . . I, sitting in the schoolroom . . . the gloom
and cheerlessness of my situation"—that like Beth's reluctant femininity makes
identification with her hero impossible. For Brontë as for Beth, imagination is
a form of motion: in visions, she is transported to another world ("I was quite
gone"). Like Beth's ride, too, her visionary experience is solitary, and her solitude mirrors and is mirrored by Zamorna's. The essence of romantic experience, for Brontë as for Beth, is the imagination going forth alone to create a
living world: what is romantic, that is, is less the content of experience than its
form, and its essential inwardness is heightened by the frequency with which it
comes to rest on a figure that mirrors the solitude of the imaginer.[15]

As the two writers matured, their imaginations took a sadder tone, reflecting
the darkening circumstances of their lives, but kept the same form. For Brontë,
the misery of school in Yorkshire was succeeded by the deeper and ultimately
more enriching miseries of a school in Belgium. Her Angrian visions—erotic,
amoral, escapist, overcharged, and unsuitable for publication—eventually became the substratum for more sober and realistic novels. When Elizabeth Barrett was about fifteen—the age at which Beth had planned to love and be Lord
Byron as well as rescue Greece—her physical strength declined under a series of
physical ailments that family tradition attributed (probably erroneously, but
with symbolic appropriateness) to injuring herself fastening a girth on her
pony. She worked for a long time on a poem in the vein of Byronic self-consciousness, moodiness, aspiration, and nameless guilt called "The Development of Genius," but her father—who was usually extremely proud of her
writings—cruelly ridiculed it, and she never completed it.

Byronism was a phenomenon of Romanticism and adolescence, and when
writers whose youth he had enchanted grew into sober and serious Victorians
he came to seem inauthentic and even a little silly. For men, outgrowing Byron
was part of growing up. For women, though, his potency was more enduring.

When Fanny Kemble was about eighteen, she resolved to stop reading his poetry.

> It was a great effort and a very great sacrifice, for the delight I found in it was intense. . . . "Cain" and "Manfred" were more especially the poems that stirred my whole being with a tempest of excitement that left me in a state of mental perturbation impossible to describe for a long time after reading them. . . . It was a severe struggle, but I persevered in it for more than two years, and had my reward; I broke through the thraldom of that powerful spell, and all the noble beauty of those poems remained to me thenceforth divested of the power of wild excitement they had exercised over me.[16]

Byron's spell bound women with an erotic force that made resistance especially imperative and especially difficult.

But for women writers Byronism was not just a stage to be outgrown: it was a psychological impulsion to be cherished and an artistic problem they had to resolve. Byron's obstinate self-assertion, his reckless defiance of tyranny and convention, gave an essential impetus to women who had to defy cultural authority and override the convention of feminine self-suppression in order to write. His example helped fire Elizabeth Barrett's translations of Aeschylus' *Prometheus Bound* (Byron being widely regarded as the modern Prometheus) and her eventual bold support of American abolitionism and the Italian Risorgimento. Her most enduringly influential work, *Sonnets from the Portuguese*, explores the situation of a woman who both is and loves a great poet: not Lord Byron now, but Robert Browning, and not in fantasy but in waking truth. What Beth could hardly formulate to dream of, Elizabeth Barrett did: she both became and married a great poet, as well as being recognized in her lifetime as the "feminine of Homer," the first and greatest of English women poets.

And Brontë's Zamorna became Mr. Rochester, against and in concert with whom Jane Eyre tests, purifies, and strengthens her passion and her sense of self. In the happy ending of *Jane Eyre*, the old story of quest and rescue is reversed: Rochester imprisoned by blindness and sorrow is saved by Jane, who travels through a landscape of fairy-tale obstacles to find him. The perplexing doubleness of the hero as self and other, subject and object of desire, is resolved not only in *Sonnets from the Portuguese* but also in the egalitarian marriages that conclude *Jane Eyre* and Barrett Browning's novel in verse, *Aurora Leigh*, in which the men (like Byron) are both socially powerful and in revolt against social convention, and the women (also like Byron) are fiercely independent and possessed of powerful artistic imaginations and bold desire. Both stories end with the union of two equally impassioned, aspiring, anticonventional characters who defy, in order to remake it, the gendered social order. But the fact that both heroines refuse to marry until the men have been tamed by the loss of their eyesight and the houses that represent their inherited authority shows how difficult it was to reach the equilibrium of this ending.

The first great literary works by Victorian women—Charlotte Brontë's *Jane Eyre* and Emily Brontë's *Wuthering Heights* in fiction, Barrett Browning's *Sonnets from the Portuguese* and *Aurora Leigh* in verse—emerged from the struggle between the Byronic impulses that defined their burgeoning imaginations and the constraints of society and literary form. Heathcliff is among the most purely Byronic characters in English fiction, but his amoral, antisocial passion is mediated for us by the timidly respectable narrator with whom we enter the violent world of *Wuthering Heights*, the robustly decent housekeeper who tells most of the story, and the diversion of our sympathies onto those whom Heathcliff hurts.[17] On the margins between male and female and between poetry and prose, between will and desire on the one side and moderation and domesticity on the other, the first great era of women's literature was born.

Those who followed the Byronic model in a simpler way were less successful. Caroline Norton and Letitia E. Landon (known as L.E.L.) specialized in quasi-Byronic narratives and sad tales of passion, and their lives like Byron's were scandalous and dramatic. Norton was a famous beauty and wit whose brutal husband sued Lord Melbourne, the prime minister, for alienating his wife's affections and exercised his legal right to control her money and her children. Like Byron, she made her notorious marital misfortunes the thinly disguised subject of verse, and her attacks on the legal system that empowered her husband exposed her, like Byron, to additional obloquy on the score of her personal life. Landon concluded a less socially exalted career of glamour and scandal and the adulation of undergraduates by marrying a man who was governor of the Gold Coast; she went to Africa with him and soon thereafter died of poison, stirring exciting rumors of suicide and murder. Closer to home, Branwell Brontë fatally enacted the Byronic dream of his and his sisters' childhood: he kept bad company, embroiled himself in an improper and hopeless love affair, squandered his talents, drank and took drugs, and died miserable and young. His sisters lived lives of rigid propriety and self-conquest, seizing imaginative control of Byronic impulse and using it to create some of the greatest novels in English literature. Elizabeth Barrett, like the Brontës, left her most Byronic work unpublished; the Byronic strain went underground and emerged transformed in *Sonnets from the Portuguese*, her great political poetry, and *Aurora Leigh*.

George Eliot left few records of her early years. Her first surviving letter was written when she was sixteen, and no juvenile compositions have been preserved. But in *The Mill on the Floss*, her one extended study of the childhood of a talented, imaginative girl,[18] Maggie Tulliver tries to enact a fantasy journey such as Beth and Brontë dream of. Fleeing an alien and restrictive world like Brontë escaping from the schoolroom into Angria, confident like Beth of her powers as pedagogue and charismatic leader, Maggie runs away to become queen of the Gypsies. The Gypsies are neither attractive nor grateful, however, and send her home again. Her return is a parody of Beth's happy dreams of adventure: instead of an androgynous hero she is a maiden who has to be rescued. "The red light of the setting sun seemed to have a portentous meaning" (179), as it would in Angria; but she rides ignominiously behind a Gypsy on a donkey, and the knight on horseback who rescues her is her affectionate father. The effect is to bind her closer to home and paternal authority; bewildered, terrified, and grateful, she promises never to run away from her father again.

A few hours before Eliot's own father, a prosperous farmer and estate-agent, died, when she was twenty-nine, she wrote: "What shall I be without my Father? It will seem as if a part of my moral nature were gone. I had a horrid vision of myself last night becoming earthly sensual and devilish for want of that purifying restraining influence."[19] Like Maggie, she felt that her father anchored her to a home she felt inadequate to her needs, which she both longed and feared to leave. Eliot's childhood seems not to have been an apprenticeship in writing, although by her late teens, at least, she wrote poetry, and she published a poem at twenty. But she read, and she daydreamed, and like Elizabeth Barrett and Charlotte Brontë she had to shake herself free from daydreams and bring herself home from imaginary distant lands. Her earliest surviving letters show her under the rigid sway of Evangelical religion and altogether disapproving of imaginative activity. Novels and romances are pernicious, she wrote to her former teacher when she was sixteen, because they arouse the imagination to solitary, self-centered fantasy.

> I shall carry to my grave the mental diseases with which they have contaminated me. When I was quite a little child I could not be satisfied with the things around me; I was constantly living in a world of my own creation, and was quite contented to have no companions that I might be left to my own musings and imagine scenes in which I was chief actress. Conceive what a character novels would give [i.e., did give] to these Utopias.

Isolation, self-centeredness, and dissatisfaction with the real world are the daydreamer's crimes, and they lead to authorship, confusion of fantasy with reality, and moral turpitude: Sir Walter Scott (her favorite novelist), Eliot adds in a postscript, "sacrificed almost his integrity for the sake of acting out the character of the Scotch Laird, which he had so often depicted."[20]

This is a singularly priggish letter. But it is not just the prudery that a provincial girl with too much religious enthusiasm would think proper to express. Victorian notions of moral hygiene condemned daydreaming, or "castle building," to which girls' restricted scope made them particularly prone and which were all too likely to be tainted by sexuality or ambition or both. Harriet Martineau blamed "exciting and vain-glorious dreams" about "bodily suffering, and . . . the peculiar glory attending fortitude in that direction"—"All manner of deaths at the stake and on the scaffold"—for injuring her nervous system and causing her to become deaf.[21] These daydreams, which began when she was eight, incorporate their own punishment. But daydreams could also be

part of a writer's apprenticeship. When Charlotte M. Yonge was little she made
up stories about a family of twenty-one children who lived in her garden, and
when she grew up she wrote novels about families almost as large located almost as close to home.[22] Anthony Trollope too beguiled his lonely childhood
with stories, carried on for months and years, by which, he says, he learned the
essentials of the novelist's trade; but even Trollope, as a man in his fifties, pays
lipservice to the conventional attitude: "There can, I imagine, hardly be a more
dangerous mental practice."[23] And Charlotte Brontë eventually forced herself
to withdraw from Angria in order to write more sober fiction. "I long to quit
for a while," she wrote in 1839,

> that burning clime where we have sojourned too long—its skies flame—the glow
> of sunset is always upon it—the mind would cease from excitement and turn now
> to a cooler region where the dawn breaks grey and sober, and the coming day for
> a time at least is subdued by clouds.[24]

Eliot's condemnation of literature as an extension of castle building is extreme but not unique. Charlotte Elizabeth Tonna, whose various writings were
all directed to religious ends, recalls with pious horror her habit in youth "of
dreamy excursiveness into imaginary scenes, and among unreal personages,
which is alike inimical to rational pursuits, and opposed to spiritual-minded-
ness"; nursery tales, Shakespeare, and the British poets in turn stored her mind
with "the glittering tinsel of unsanctified genius."[25] The idea that imagination
is isolating, amoral, and antisocial particularly afflicted Evangelicals like Mrs.
Tonna and the young George Eliot, but it also pervades Victorian literary culture as a whole. Novels and popular poetry were deplored, as television is today, for corrupting youth: exciting restlessness and desire, breeding dissatisfaction, crowding out more productive pursuits. The major Victorian poets,
moreover, worried that poetry endangered its authors still more than its readers, and writers like Dante Gabriel Rossetti and Algernon Swinburne happily
turned the idea of art as disease into a positive value in the counterculture of
aestheticism, art for art's sake, which culminated in Oscar Wilde's paradoxical
assertions that life imitates art: precisely what the young George Eliot warned,
by the example of Scott, that imagination inexorably leads to.

Fear of the effects of art on its producers (as opposed to readers) was particularly acute in regard to poetry but affected novelists as well, many of
whom, including Eliot and the Brontës, published poems before they published
prose. Victorian poetry in its major phase begins with Tennyson's volumes of
1830 and 1832, which include several quasi-allegorical depictions of solitary
figures, mostly female, who seem to represent artists cut off from life and love.
In Tennyson's "The Palace of Art" the poet builds a glorious palace for his soul
to dwell in; but the soul, living there alone, is struck by madness and despair
and moves to a humble cottage instead. What she renounces, though, is the
sinful isolation of her art, not the palace itself, and the poem ends hopefully:

"Perchance I may return with others there / When I have purged my guilt." "With others": the primary function of art, most Victorian writers and critics agreed, was to affirm human community by arousing in the reader the emotions common to all humanity. For a society that saw itself as increasingly mechanical, industrial, urban, fragmented, and inhuman, with very little idea how to ameliorate the increasingly visible suffering of the poor, the one antidote seemed to be sympathy, or love. The source, model, and sanctuary of love was the family; and within the family its guardian was woman. Art at its moral worst, then, violated everything highest and best in woman; while at its best it only did indirectly and diffusely, although with more beneficiaries, what a woman should do immediately and directly in her own person.

Tennyson did not intend actually to move into a humble cottage, either in verse or in fact. As is frequently the case, however, what was metaphor for a male writer was only too literally applied to women. In 1837 Charlotte Brontë sent some poems to Robert Southey, the poet laureate, with a request for advice; and Southey in return issued a warning that accorded all too well with Brontë's own accounts of her experience and resonates closely with Eliot's fears. "The day dreams in which you habitually indulge," he wrote, "are likely to induce a distempered state of mind; and, in proportion as all the ordinary uses of the world seem to you flat and unprofitable, you will be unfitted for them without becoming fitted for anything else." Brontë's Angrian visions as recorded in her Roe Head journal are indeed inseparably bound up with her alienation from the people she lived among and despised. But it is precisely in the "ordinary uses of the world," Southey reminds her, that woman's destiny lies: "Literature cannot be the business of a woman's life, and it ought not to be. The more she is engaged in her proper duties, the less leisure will she have for it even as an accomplishment and a recreation."[26] Eliot at eighteen wrote similarly of singers: "I ask myself can it be desirable, and would it be consistent with millenial holiness for a human being to devote the time and energies that are barely sufficient for real exigencies on acquiring expertness in trills, cadences, etc.?"[27]

Women writers made a point of insisting that their work did not interfere with their domestic responsibilities. In *The Life of Charlotte Brontë* Mrs. Gaskell repeatedly depicts Brontë sacrificing herself to filial responsibility, caring for her sisters, and being ruled by domestic affection and "the sense of the supremacy of that duty which God, in placing us in families, has laid out for us." Gaskell gave definitive expression to the dilemma this entails:

> When a man becomes an author, it is probably merely a change of employment to him. . . . [A]nother merchant or lawyer, or doctor, steps into his vacant place, and probably does as well as he. But no one can take up the quiet, regular duties of the daughter, the wife, or the mother, as well as she whom God has appointed to fill that particular place. . . . And yet . . . [the gifted woman] must not hide her gift in a napkin; it was meant for the use and service of others. In a humble and faithful

spirit must she labour to do what is not impossible, or God would not have sent her to do it.[28]

So put, or even as Southey put it, the conflict need not be irreconcilable. But what if the writer is not quite sure that she is laboring in a humble and faithful spirit to serve others? What if she wants the traditional reward of the artist, fame?

Southey assumes, in fact, that his young correspondent is inspired by ambition for fame, not service. "Write poetry for its own sake," he exhorts her, "not in a spirit of emulation, and not with a view to celebrity; the less you aim at that, the more likely you will be to deserve, and finally to obtain it." Brontë swallowed her mortification as best she could and accepted the lesson in its starkest form: "I trust I shall never more feel ambition to see my name in print; if the wish should rise, I'll look at Southey's letter, and suppress it."[29] For men, the desire for glory has traditionally been considered a spur to virtue, at worst what Milton called it in "Lycidas," the last infirmity of noble minds. But in women it has been seen as a vice. "I feel that my besetting sin," Eliot wrote in 1839, "is the one of all others most destroying, as it is the fruitful parent of them all, Ambition, a desire insatiable for the esteem of my fellow creatures." A year later she bemoaned her compliances with "that traitor within, the love of human praise." The besetting sin of Maggie Tulliver's childhood, which Eliot treats more kindly in Maggie than she had in herself, is a burning desire to have her superiority recognized; Maggie daydreams of being a queen among children or Gypsies. Elizabeth Barrett thought at thirteen that she had learned "to throw away ambition," but her first published volume of poems has it both ways: it concludes with "A Vision of Fame," a grandiose renunciation of the ambition that presumably inspired publication in the first place.[30]

Self-contradictions like "A Vision of Fame" were nourished by an atmosphere in which women were judged as much by their presumed motives for writing—a woman author being a phenomenon that always required explanation—as by what they wrote. In a dialogue written by Anna Jameson a man says, "female authorship is in danger of becoming a fashion,—which Heaven avert!" Jameson's spokeswoman replies:

> It is too true that mere vanity and fashion have lately made some women authoresses;—more write for money, and by this employment of their talents earn their own independence, add to the comforts of a parent, or supply the extravagance of a husband.

The "mere energy of intellect and will" is also an acceptable motive, and "some few" women write "from the pure wish to do good, and to add to the stock of happiness and the progress of thought." But the desire for fame (which Jameson shared) is another matter.

> Some, who are unhappy in their domestic relations, yet endowed with all that

feminine craving after sympathy, which was intended to be the charm of our sex, the blessing of yours, and somehow or other has been turned to the bane of both, look abroad for what they find not at home; fling into the wide world the irrepressible activity of an overflowing mind and heart, which can find no other unforbidden issue,—and to such "fame is love disguised."[31]

The woman writer seeks from the public, that is, what only a husband should give.

"Love disguised" has a coarse connotation when writing is conceived as performance or self-display. This conception goes back in England at least to the seventeenth century and is established as the norm in nineteenth-century women's writing by Mme de Staël's *Corinne*, in which the heroine is an *improvisatrice*, an improvisor of song and story and also on occasion a dancer, a beautiful woman whose intellectual and creative power is expressed in public performance. A basic assumption of Victorian reviewing (not extinct today) is that the best writing comes directly from personal experience, and that what moves the reader is what the writer most deeply felt. So it is appropriate that in Victorian women's writing the central figure for female ambition and for the woman artist, almost always, is not a writer but (in order of decreasing respectability) a singer, actress, dancer, or circus performer: women, that is, who put themselves literally on display, whose bodies are the material of their art. A disagreeable man in Geraldine Jewsbury's 1848 novel *The Half-Sisters* explains what they have in common:

> I would never marry an artiste of any grade. A woman who makes her mind public, or exhibits herself in any way, no matter how it may be dignified by the title of art, seems to me little better than a woman of a nameless class [i.e., a prostitute]. I am more jealous of the mind than of the body; and, to me, there is something revolting in the notion of a woman who professes to love and belong to you alone, going and printing the secrets of her inmost heart, the most sacred workings of her soul, for the benefit of all who can pay for them. What is the value of a woman whom every one who chooses may know as much about as you do yourself? The stage is still worse, for that is publishing both mind and body.[32]

The author is satirizing the speaker, but she does not deny the self-revelatory nature of writing; and in fact the actress this gentleman scorns, although she triumphs over such prejudice by marrying a very nice nobleman, upon marriage retires from the stage.

The conception of art as self-display prompted by vanity and seeking an erotic response crucially differentiates women writers' sense of themselves and their work from that of their male counterparts. The great example of celebrity in English literature was Byron, whose poetry brazenly exploited the known facts of his life and his scandalous reputation. Most Victorian writers, however, both female and male, avoided such blatant self-exposure. Matthew Arnold dismissed it as futile: "What helps it now," he asked in plaintive verse, that

Byron carried across Europe the "pageant of his bleeding heart?" ("Stanzas from the Grande Chartreuse," 133, 136) Female emulation of Byron in this respect would seem not just futile, however, but immodest, impure, unwomanly. For a woman to appear in public, to be publically known or spoken of at all, was still, as it had been in England for centuries, morally suspect; for women, all fame was ill fame.

Not surprisingly, then, the writings of English women from the seventeenth century onward exhibit moments of intense revulsion or fear in connection with the art of writing or with artistic performance in general.[33] An anecdote Eliot told in illustration of her childish conviction that she was going to be "a personage in the world" locates ambition in musical performance. "When she was only four years old, she recollected playing on the piano, of which she did not know one note, in order to impress the servant with a proper notion of her acquirements and generally distinguished position"; but when she did become an accomplished pianist and performed for visitors at her school, she "suffer[ed] agonies from shyness and reluctance" and later would often "rush to her room and throw herself on the floor in an agony of tears."[34] At eighteen she declared her revulsion against a performance of an oratorio in terms which emphasize bodily display: "I think nothing can justify the using of an intensely interesting and solemn passage of Scripture, as a rope-dancer uses her rope, or as a sculptor the pedestal on which he places the statue, that is alone intended to elicit admiration."[35] "To elicit admiration"—what might strike a man as laudable ambition is deplorable vanity for a woman.

And so women were anxious to redefine their art as womanly service: selfless in intent, self-effacing in execution, enhancing rather than replacing womanly responsibility, and if possible attributable to the impetus of a man. Elizabeth Barrett's early poems and prefaces ignore the substantial help and encouragement she received from her mother and suggest, not quite truly, that she became a poet at her father's impulse and for his pleasure. Elizabeth Gaskell began writing fiction, she said, when her husband suggested that it might ease her grief for her dead son. Eliot did not write fiction until George Henry Lewes, whom she considered her husband, encouraged her to. The Brontës could have used as an excuse their absolute need of money: their father could make no provision for them after his death and they had no other resource except the badly paid and uncongenial one of teaching. And they all (except perhaps Emily Brontë, who would have scorned self-justification of any sort), intended their books to do moral good. Christina Rossetti's astonishing allegory of sexual fall and redemption, *Goblin Market,* for instance, masquerades as a moral lesson for children, and Rossetti turned increasingly to devotional poetry and didactic prose.

A particularly telling depiction of the ideal subordination of art to womanliness comes from Charlotte M. Yonge, whose best-selling novels (still eminently readable today) inculcate a high-minded pious ideal of family life. Yonge's books were corrected and approved in manuscript by her father and the Reverend John Keble, the venerated poet and religious leader. Geraldine, the crippled artist-heroine of *The Pillars of the House*, paints pretty, sentimental pictures in her spare time which are exhibited and acclaimed at the Royal Academy, but the pleasure of success is spoiled by the failure of her brother Edgar, who has occasionally instructed her in art but (like another aspiring painter and brother of artists, Branwell Brontë) threw his own talents and chances away. Even when the orphaned family desperately needs the money she could make by selling her paintings, her first responsibility is to give more immediate service to her siblings. "It took some resolution not to attend exclusively to her art, and she was forced to make it a rule never to touch a pencil" (2: 69) until she had given the younger children their lessons. She devotes the money from her Academy pictures to paying Edgar's debts. Geraldine evades the onus of ambition by subordinating it to the service of her family, and escapes the onus of sexuality by bodily mutilation: since a rheumatic foot impedes her participation in the work of the parentless household, she has the foot amputated. She is allowed to attend to her painting only at the end of the novel when, selfless, sexless, and essentially self-mutilated, she devotes herself primarily to raising Edgar's son, whom Edgar's death makes the heir to the family's recovered estate.

Geraldine's most ambitious painting is an allegory of womanhood that mocks female ambition. The stringent restrictions Yonge places on the woman artist — her own strict avoidance of all temptations to vanity or self-assertion, the steady didacticism of her very entertaining books, and not least the shocking violence of Geraldine's amputation, which like Martineau's fantasies of martyrdom pays for glory with the loss of bodily integrity — carry into mature adulthood the inhibitions and terrors with which other women's careers began.

2. Travel, Trials, Fame

Renouncing ambition did not, of course, prevent Elizabeth Barrett, Charlotte Brontë, and George Eliot from producing the works that made them famous, although Eliot began her fiction-writing career when she was already an experienced reviewer, editor, and translator, thirty-six years old. All three were inspired and emboldened, moreover, by the example of George Sand, whom they all read in early adulthood and who offered a radical new model of female authorship. Sand was a French, female, feminist version of Byron, by whom she was greatly influenced. Her novels vibrate with sexual passion and passionate protests against the subjection of women. She dressed as a man and lived with a man's freedom: left her husband, smoked cigars, took lovers. Her artist-heroine Consuelo, unlike Mme de Staël's Corinne who wins fame but loses her lover, manages to have everything: exciting travels, heroic adventures, triumph as a singer, a grand marriage, fame, and a good deal more besides. Like Byron, George Sand was immensely famous, and she and her books, which were regarded in many quarters (by Elizabeth Barrett's father, for instance) as unfit for women to read, were attacked in the British press as profligate and poisonously dangerous. For women she exemplified, more immediately than Byron, both the scandal attached to fame and an exhilarating freedom.[1]

The idea of fame as a kind of sexualized self-exposure profoundly affected women writers' sense of themselves and their work. Lady Godiva was the standard by which Elizabeth Barrett condemned her own failure of courage when she declined to write a poem supporting popular agitation against tariffs on grain because her father and brothers objected, and after her marriage she tried to live up to Godiva's example. She borrowed the image from Harriet Martineau, whose eagerness to make known the beneficent powers of mesmerism led to public discussion of her uterine tumor that mesmerism, she claimed, had cured; sexual display by words alone could hardly go farther. When Elizabeth Barrett expressed sympathy, Martineau replied,

> I took my part deliberately, — *knowing privacy to be impossible*, & making up my mind to *entail* publicity as the only course faithful to truth & human welfare. I cannot tell you how the thought of *Godiva* has sustained and inspired me.

Years later Martineau lent her name to the campaign against the Contagious Diseases Act, which enforced examination for venereal disease of women suspected of prostitution, and when she was told "that American ladies were shocked to think of such personal exposure" as a campaign on this subject entailed, she replied, "English ladies think of the Lady Godiva!" Elsewhere she invoked the example of "that representative Englishwoman, Godiva of blessed memory."[2] In Godiva, a woman writer's virtue is one with transgressive power.

The best-known nineteenth-century version of the legend is Tennyson's 1842 poem "Godiva," which resonates closely with women's use of it as an image of their boldness and their social goals in writing. Tennyson's heroine exposes herself to be seen after sending word to the people to ensure that no one will look: the only offender is Peeping Tom, whose eyes shrivel and drop out before they see her and of whose presence and punishment she is unaware. She is protected by her virtue—naked, Tennyson twice remarks, she is "clothed on with chastity" (53, 65)—and by "the Powers, who wait / On noble deeds" (71-72) and the people's grateful love. Her actual ordeal takes place in her imagination, which transforms the familiar city into a surreal world alive with inhuman observers, and through this imaginative experience she achieves two apparently contradictory goals: social amelioration and personal fame. "[S]he took the tax away," Tennyson concludes, "And built herself an everlasting name" (78-79).

Women writers often figure imagining, writing, and publishing as a kind of solitary travel, like Godiva's ride through the streets of Coventry, into a new realm of experience, an imaginatively transformed world. The heroines of Charlotte Brontë's, Gaskell's, and Eliot's first published novels, *Jane Eyre*, *Mary Barton*, and *Adam Bede*—the books that made them famous—and of *Villette*, which incorporates Brontë's actual experience of fame, undertake journeys that expose them to insult and contempt and culminate in a trial or other scene of self-display. And each emerges, like Godiva, with her virtue intact and acknowledged. Jane Eyre, penniless and friendless, blindly flees Rochester's proposal that she become his mistress. Lucy Snowe in *Villette* seeks her fortune abroad in almost the same condition. Mary Barton rushes from Manchester to Liverpool to prevent the man she loves from being convicted of murder. Dinah Morris is an itinerant preacher, and her fallen cousin Hetty Sorrel roams the countryside seeking escape from shame. These journeys mark transitions to utterly unfamiliar worlds where old constraints dissolve and new possibilities, both horrific and glorious, both desired and feared, take form. Jane Eyre sleeps in a field, alone with nature. Lucy Snowe finds the city of Villette utterly foreign and mostly repulsive, but her sojourn there lets her imagination and desire flourish. Mary Barton's increasingly hallucinatory chase includes her first train ride, her first sight of a seaport, and a trip out to sea in a small boat. Dinah leaves industrialized, impoverished Stoniton to preach and find love in Edenic rural Hayslope, and illegitimate pregnancy impels Hetty out of Hayslope through increasingly alien and hostile territory to the Stoniton gaol. And they all move toward climaxes of self-exposure. Jane humiliates herself by begging from strangers;

on her first night abroad Lucy is rudely followed by men who later reappear for a kind of mock trial of her abilities; Mary reveals her amatory secrets in a crowded courtroom; and Dinah and Hetty are carried through crowded streets in a prison-cart to the place of public execution.[3]

The paradigm of these experiences can be found in Charlotte Brontë's visions of Angria, in which self-exposure comes into question even though—or perhaps because—she seems deliberately to preclude it. She watches her characters, but they do not see her, and until almost the very end of the Angrian saga she created no characters who in any obvious way resemble herself. "I know nothing of people of rank and distinction" (she writes in the Roe Head journal), "yet there they are before me; in throngs, in crowds they come, they go, they speak, they beckon."[4] The Angrians, of whom Branwell was co-creator, seemed to have an existence coextensive with her own and beyond her control. She writes in her journal: "I wonder if Branwell has really killed the Duchess. Is she dead? Is she buried is she alone in the cold earth on this dreary night? . . . I hope she's alive."[5] But since the duchess inhabits the same time and place ("this dreary night") as Charlotte Brontë, the separation between Angria and England, at any rate, is not absolute. The fiction of her characters' independent reality, like her own invisibility in their world, implicitly asserts that they are not expressions of herself—an assertion that is especially necessary because many of her visions (which generally occur in solitude, frequently in or on her bed) are amoral and profoundly erotic. But her hero Zamorna is an object not only of vision but of desire, and he is also another self. And since her visions are material for writing, even if not for publication, they inevitably imply an audience. Her Angrian stories always assume a reader, and the concept of audience is literalized when, writing in the schoolroom at Roe Head with her eyes shut, she describes herself surrounded by "staring, gaping" onlookers who see not her visions but herself, and whom she detests ("stupidity the atmosphere, school-books the employment, asses the society!").[6] Imagining, she sees; writing, she presents herself to be seen—but only because she cannot help it.

The first-person narrators of Brontë's *The Professor*, *Jane Eyre*, and *Villette*, similarly, are conceived as both subjects and objects of vision. They travel to places which in *Jane Eyre* and *The Professor* are ostensibly in England but much resemble Angria, Mr. Rochester being a quasi-domesticated Zamorna and his imprisoned wife and beautiful, haughty Blanche Ingram quintessentially Angrian characters. All three protagonists, moreover, commence their voyages twice (William Crimsworth from school and his brother's business, Jane Eyre from Gateshead and Lowood, Lucy Snowe from Mrs. Bretton's and Miss Marchmont's houses), each time wanting to go and yet waiting for external impulsion, reflecting the doubling of desire and innocence, will and involuntary inspiration, action and passivity, with which Brontë, like Gaskell and Eliot, describes her own imaginative ventures.

When Jane Eyre goes to Lowood she is called a liar and "exposed to general

view on a pedestal of infamy" (99) for having threatened to tell the truth about
her aunt's mistreatment of her—to publish, so to speak, what she has seen.
Later, at Thornfield, like Brontë summoning visions of Angria, she would

> allow my mind's eye to dwell on whatever bright visions rose before it—and, cer-
> tainly, they were many and glowing; to let my heart be heaved by the exultant
> movement, which, while it swelled it in trouble, expanded it with life; and, best of
> all, to open my inward ear to a tale that was never ended—a tale my imagination
> created, and narrated continuously; quickened with all of incident, life, fire, feel-
> ing, that I desired and had not in my actual existence. (141)

But when "incident, life, fire, feeling"—all the melodrama concerning Rochester's mad wife and his proposal that Jane become his mistress—do erupt into
her "actual existence," she runs away. In her flight she becomes agonizingly
"conscious of an aspect in the last degree ghastly, wild, and weather-beaten"
(362), and of arousing aversion and scorn in the people she speaks to. As at
Lowood, however, her virtue is soon recognized. The pattern of a journey into
the unknown, with exposure sometimes to nature's harshness (the girls at
Lowood are racked by cold and hunger, and when Jane flees Thornfield she
sleeps outdoors and almost starves) and always to social scorn—that is, to a
situation in which the heroine's body is weak and vulnerable, not under her
control—followed by her triumphant vindication, is perhaps the central paradigm of the Victorian woman writer's sense of her own experience.

For Brontë this paradigm of fear and triumph was enacted in reality when
she published *Jane Eyre* and became the object of excited scrutiny. The distinction between creator and creation all but vanished under the reviewers' assumption that effective writing and convincing characters come only from personal experience. "The characters are too life-like to be the mere creations of
fancy," wrote George Henry Lewes (the future guide and guardian of George
Eliot's career) in a review of *Jane Eyre,* and in another review of the same novel
he said, "the authoress is unquestionably setting forth her own experience.
This gives the book its charm." Most Victorian reviewers, moreover, assessed
novels in terms of how much the characters attracted them. There was dis-
agreement about Jane Eyre: one reviewer declared that she would not arouse
his own passion, but others said they loved her. A reviewer of *Villette* complained: "Nor can we, with every desire to do so, fall in love with the heroine
herself." Since the author is assumed to be one with her heroine, she seems herself to be courting admiration, soliciting love.

Like Jane Eyre, Brontë was accused of being a liar and an ingrate, and her
novels evoked accusations that she and her characters were coarse, impure, and
unladylike. From the powerful expression of sexual passion ("The love-scenes
glow with a fire as fierce as that of Sappho, and somewhat more fuliginous") it
was inferred that the writer, if a woman, was in Elizabeth Rigby's memorably
vicious words "one who has, for some sufficient reason, long forfeited the so-

ciety of her own sex." Like the women Anna Jameson described, she seemed to
have solicited love by courting fame. Her pseudonym ("Currer Bell") instead of
shielding her offered an invitation to speculate on the author's identity, especially her gender, and gave an additional justification for the highly sexualized
cast of public scrutiny and judgment.[7]

Her experience was not unlike Byron's as described in a review the Brontë
children would have read in *Blackwood's* in 1825:

> We tell [the poet] . . . that the great and distinguishing merit of his poetry is the
> intense truth with which that poetry expresses his own personal feelings. — We
> encourage him in every possible way to dissect his own heart for our entertain-
> ment . . . to plunge into the darkest depths of self-knowledge, to madden his brain
> with eternal self-scrutinies . . . and the moment that, by habits of . . . our own
> encouraging and confirming, he is carried one single step beyond what we happen
> to approve of, we turn round with all the bitterness of spleen, and reproach him
> with the unmanliness of entertaining the public with his feelings in regard to his
> separation from his wife. . . . The public had forced him into the habits of famil-
> iarity, and they received his confidence with nothing but anger and scorn.[8]

Here too Byron was an example and a warning.

When Brontë ventured forth to London as an acknowledged author she was
stared at, gossiped about, referred to as "Jane Eyre" — the same name standing for
book, character, and author — and found morally superior to her heroines but sexually unattractive. Thackeray, the contemporary writer whose works she most
admired — although without entirely approving of them — and who of all people
should have known better, read her novels as transparent screens for desire.

> It amuses me to read [in *Villette*] the author's naive confession of being in love
> with 2 men at the same time; and her readiness to fall in love at any time. The
> poor little woman of genius! the fiery little eager brave tremulous homely-faced
> creature! I can read a great deal of her life as I fancy in her book, and see that
> rather than have fame, rather than any other earthly good or mayhap heavenly
> one she wants some Tomkins or another to love her and be in love with. But you
> see she is a little bit of a creature without a penny worth of good looks . . . a ge-
> nius, a noble heart longing to mate itself and destined to wither away into old
> maidenhood with no chance to fulfil the burning desire.

"Not that I should say burning," he adds; "les demoiselles ne brûlent pas."[9] As
a novelist she was at least his equal, but masculine condescension allows him to
strip her of art, dignity, and even the pleasures of success. Her shyness of lion-
izing strangers reflects her terror as a woman of the judgment that as an author
she fearlessly invoked. But admiration came too, of course, once even in a kind
of public apotheosis that could serve as the climax of a woman writer's fiction.
In one of her rare appearances in public, at a lecture in London, the audience
having learned of her presence lined the aisle at the end to watch her trembling
departure; the outshone lecturer, one is pleased to note, was Thackeray.[10] Hu-

miliation and triumph inextricably mingled in Brontë's experience of fame, and both were painful.

Her next novel after *Jane Eyre, Shirley*, distances the author from her characters by returning to the third-person narrative mode of the Angrian tales, but it also evoked accusations of coarseness, especially in regard to the heroines' readiness to feel unsolicited love. *Villette* uses first-person narrative again, and the plot incorporates Brontë's experience of imaginative creation as movement from a hidden existence at home to public exposure in a strange land. Lucy Snowe describes her childhood through observations of people who hardly bother to look at her, and she not only conceals feelings and events from the reader but is sometimes deliberately deceptive; both as character and as narrator she hides her own life, making reticence and self-revelation explicit issues in the novel. Having decided to leave England for Labassecour (that is, Belgium), she summons a panorama of the world that recalls Brontë's visions of Angria:

> In my reverie, methought I saw the continent of Europe, like a wide dream-land, far away. Sunshine lay on it, making the long coast one line of gold; tiniest tracery of clustered town and snow-gleaming tower, of woods deep-massed, of heights serrated, of smooth pasturage and veiny stream, embossed the metal-bright prospect. (117)

Like most of the visions recorded in Brontë's Roe Head diary, Lucy's ends with a nasty collapse into reality: interrupted by a pupil at school when she was starting to record her vision, Brontë had written, "I thought I should have vomited,"[11] and Lucy succumbs to sea sickness.

The first effect of Lucy's journey is to make her visible. When John Graham, a revenant from her life in England, appears in Labassecour he notices her no more than the furniture (162) and totally misapprehends her: "he did not read my eyes, or face, or gestures" (404). But Labassecourians greet her with intent and usually erotic scrutiny, from the rudeness of men who follow her in the streets and the jealous surveillance of Madame Beck, director of the school she teaches in, to the pedagogical-amatory inquisitions of M. Paul; and she tells us more than before (though never all) about herself. Summoned by Madame Beck to read Lucy's countenance, M. Paul "fixed on me his spectacles," his expression "seem[ing] to say that he meant to see through me, and that a veil would be no veil for him" (128); and indeed he detects and arouses her hidden passions. Her venture into the world exposes her to scrutiny she both fears and desires; within this novel as in the publication of novels, to court observation is to court desire. The tension amounting almost to terror that the link between art, observation, and desire arouses in Lucy is enacted in three set-pieces: Lucy's participation in a school play, the performance of the great actress Vashti, and M. Paul's attempt to display Lucy's intellectual accomplishments to his friends.

M. Paul forces Lucy to act in the play despite her terror of "public display" (203). He locks her in the attic, where "Perfectly secure from human audience"

(204) she enjoys learning her part. She costumes herself (as the Brontë sisters did with the ambiguous pseudonyms Acton, Currer, and Ellis Bell) in a gender compromise: male above the waist, female below. Once actually on stage, she throws herself zestfully into her role and uses it to express feelings too complex and dangerous to be otherwise acknowledged. Afterward she resolves never to act again, precisely because she had enjoyed it so much: "A keen relish for dramatic expression had revealed itself as part of my nature; to cherish and exercise this new-found faculty might gift me with a world of delight, but it would not do for a mere looker-on at life." The pleasure she renounces is like the novelist's own: Brontë herself always cared more about character than about plot, and her first-person narratives were a form of "dramatic expression." And so, like Brontë watching Angrian revels, Lucy withdraws "to a quiet nook, whence unobserved I could observe—the ball, its splendours and its pleasures passed before me as a spectacle" (211).

Lucy's visit to the theater with John Bretton repeats this episode in a deeper tone. The great actress Vashti transcends androgyny ("something neither of woman nor of man: in each of her eyes sat a devil" [339]) as much as she transcends the frivolous emotions of the school play. She is "Hate and Murder and Madness incarnate" (339), angel and demon, filled with "unholy force" (340). But John Bretton is oblivious to Vashti's power, unmoved by her agony. He admires women who are "bright, soft, sweet" (341); "for what belonged to storm, what was wild and intense, dangerous, sudden, and flaming, he had no sympathy" (341). He "judged her as a woman, not an artist: it was a branding judgment" (342)—a judgment marked (branded), as it were, on her exposed body. Artistic expression being once again forbidden, Lucy concludes that she must lock up her emotions and herself (348) even though she is then like a prisoner who goes "mad from solitary confinement" (356).

But M. Paul will not allow this. Himself a happy and unabashed performer on all available platforms, he recognizes her repressed ambition and urges her to display her imaginative power by publicly improvising a composition in French. She refuses on the grounds that she is "in public . . . by nature a cypher" (445) and that the "Creative Impulse" cannot be summoned on demand. That "Impulse" is strongly gendered: "the most intractable, the most capricious, the most maddening of masters (him before me always excepted)" (445)—which is all the more reason for not wrestling with it in public. So M. Paul takes her by surprise, summoning her to the presence of "two fine, braided, moustachioed, sneering personages" (493) and demanding that she answer their questions. "Here was the show-trial, so long evaded" (492), the schoolroom equivalent of the trials in *Mary Barton* and *Adam Bede*. She is obstinately silent: "I either *could* not, or *would* not speak—I am not sure which" (493); but unwilling tears express her rage: "it *was* emotion, and I would rather have been scourged, than betrayed it" (494). Like the hysterical women treated by Freud, her body speaks what she refuses to give voice to. The sexual nature of this exposure is underlined by her realization that the grossly male beholders "looking out of the forest of long hair, moustache, and whisker" (495) are the same who insolently accosted her on her first night in Labassecour. Like Elizabeth Barrett and Harriet Martineau when they thought of Godiva, however, Lucy finds strength in her vulnerability: unable to speak, she can write. She dashes off an essay describing a crude, lawless female figure — "a red, random beldame with arms akimbo" (495) — as the punitive, parodic emblem of human justice. The pain of public exposure issues in writing that outfaces hostile eyes; like Peeping Tom, the men are punished for looking at her.

But although Godiva represented intense and apocalyptic moments of the woman writer's experience, Brontë like other Victorian writers, both male and female, fought against the prevalent critical notion that one's works did or should simply reveal one's naked self. Against Lewes's injunction to keep to her own experience, she objected: "is not the real experience of each individual very limited? . . . [I]magination is a strong, restless faculty, which claims to be heard and exercised."[12] *Villette*, however, is the story of a woman whose real experience consists almost entirely of deprivation and loneliness and whose imagination erupts in hallucinatory terror as well as dreams of impossible bliss, and its open-endedness — does M. Paul come back and marry her, or does he die at sea? — leaves the question open as to whether imagination or reality rules the novel's world.

Gaskell's *Life of Charlotte Brontë*, the greatest biography of the nineteenth century and the work that did the most to establish the ideal picture of a Victorian woman writer, presents for judgment the woman rather than the books. "I find that some are apt to imagine, from the extraordinary power with which she represented the passion of love in her novels," Gaskell says, "that she herself was easily susceptible of it,"[13] and she set herself the task of erasing this misconception. She excuses Brontë's "coarseness" on grounds of ignorance, blaming Branwell and the rough manners of Yorkshire for what seemed excessive in Brontë's feelings or unladylike in her books. Setting out to win Brontë her readers' love, Gaskell deflects attention from her books onto the pathos of her deprived and sacrificial life, her womanly virtues, and her feminine charm. She conceals evidence that might repel affection, such as Brontë's unrequited passion for her Brussels schoolmaster (the model for M. Paul), details about the wild imagination revealed in her juvenilia, her coarse complexion, and her missing teeth. Gaskell's biography brought Brontë a triumphant posthumous vindication, but she vindicated the woman by concealing most of the qualities that made her a writer. Like *Villette*, *The Life of Charlotte Brontë* performs an intricate dance of revelation and concealment.

Gaskell herself had been deeply wounded by the censure of friends, acquaintances, and some reviewers that accompanied the otherwise gratifying success of her first novel, *Mary Barton*, and fell with still greater force on *Ruth*, which sympathetically portrays the mother of an illegitimate child. *Mary Barton* was considered unfair to industrialists, and both novels were daringly open and sympathetic in their portrayal of illicit sexuality. But Gaskell was a pretty, charming, sociable, thoroughly respectable woman with a husband and children to prove her womanliness (even now, one calls her "Mrs. Gaskell"), and was therefore less vulnerable than most women writers to sexual shame. Her novels, moreover, would have been hard to read as autobiographical: no one could have mistaken the author for Mary Barton or Ruth, poor young working girls.[14] Still, she said things about class, economics, the social structure, and especially sex that outraged many people and exposed her even to herself in a strange new light. "I think I must be an improper woman without knowing it, I do so manage to shock people." She felt in her own body—literally, as fever and "a quiver of pain"—the "painful & stinging" responses to *Ruth*, which made her feel like "St Sebastian tied to a tree to be shot at with arrows": Sebastian, the saint depicted in paintings as naked or nearly so, a male Godiva. As with the writers who thought of Godiva, however, her expressions of distress display some self-satisfaction (it's rather grand, after all, to be a handsome young martyr); and like Lucy Snowe writing about beldame Justice she was bolder as a novelist than as her ordinary self. "Do you think I cd say or write in a letter (except one that I was sure wd be regarded as private by some dear friend) what I have said both in M[ary] B[arton] & Ruth? It may seem strange & I can't myself account for it,—but it *is* so."[15]

The plot of *Mary Barton* enacts Gaskell's sense of daring and danger as she embarked on a novelist's career of saying the unsayable. In the latter part of the book Mary frantically travels from Manchester to Liverpool to find an essential witness for the trial of Jem, who has been accused of a murder actually committed by Mary's father, and she herself testifies at the trial. This episode has seemed to many critics an evasion of the novel's political concerns, an irrelevant divagation into the threadbare clichés of romance. The melodramatic last-minute rescue—the crucial witness, having been taken off an outbound ship, leaps into the courtroom exactly in the nick of time—seems a particularly egregious lapse from seriousness. But in this episode Gaskell works out the issues involved, not in the industrial politics that are the novel's main subject matter, but in writing the novel itself. Mary's journey, like those of Brontë's heroines, is both desired (she wants to save Jem) and involuntary (she goes because someone must and no one else can), and exposes her to insult and doubts of her virtue. The culmination of her journey, moreover, is her public confession that she loves Jem. Having refused him because she did not know her own feelings, she had been restrained by the demands of maidenly modesty—demands insisted on by characters and narrator in defiance of all common sense—from telling him she had changed her mind; but on the witness stand she is forced to expose her erotic history: her secret flirtation with rich Harry Carson, the murdered man, and her love for Jem.

She does this willingly but at first almost unconsciously. In public situations as in sexual ones, a Victorian woman's virtue is marked by her unself-consciousness, her unawareness of her sexual body. Before being called to testify Mary is almost in a trance, sitting motionless for almost two hours and called by the touch of the court officer as if by a mesmerist: "She started up in an instant, and followed him with a kind of rushing rapid motion into the court, into the witness box" (388). Looking out at the spectators, she sees only the judge and Jem; but everyone sees her:

> The mellow sunshine streamed down that high window on her head, and fell on the rich treasure of her golden hair, stuffed away in masses under her little bonnet-cap; and in those warm beams the motes kept dancing up and down. . . . Many who were looking for mere flesh and blood beauty, mere colouring, were disappointed: for her face was deadly white, and almost set in its expression, while a mournful bewildered soul looked out of the depths of those soft, deep, grey eyes. But, others recognized a higher and stranger kind of beauty. (389)

She is unconscious of her bodily beauty, which is now purified and sanctified by nature, although she had known it well enough when it fueled her dreams of a rich marriage. But when she becomes aware of the hundreds of onlookers, "Her face flash[es] scarlet, and then paler than before" (389). For the audience she is a notorious young woman for whom a rejected lover is accused of murdering his apparently successful rival, and when the prosecutor asks her sneeringly which man she preferred her body acknowledges by blushing—always the sign in Gaskell and Eliot of sexual awareness—what her words confess. "She covered her face with her hands, to hide the burning scarlet blushes, which even dyed her fingers" (391). After she testifies, the blush becomes a deadly fever—she is "so hot, and first white and then red" (392)—a delirious state in which the danger is both that she will die and that she will speak.

The plot gives a reason for this—she knows her father is the murderer, and her illness is induced partly by the strain of suppressing that secret—but the logic of narrative sequence suggests that having once lost control of body and speech, she might never regain it. She might say anything. After her testimony she is "flushed and anxious, . . . moving her lips incessantly, as if eagerly talking" (394), terrified that she will go mad and tell the truth about her father, until she collapses in convulsions. "[H]er poor brain had lost all guiding and controlling power over her words" (402). In her ensuing delirium she does indeed reveal the secret, although only to Jem, who already knows it, and to those who don't understand. The coercion, the prurient crowd, the loss of control over language, the half-voluntary revelation of feelings she has longed to express, and the terror of a further and much worse revelation prefigure Lucy Snowe.[16]

Mary's erotic secret is published in the newspapers. "You can't hide it now, Mary, for it's all in print" (426). Whereas Lucy knows perfectly well that she both wants and fears to perform in public, Gaskell guards her heroine from censure by insisting that Mary detests what others might enjoy: her workmates are "almost jealous of the fame that Mary had obtained; to herself, such miserable notoriety" (426). Mary's performance and publication are redeemed by being involuntary: she is impelled by moral duty and civil authority, barely conscious of her situation or herself, and only intermittently in control. Her enforced publication recalls Gaskell's account of how she herself began to write, impelled by her child's death and her husband's authority, justified by the wish to help others. Gaskell first conceived *Mary Barton*, she said, entirely in terms of John Barton, Mary's father,[17] who carries the weight of parental bereavement and social protest. Mary's tale, especially in the second part of the book, adds to the novel as originally conceived a representation of Gaskell's feelings about writing it.[18]

When George Eliot published her first novel, *Adam Bede*, in 1859, she had witnessed the reception of Brontë's novels and *Mary Barton*. She had more to fear than Brontë and Gaskell did, since her life, unlike theirs, was not fit for public scrutiny. Much had happened since her youthful abjurations of ambition. She had left home to live and work in London; she had published a translation of Johann Strauss's *Life of Jesus*, a book generally considered blasphemous and outrageous; and she was openly living with a married man, George Henry Lewes, the very person who had lectured Charlotte Brontë on the necessity of writing only from experience. She could expect much worse treatment than Brontë or Gaskell if her authorship became known. So it is not surprising that through its female protagonists *Adam Bede* explores the dangers of public exposure. As an itinerant Methodist preacher, Dinah Morris has a public career that is acceptable—to the narrator, to characters whose judgment matters (with the significant eventual exception of Dinah's husband, the eponymous hero), and presumably to readers—because its motive is purely religious and sexuality is repeatedly and emphatically put out of question. Such a career could be all the more safely tolerated because it was no longer possible, the Methodists having banned women from preaching in 1803; at the end of the novel Dinah has retired. We first hear of Dinah through an argument between two young men about whether she should be thought of as a "prophetess" or just "a uncommon pretty young woman" (52). When we first see her, she climbs up on a cart to be seen and to preach, and the narrator insists on her "total absence of self-consciousness" (66) and the sexlessness both of her appearance and of the response she inspires. In this novel as in *Mary Barton*, blushing is the body's way of asserting its presence to a modest consciousness, and Dinah does not blush until much later in the story. And yet there is a telling ambiguity right from the start.

> [Dinah is asked,] "And you never feel any embarrassment from the sense of your youth—that you are a lovely young woman on whom men's eyes are fixed?"
>
> "No, I've no room for such feelings, and I don't believe the people ever take notice about that. I think, sir, when God makes his presence felt through us, we are like the burning bush; Moses never took any heed what sort of bush it was—he only saw the brightness of the Lord." (136)

The burning bush is a transparent vessel through which Moses sees divine glory, but for the "prophetess" it is her own body, set on display and "burning" as if with a blush.[19]

Like Lucy Snowe and Mary Barton, Dinah speaks in public only under compulsion, which in her case is a divine vocation. Like Mary, she is moved by a selfless desire to help others and her words come without volition. She speaks simply, "directly from her own emotions" (72), looking at her hearers rather than thinking of herself, describing the visions present to her own eye. Her imagination, like Brontë's seeing Angria, summons scenes in which she herself does not appear, in significant contrast to the daydreams Eliot had extravagantly deplored in which she was herself "chief actress."[20] Like Brontë's Vashti, however, she exerts compulsion over susceptible hearers: the sophisticated traveler through whose eyes we initially see her is "chained to the spot against his will by the charm of Dinah's mellow treble tones" (71). Like Vashti's and Mary's her power comes from revealing profound feeling; the traveler follows her sermon "as if it had been the development of a drama — for there is this sort of fascination in all sincere unpremeditated eloquence, which opens to one the inward drama of the speaker's emotions" (76). Like Gaskell and unlike Brontë, however, Eliot finds it necessary to insist, over and over, that the display is indeed sincere and unpremeditated.

Unself-conscious sincerity is an ideal that during the Victorian period is applied equally to women and to art, and thus exerts a doubled force on women writers. In "Characteristics," an essay published in 1831 that introduces one of the master-themes of the century, Thomas Carlyle begins:

> The healthy know not of their health, but only the sick: this is the Physician's Aphorism; and applicable in a far wider sense than he gives it. We may say, it holds no less in moral, intellectual, political, poetical, than in merely corporeal therapeutics; that whatever, or in what shape soever, powers of the sort which can be named *vital* are at work, herein lies the test of their working right or working wrong.
>
> In the Body, for example, as all doctors are agreed, the first condition of complete health is, that each organ perform its function unconsciously, unheeded; let but any organ announce its separate existence, were it even boastfully, and for pleasure, not for pain, then already has one of those unfortunate "false centres of sensibility" established itself, already is derangement there.[21]

The same rule applies to female virtue.

Unself-consciousness, however, cannot be consciously striven for: setting it as a goal makes its attainment impossible. Male writers of the period made good artistic use of this paradox even while they deplored it. We see it in Carlyle's own self-consciously convoluted prose, for instance, or Arthur Hugh Clough's self-reflexive irony, or Browning's dramatic monologuists when they try to prove themselves sincere. Matthew Arnold deplored such "derangement" in literature, calling it "the dialogue of the mind with itself."[22] But for a

Victorian woman self-consciousness comes down in the end to consciousness not of her mind but of her body. She cannot exploit the paradox as men do, since acknowledging its existence would mean acknowledging her own sexuality, which a modest woman—by definition—never does.

Late in the century Augusta Webster describes women's dilemma in everyday terms:

> People think women who do not want to marry unfeminine: people think women who do want to marry immodest: people combine both opinions by regarding it as unfeminine for women not to look forward longingly to wifehood as the hope and purpose of their lives, and ridiculing or contemning any individual woman . . . whom they may suspect of entertaining such a longing. . . . [Marriageable women] must wish and not wish; they must by no means give, they must certainly not withhold, encouragement; they must not let a gentleman who is paying attention think them waiting for his offer, they must not let him think they would admit the careless homages of a flirtation and are not waiting for his offer; they must not be frank, they must not be coy; . . . so it goes on, each precept cancelling another, and most of them negative. How are the girls to get themselves married and escape censure in the process?

If a girl gets "'talked about,' as the phrase is," Webster adds, her chances are over. Novelists seeking to get themselves published and escape censure have similar problems.[23]

Self-consciousness implies the existence of two selves, one of them the object of the other's awareness. In order to influence others—as Dinah does, as novelists want to—a woman needs, according to the conduct book *Woman's Mission*, which Eliot had much admired when she was younger, "consistency, simplicity, benevolence, or love": "consistency of character . . . consistency of action with principle, of manner with thought, of *self* with *self*."[24] Women's unique power, books like *Woman's Mission* insisted, was exerted through influence, and stemmed from wholeness of character. Tom in *The Mill on the Floss*, whose masculine hardness is impervious to his sister's influence, complains: "I can't trust you, Maggie. There is no consistency in you" (445). Self-division is a persistent theme in *The Mill on the Floss*, which was written right after *Adam Bede*. Maggie's doubleness of character, which contrasts sharply with Dinah's tenuously held simplicity, is conceived partly in temporal terms. "The sense of contradiction with her past self in her moments of strength and clearness, came upon her like a pang of conscious degradation" (648). But doubleness is also bound up with the power of language. There are "dangerous moments," the narrator says, "when speech is at once sincere and deceptive— when feeling, rising high above its average depth, leaves flood-marks which are never reached again" (437)—a metaphor that points forward to the actual flood in which Maggie and Tom, united in feeling at last, drown. An essential part of Maggie's fatal superiority to Tom is her recognition that language is always multivalent: a word, she points out to him when he scorns her for not being allowed to study Latin, "may mean several things. Almost every word does" (214). Maggie's command of language carries with it her undoing as a woman.

The self-contradiction in the ideal of unself-consciousness explains, no doubt, why Eliot and Gaskell press it so often and so unconvincingly. It is a problem looming on the threshold of their careers that they can neither resolve nor let be. Mary Barton and Dinah affect audiences by means of artless spontaneity. Dinah is unaware of either her physical presence or the sources of her speech—she thinks she preaches by divine inspiration, but the divinity whose impulsion she relies on, the author makes clear, is the reflex of her own nature. Eliot herself wanted her books to do as much moral good as Dinah's preaching, and she often composed in a state of fervid self-forgetfulness; but her books were carefully researched and planned, and she did not believe in divine inspiration. The ideal of unself-conscious art was one of many inheritances from the Romantics that proved difficult for their successors to sustain, and it was especially difficult for women. Shelley in "To a Skylark" celebrated "unpremeditated art" (5) incarnate in the near-disembodiment of a bird; but nineteenth-century women found it impossible to define themselves as artists in disregard of their gendered bodies. And the identity behind the mask of "George Eliot" was not only incarnate and gendered, but scandalous.

And so Dinah has a shadow side, a dark double: her earthbound, trivialminded cousin, Hetty Sorrel, who is schematically presented as Dinah's opposite. Hetty gets pregnant and travels alone through the countryside, like Dinah but without Dinah's impunity, until she is arrested for killing her baby. Like Dinah, but without her self-forgetfulness, she becomes the object of formal public scrutiny. On trial and in prison, she refuses to speak, but her body confesses: although she is not innocent enough for Mary Barton's modest blushes, she is convicted by medical evidence that she has borne a child. She is the polar opposite of Dinah, whose speech is open, her body silent. Hetty's character is framed in terms of self-display: vain and ambitious, she had courted observation ("a hidden life . . . would have had no delights for her" [417-18]), and like Mary Barton she fell in love with a vision of social advancement. The other side of her vanity is her terror of shame: "she would have borne anything rather than be laughed at, or pointed at with any other feeling than admiration" (244). Dinah terrifies her into confession by telling her that she is being watched by God, "who has known every thought you have had—has seen where you went, where you lay down and rose up again, and all the deeds you have tried to hide in darkness" (495). For the woman who wants to be seen and admired, God's surveillance is a kind of revelation of secrets, exposure to shame.

The climactic encounter between Dinah and Hetty was the origin of *Adam Bede*, the point toward which the novel moved. It was based on a true story.

The germ of "Adam Bede" was an anecdote told me by my Methodist Aunt Samuel. . . . We were sitting together one afternoon during her visit to me . . . when it occurred to her to tell me how she had visited a condemned criminal, a very ignorant girl who had murdered her child and refused to confess—how she had stayed with her praying, through the night and how the poor creature at last broke out into tears, and confessed her crime. My Aunt afterwards went with her in the cart to the place of execution, and she described to me the great respect with which this ministry of hers was regarded by the official people about the gaol. The story, told by my aunt with great feeling, affected me deeply, and I never lost the impression of that afternoon and our talk together. . . . I was very fond of [my aunt], and enjoyed the few weeks of her stay with me greatly. She was loving and kind to me, and I could talk to her about my inward life, which was closely shut up from those usually round me.[25]

This story was seminal both in its content and, more significantly, in its relevance to Eliot herself. Eliot's relation to her Aunt Samuel precisely parallels both the condemned girl's to Aunt Samuel and Hetty's to Dinah. Aunt Samuel is visiting Eliot, as she visited the girl in prison and as Dinah visits Hetty. It "occurred" to her to tell her niece the story, just as the right words to say to Hetty come to Dinah without conscious choice or volition. The "great feeling" of both speakers makes a deep and permanent impression on their hearers. Her aunt's love and kindness, like Dinah's to Hetty, enabled Eliot to talk about her inward life, which like Hetty's had been "closely shut up" from others, and no doubt she talked to her aunt about what she confessed to her in letters: her "besetting sin, which is an ever struggling ambition," and "that traitor within, the love of human praise."[26] In the "germ" of the book, then, Eliot took the role of Hetty: the woman whose love of praise led to public shame, who like Eliot herself was cut off from home and family by an illicit sexual liaison. Appropriately, Eliot's description of the physical manifestations of Hetty's disgrace—seduction, pregnancy, and childbirth—brought censure on the author herself,[27] although the book, which was at first assumed to have been written by a man, was very well received.

Still, Dinah is the novel's primary figure for Eliot's exploration of a writer's circumstances—she travels freely, preaches, has (so to speak) a career—and the respect Aunt Samuel inspired at the scene of shame is an essential part of the germinal tale: the equivalent of Jane Eyre's vindications, Lucy Snowe's sour triumphs, Mary Barton's acknowledged virtue. The culminating scene, which like Mary's appearance at Jem's trial necessitates the tawdry melodrama of a last-minute rescue, is Dinah and Hetty's joint appearance in public on the way to the place of execution. When we first saw Dinah, she mounted a cart to preach and pray, and she is praying again; but now Hetty is on the cart with her, the two women clinging together. Again, and with the same insistent repetition, Dinah is said to be "hardly conscious" of the "gazing crowd" that terrifies Hetty—not just a few villagers now, but a "waiting watching multitude"; Dinah "did not know that the crowd was silent, gazing at her with a sort of awe" (507). Hetty's searing apotheosis of shame is Dinah's unconscious glory: the worst debasement of female flesh (illicit sexuality, illegitimate pregnancy, infanticide, abject fear of death) paired with the triumph of pure spirituality. It is an apotheosis of opposites; but it is a joint apotheosis nonetheless.

In the last part of the novel, which like the trial episode in *Mary Barton* has seemed to many critics an unfortunate and irrelevant divagation from the main theme, qualities of the banished Hetty surface in Dinah. Adam had loved Hetty, but when Hetty is degraded and gone Dinah falls in love with him and he, eventually, with her. Like the Brontë heroines who shocked delicate-minded reviewers, Dinah falls in love first; and like Brontë's and Gaskell's heroines performing in public, and Gaskell writing her first novel, Eliot conceived this turn of the plot at the impulsion of male authority: "Dinah's ultimate relation to Adam was suggested by George . . . I accepted the idea [as one "accepts" a proposal of marriage] at once."[28]

Like Hetty's and Mary Barton's, Dinah's body confesses her secret: she blushes (521) and trembles (545). Long before Hetty's disgrace, when Adam looked at Dinah with a "concentrated, examining glance," she had "for the first time in her life, felt a painful self-consciousness. . . . A faint blush came, which deepened as she wondered at it" (162). This first awareness of her body is "painful," but she does not understand it. An odd little episode after Hetty is gone, however, suggests deeper feeling and fuller comprehension. At the Hall Farm (the home of Dinah's aunt and her family, where Hetty used to live), Dinah and Adam clasp hands in greeting. Adam, not yet awakened to love, seems unaware that he is holding her hand, but Dinah blushes. In the superficially inconsequent bit of family conversation that follows, one of the children remarks that "Dinah hasn't got a husband," while another amuses himself with his sister's doll, "turning Dolly's skirt over her bald head, and exhibiting her truncated body to the general scorn" (522). And Dinah keeps blushing; like Hetty, she suffers the crude exposure of female sexuality (or the place it would be if dolls had any) and the lack of a husband to justify what her body blazons forth. Dinah could travel freely, speak in public, enact her ambition, while awareness of self as desiring or arousing desire was displaced and reprehended in Hetty; but now Hetty is gone. Having acknowledged in herself the self-consciousness that Hetty embodied, and having married Hetty's lover, she soon stops preaching and stays at home.[29]

Eliot eventually dealt with the issue of authorial self-display by creating a narrator who is a genderless, bodiless seer, an invisible observer: what Mary Ann Evans turned herself into when she became "George Eliot." "The Lifted Veil" gives a nightmare version of such a transformation, the worst of both worlds: the narrator is a man cursed with the ability to read other people's minds, and what he sees in them is the contempt with which others see him. *Middlemarch* is its apotheosis, aligning the novelist's vision, austere and impersonal, with that of a scientist. Artistically this was a triumphantly successful strategy. Still, like Brontë the unobserved observer of Angria, Eliot knew that the writer cannot in the end separate herself from her fictions. The world will not let her: readers then and now, misogynist and feminist alike, look (as I am looking now) for the woman in the work.

According to Eliot's most famous image, moreover, the world is right. *Middlemarch* declares that the writer is merely, if arduously, tracing the web of relationships that constitutes all life, but it also tells us that the patterns we see in human affairs are produced by our own egotism.

> Your pier-glass or extensive surface of polished steel . . . will be minutely and multitudinously scratched in all directions; but place now against it a lighted candle as a centre of illumination, and lo! the scratches will seem to arrange themselves in a fine series of concentric circles round that little sun. It is demonstrable that the scratches are going everywhere impartially, and it is only your candle which produces the flattering illusion of a concentric arrangement, its light falling with an exclusive optical selection. These things are a parable. The scratches are events, and the candle is the egoism of any person now absent. (297)

A pier-glass is a mirror, in which we see — and show — ourselves.[30]

The narrator of *Adam Bede* defends her story-telling in a passage that joins mirrors and trials to suggest the combination of selflessness and compulsion that justifies the self-display of heroines:

> I aspire to give no more than a faithful account of men and things as they have mirrored themselves in my mind. The mirror is doubtless defective; the outlines will sometimes be disturbed; the reflection faint or confused; but I feel as much bound to tell you, as precisely as I can, what that reflection is, as if I were in the witness-box narrating my experience on oath. (221)

As images of the gaze turned outward and of involuntary speech, mirror and witness box align the narrator with Dinah, whose preaching shows others their vanity. Like Dinah, Eliot wants to mirror her audience to themselves so that they will be moved to radical self-transformation. Still, to *be* a mirror is to be looked at; and the witness box, for women writers, is the place where the secrets of the female body are exposed to view. For women who grew up in early and mid-nineteenth-century England, womanly decorum and artistic expression were ultimately irreconcilable; but for the greatest of them, the struggle for reconciliation gave their works a distinctive tension and a formidable energy. What may have inhibited other women from writing became for them, as for Godiva, a source of transformative power.

Except for Florence Nightingale and the queen, the most famous women in Victorian England were famous for being writers. With Nightingale, and perhaps a few actresses, they were the first women in British history to achieve great renown by their accomplishments rather than by birth, marriage, or scandal — a fact that does much to explain the initial dread of the pioneers. At the end of the century Margaret Oliphant, wryly conscious of her own obscurity despite a long and immensely prolific literary career, reflected on the Brontës:

> The effect produced upon the general mind by the appearance of Charlotte Brontë in literature, and afterwards by the record of her life when that was over, is one which it is nowadays somewhat difficult to understand. . . . No one else of the century, I think, has called forth this persevering and lasting homage. . . . No group of women, undistinguished by rank, unendowed by beauty, and known to but a limited circle of friends as unimportant as themselves have ever, I think, in the course of history—certainly never in this century—come to such universal recognition.[31]

Brontë's fame was unprecedented except by Byron's, and the story of her life, as told by Mrs. Gaskell and frequently retold since, was in its way as compelling as her books. The cast of supporting characters helped: Emily, whose genius appalled her contemporaries (including not just Gaskell but Charlotte herself); patient, sweet-natured Anne; Branwell, the flamboyantly self-destructive profligate; and the terrible old father who outlived all his children. The doom-laden family was fit for Greek tragedy, with the bleak Yorkshire moors in the background, genius standing in for noble birth, and the strange, grim natives of Yorkshire as a chorus. As with Byron, a kind of flickering double image forms in the minds of readers: Jane Eyre's suffering and triumph, Brontë's suffering, triumph, and tragedy. The unremitting deprivation, selflessness, and purity of the woman lovingly depicted by Gaskell counteracted the ferocity of desire and self-assertion in Brontë's novels, and what had been condemned as coarseness was reinterpreted as the innocent reflection of crude surroundings. And while Gaskell did not say it, readers could not help noticing that Brontë's sins against convention, like Byron's, were a kind of Promethean revolt against an oppressive society; the "furious love-making" in her novels, Mrs. Oliphant asserted in disgust, "was but a wild declaration of the 'Rights of Woman' in a new aspect."[32]

Part of Brontë's appeal to restless, aspiring young women must have been that she both depicted female ambition and embodied (at least as Gaskell described her) a guiltless success. When *Jane Eyre* was published she denied to her closest friend in England being the author, asserting that "The most profound obscurity is infinitely preferable to vulgar notoriety."[33] But the words barely conceal desire for what they forswear: "*even* a *profound* obscurity is better than *vulgar* notoriety." Samuel Johnson's remark that while marriage has many pains, celibacy has few pleasures, can be applied to Victorian women's feelings about fame. Even for Brontë the pains of notoriety were more than counterbalanced by its pleasures, although she was usually too sad or too shy fully to enjoy them. Her friend Mary Taylor told Mrs. Gaskell:

> Of course, artists and authors stood high with Charlotte, and the best thing after their works would have been their company. She used very inconsistently to rail at

money and money-getting, and then wish she was able to visit all the large towns in Europe, see all the sights, and know all the celebrities. This was her notion of literary fame—a passport to the society of clever people.[34]

Aside from financial independence and the satisfaction of having one's work recognized, successful publication brought women into contact with the great world and a broader circle of correspondents and friends, especially other famous women. Brilliant young men formed sustaining friendships at school and university that were augmented in literary London. But for brilliant women of the same social background, educated at home or in small provincial schools, restricted to whatever social circles their families happened to frequent, such friendships were generally initiated by publication and carried on largely in letters. They sent their first books to those whose books they admired, and good work received an eager welcome. Even Charlotte Brontë, whose brief years of fame were darkened by her sisters' deaths and whose shyness made visiting exquisitely painful, spent some of her happiest days at the homes of Gaskell and Martineau, and Gaskell's careful and loving biography is her tribute to their mutual affection.

Other writers profited still more from success. Gaskell was quiveringly sensitive to criticism, but she thoroughly enjoyed her friendships with distinguished men and women. And Eliot, who had most to fear from becoming known, may have gained the most too. Living with a man who couldn't marry her, disowned by her censorious brother and alienated from old friends, she could not expect to reenter respectable society. So she created a unique position for herself as wise woman, prophetess, and seer. *Middlemarch* ends with an elegiac tribute to those whose influence is "incalculably diffusive" but who never achieve a "great name on earth," and the very last words of the novel ring with pathos for those "who lived faithfully a hidden life, and rest in unvisited tombs" (896). This fate she avoided.

Poetry brought more prestige although usually less money than fiction did. The most dubious aspect of a woman writer's career, the implication that to publish was in effect to be looking for a lover, became part of Elizabeth Barrett's magically happy enactment of the paradigmatic Victorian myth. An invalid who hated meeting strangers, she corresponded with admirers of her work, and then one day she received a letter from Robert Browning that said, "I love your verses with all my heart, dear Miss Barrett . . . and I love you too."[35] An extremely popular minor poet, Jean Ingelow, wrote nicely to Henry Wadsworth Longfellow: "I always feel that the most valuable advantage which comes from authorship is its having brought me into communication with persons like yourself."[36] Ingelow was shy and reclusive but she visited the Tennysons and met some other women poets, including Rossetti. Rossetti had access to literary circles through her brothers and tended toward reclusiveness too, but she enjoyed meeting women poets and being admired by discriminating readers.

In fact fame proved no worse for women than for men. Tennyson retreated to the Isle of Wight to avoid literary tourists, but they came and stared in his windows. Dickens wore himself out in public readings to assure himself of his audiences' love. For the most eminent women writers, fame validated the virtues it seemed at first to imperil. They were subjected to bodily scrutiny, but admirers (like Mr. Rochester with Jane Eyre, and Mrs. Gaskell with Jane's creator) disregarded defects of form and saw only expressive eyes, a low and musical voice, and a pleasantly unselfconscious demeanor. If at first their writings seemed tainted with bodily presence, in the end the virtues of the writings were read back into their bodies. Those with less exalted reputations and more scandalous private lives, like Letitia Landon and the sensation novelist Mary Braddon, were less safe from scorn; but the demonstration that women of genius could achieve fame and escape its penalties—could even, in the case of Barrett Browning and Gaskell, be happy wives and mothers—was one of their most important gifts to the female literary tradition.

❧ ❧ ❧ *Part Two*

3. Entering the Literary Market

❦ ❦ ❦

The pleasures fame brought women writers show not only the gap between premonitory terror and a realized fact but also changes occurring in the literary world. It has been estimated that half the novels published in England in the eighteenth century were written by women, but the prestige of the genre was low, in large part because of its female associations. In the Victorian period, however, it became the dominant literary form. As the status of the novel rose, the status of women writers rose with it. Of the 878 novelists included in John Sutherland's *Stanford Companion to Victorian Fiction*, 312 are women, who published an average of 21 novels each, while 565 men published on average 17.7. And for the first time in the history of any literary genre women authors were a significant proportion of those most highly esteemed. The low prestige of novel writing allowed women to enter the field; later in the century fiction became defined as high art and women were pushed to the periphery.[1] But in the middle decades of the nineteenth century they flourished.

Women poets had also become more numerous during the eighteenth century, but poetry remained at the apex of the literary hierarchy and was wholly dominated by men. Still, change was beginning here too. The Romantic movement listened for new voices—the poor, the mad, children, women—although such voices found canonical utterance through male poets. In the nineteenth century women's devotional, didactic, and descriptive verse, lyric laments, poems for or about children or the poor, and quasi-novelistic narratives were published in vast quantities and often reviewed favorably if with considerable condescension. Amatory verse, however, especially with audible sexual overtones, was problematic, and anything political, apart from effusions of sympathy, was touchier still: Barrett Browning's sentimental verses about poverty-stricken children were admired, but her fierce incursions into politics provoked outrage. Drama had entered a long decline, so that the paucity of female playwrights did not materially affect the literary landscape. But a plenitude of periodicals and readers eager for edification produced an enormous demand for nonfictional prose, much of which women supplied. About 20 percent of published writers in the nineteenth century, it is estimated, were women.[2]

The shifting status of literary genres and the opening of new literary markets

were facilitated by an increase in the reading public, cheaper methods of printing, better transportation and communication, and new modes of distribution.
The spread of elementary education made basic literacy more common; Richard Altick estimates that by mid-century perhaps 60 percent of the adult population could read at least minimally, creating for the first time what might be
considered a mass literary audience.[3] Cheap newspapers catering to an interest
in politics spurred by agitation for Reform, cheap magazines, fiction sold by
the penny, and edifying materials distributed by religious and philanthropic
groups were available for the newly literate. Harriet Martineau's *Illustrations
of Political Economy*, published from 1832 to 1835 in monthly parts at a very
low price and designed to teach the working classes practical lessons about
such matters as trade, commerce, and banking, sold in 1834 at the rate of
10,000 a month.[4] Books, which were expensive, were available to a higher social class through the circulating libraries for a small annual fee, and also in
cheap reprints and in serial publication. The greatest single purchaser of new
books was Mudie's Circulating Library, begun in 1842 and surviving in diminished form into the next century, which exercised an influence on what was
published that authors and publishers resented but could not effectively resist.
Mudie's preference for three-volume novels (since each volume could be loaned
out separately) encouraged prolixity; and since his subscribers were mostly
families, the books he bought had to meet his standards for family reading. The
censorship exercised by Mudie and reinforced by many reviewers helped ensure
fiction's social respectability, if not its artistic quality.

There were also periodicals at all levels and for many audiences, intellectual
or frivolous: for men, women, children, or particular religious groups; dealing
with literature, art, politics, science, religion, travel, and many other subjects;
and publishing reviews, essays, poems, stories, and serialized novels. For many
women, journalism served as an entrance to a literary career or augmented income from poetry or fiction. All sorts of journals were happy to accept poems
from unknown writers, and Elizabeth Barrett and George Eliot first achieved
publication in this way—not very prestigious, but encouraging to the young.
The most prestigious journals that printed new literary works were edited by
men, including Dickens, Thackeray, and Trollope, but women could be editors
too, particularly of journals for women and children, or, like Geraldine Jewsbury, exercise similar power as publishers' readers. Mary Howitt's varied,
wide-ranging literary career, for instance, included *Howitt's Journal*, a joint
venture with her husband, and Eliza Cook, a poet, published *Eliza Cook's
Journal* from 1849 to 1854. Anonymous reviewing and the constant demand
for fiction and poetry to fill the journals created even more openings for
women. Before she became a novelist George Eliot regularly wrote reviews and
essays for the *Westminster Review* and served for a while as its *de facto*
editor—secretly, though, letting the publisher and official editor, John Chapman, take the credit, and without pay. It was hard but not impossible to make

a living writing nonfiction for periodicals, but at worst it was a kind of participation in the literary world.

In the nineteenth century many women became writers because there was nothing else for them to do. Many began writing in childhood, literary composition being one of the few amusements, like "castle building," as available to girls as to boys. And at mid-century there were very few ways for a middle-class woman to earn a living or enjoy the satisfactions of work outside her home or the unpaid, unprofessional rounds of church and charity. If she were talented and enterprising she might become an actress; but at a time when many people still disapproved even of attending the theater her family would almost certainly disapprove. She could be a governess or a teacher, with low status, few pleasures, and little financial reward. Lower still on the social and economic scale, she could be a seamstress or milliner, but would probably not earn enough to live on and might easily drop into the working class or the moral abyss of prostitution. Florence Nightingale was almost maddened by the uselessness of her life before she made herself a unique career as a hospital administrator and reformer and created nursing as a reputable occupation; but Nightingale's aristocratic family and friends were essential to her success, and she was never constrained by the need to earn money.

Writing, however, required no training or special skills. Georgiana Fullerton and Geraldine Jewsbury achieved print and popularity despite a shaky command even of English grammar. Augusta Webster, pointing out that an astonishingly large number of women with little talent or education wrote "light literature" successfully, suggests that their mental worlds had been so thoroughly formed by novel-reading that they were as much at home in the conventions of the novel as in their actual lives.[5] Writing did not require money or materials beyond the books and paper that would be available in most middle-class homes. Social connections were not necessary either, although having writers or publishers among one's friends and relations certainly helped. The fact that poetry was usually less remunerative than fiction meant that it did not imply humiliating financial need, and its generic prestige could educe family pride and encouraged precocious publication. Elizabeth Barrett's father and Christina Rossetti's grandfather had the girls' poems privately printed when Barrett was fourteen, Rossetti seventeen.

Male writers were afraid that the apparent predominance of women as producers and audience (a predominance much magnified in nervous imaginations) would feminize—that is, degrade—the profession of literature. Their fears were all the stronger because by mid-century literature already seemed to be in some alarming ways intrinsically feminine. Male superiority in poetry remained unchallenged, despite a few partial exceptions to the rule of female incapacity, but writing poetry seemed unpleasantly similar to women's work as the early Victorians, following the Romantics, defined it: apart from and opposed to the public world of business and power, trafficking only in the most delicate feelings and perceptions, speaking from the heart to touch the hearts of others. Critics liked simple, homely poetic themes and language and sincere, spontaneous expressions of feeling: the artless spontaneity Jameson's *Ennuyée* enacts, which was assumed to be natural to women. And insofar as prose fiction examined domestic matters and the inner life, it too was in the feminine domain.[6] The novel did not have a long male tradition, as poetry did, to ward off feminine intrusion. There were more women novelists than women poets, and they took indisputably higher rank and were harder to ignore or explain away.

It was taken for granted by writers, reviewers, and publishers that many, perhaps most, readers of novels were female.[7] Middle-class women, and especially young girls, were likely to be confined to home, with a lot of free time and little to fill it. Fiction concentrated on personal relationships and the minutiae of social life—the material of their own existences—while also allowing them a sense of experiencing a wider world. (French novels, being by English definition wicked and corrupting, were particularly rich in worldly knowledge, but relatively few girls had access to them.) A predominantly young and female audience was thought to require love stories, which almost every novelist duly provided. Whereas (presumably male) reviewers assessed the attractiveness of heroines, female readers were expected to fall in love with the hero, and a common objection to novel-reading was that it fueled erotic daydreams.

Such an audience was naturally the object of satire, especially by men. Within fiction itself the housemaid dreaming of love while reading cheap romances and the idle young lady lounging on a sofa devouring novels and chocolate are objects of contempt left over from the eighteenth century. Jane Austen mocked this habit of derision in *Northanger Abbey* without being able to laugh it away. Poets and their reviewers, in contrast, apparently assumed the existence of a fairly serious and intellectual male audience, with a substratum of sentimental female readers (best ignored) somewhere below. But the identification of poetry's readers with young women and aesthetic young men was becoming established in the general consciousness, comically exemplified by the effete poet and his chorus of female adorers in Gilbert and Sullivan's *Patience*.

The multisided threat of femininization in literature provoked a vigorous satiric counterattack in Thackeray's *Pendennis*, published just at mid-century. Arthur Pendennis (whose nickname, "Pen," is as appropriate as the combined first and last syllables of his surname) becomes a successful novelist after encountering and resisting various feminine corruptions of literature. First he is ensnared by a good-natured provincial actress whose only artistic gift is her ability to follow male direction. Later he attracts the affection of a nice but silly girl, a porter's daughter, who has "heated her little brain with novels, until her whole thoughts are about love and lovers, and she scarcely sees that she treads on a kitchen floor" (142). And he has both an object of infatuation and a parodic opposite in beautiful, wily Blanche Amory. Blanche's sexual corruption is demonstrated if not caused by the fact that she read all the novels of Balzac and George Sand before she was sixteen. She represents everything that is insincere, disreputable, and false about the feminine in literature: she is self-named, full of genteel pretensions but in fact a convict's daughter, given to uttering the highest sentiments for public effect while being unpleasant and spiteful at home. Worst of all, summing it all up, she is a genuinely sentimental poet. She "indeed loved poets and men of letters if she loved anything, and was sincerely an artist in feeling" (429).

Blanche's volume of (unpublished) verses in English and French, entitled "Mes Larmes," foreshadows the sentimental effusions of Mark Twain's Emmeline Graingerford.

> It appeared from these poems that the young creature had indeed suffered prodigiously. She was familiar with the idea of suicide. Death she repeatedly longed for. A faded rose inspired her with such grief that you would have thought she must die in pain of it. It was a wonder how a young creature should have suffered so much—should have found the means of getting at such an ocean of despair and passion (as a runaway boy who *will* get to sea), and having embarked on it, should survive it. What a talent she must have had for weeping to be able to pour out so many of "Mes Larmes"! (250)

Blanche embodies both the corruption and the absurdity of the feminized notion of poetry: that it should express deep (and mostly painful) feelings, that its greatest virtue is sincerity, and that it should emerge as a kind of involuntary effusion or indeed (her poems are tears, "Mes Larmes") bodily secretion. Thackeray mocks Blanche's writing in precisely the terms women most feared: as an expression of vanity, a manifestation of an ambition that destroys filial affection and parental authority (her intellectual superiority allows her to terrorize her stepfather and bully her good-natured, vulgar mother), and a tool of seduction.

Pen likes Blanche's verses—he "thought them very well for a lady" (250)—and composes his own in reply, but he soon outgrows both poetry and Blanche and becomes a successful novelist. The most admirable man in the book, however, is George Warrington, who is entirely cut off from the feminine element in literature and indeed from women, since after being seduced into an unfortunate early marriage he has lived apart from his wife but cannot remarry. Warrington is a professional writer, but only of nonfiction. He scorns everything that is self-expressive and self-dramatizing in art. "All [modern] poets are humbugs, all literary men are humbugs; directly a man begins to sell his feelings for money he's a humbug" (434), says Warrington, and while he does not give a name to a *woman* who sells her feelings one can guess what it would be. Literary life as *Pendennis* satirically and affectionately depicts it is a masculine world of comradeship, drink, debt, and harmless raffishness, with no women except a few poor desexualized hacks. Miss Bunion, author of "Passion Flowers," is "a large and bony woman in a crumpled satin dress, who came creaking into the room with a step as heavy as a grenadier's" (368). It is not an exalted world, socially or morally, but the growing power and tawdry glamour of the press, along with the income and modest degree of fame it offers to those with no special skills or connections, make it attractive; and it is safe from Blanche Amory.

Anthony Trollope (whose mother's writings supported the family for many years) and Thomas Hardy (whose impoverished background was a barrier as hard to cross as that of gender) treat female aspirants to literature more kindly than Thackeray does, but still as figures of comedy. Trollope's Lady Carbury in *The Way We Live Now* works hard, manipulates the reciprocal-flattery system of reviewing, publishes a feeble work of romanticized history called *Criminal Queens*, and begins a novel. Her literary ambitions are amiably preposterous, based on vague ambition and a desperate need for money to support her profligate son, and when she marries a powerful editor she no longer has to write—indeed, he will not let her. Hardy's heroine in *The Hand of Ethelberta*, a pleasant and highly improbable comedy, is nicer and more sensible than Lady Carbury. She publishes a volume of bold, unsentimental poetry and then sets herself up as a kind of Corinne, telling stories in public performance to make money and catch a husband so that she can provide for her numerous siblings. Like Blanche Amory, Lady Carbury and Ethelberta are decidedly unromantic in the actual conduct of their lives, and their literary efforts, while justified by altruistic familial ends, are in reality little more than husband-hunting—although Ethelberta after ensnaring an elderly, debauched, disagreeable, but very rich nobleman is reported as the novel ends to be composing an epic poem.

Women who did not want to be dismissed as a Blanche Amory or Lady Carbury or even a talented but lowborn husband-hunter like Ethelberta often hid behind anonymous or pseudonymous publication. Female novelists' use of male pseudonyms has been said to characterize the period from the 1840s to 1880.[8] In this as in other ways, women's entrance into literature was facilitated by an established convention which they used with special intensity and an inflection peculiar to themselves. Anonymous reviewing (including long essays only nominally connected to the books ostensibly in question) remained customary throughout the century, allowing women to assume an authoritative tone that a gendered signature would undermine. Most male poets inaugurated their careers without disclosing their identities, testing the waters while following a tradition going back to Renaissance poets' eagerness to define themselves as gentlemanly amateurs; such poets, the venerable convention went, wrote for their own and their friends' amusement, published more or less inadvertently, and were indifferent to reward—a useful pose for women too. Tennyson, Browning, and Arnold, like Elizabeth Barrett and the Brontës, sent their first books forth anonymously. Disguising gender is most difficult in lyric poetry, and was rarely attempted, although the Brontës' first book was *Poems*, by "Currer, Ellis and Acton Bell," and Augusta Webster published her first volume of poetry in 1860 with a name that left the question open, "Cecil Home." (In the last decades of the century the joint compositions of Katherine Bradley and Edith Cooper appeared under the name of "Michael Field" and William Sharp published as "Fiona Macleod.") Novelists had Austen and Scott as precedents for anonymity, the latter of whom guarded his secret with unusual pertinacity, and Dickens and Thackeray used pen names although without any real attempt at concealment. But the Brontës dropped their disguise only when an unscrupulous publisher made it seem absolutely necessary, and Gaskell, who had considered using a male name, published *Mary Barton* anonymously and submitted to be known with real reluctance. Mary Ann Evans is still called George Eliot.

Eliot's persistence in that name is sufficiently accounted for by the fact that she had no "real" one. Her publisher John Blackwood wanted as desperately as she did to preserve the secret, since there seemed no safe way to disclose it. "Mary Ann Evans" was the name of the translator of notoriously heretical books on religion and of a woman living openly with another woman's husband, and in any case she insisted on being called by still another assumed name, "Mrs. Lewes." Eliot's two pseudonyms were not just protective—they represented deliberately chosen identities, and she forced the world to acknowledge them—but they served first of all to cover moral and sexual irregularities. Similarly, the Brontës would have been spared many insults if Currer, Acton, and Ellis Bell had been taken to be men. A man's name could ward off sneers at unladylike writing, as the sensation novelist Mary Braddon explained:

> Did you see what the ——— ——— says about *Aurora Floyd* and my philosophy in the matter of beer, brandy, and cigars and tobacco? It is all Mr. Tinsley's fault for advertising me as "Mary Elizabeth." I used to be called *Mr.* Braddon, and provincial critics were wont to regret that my experience of woman had been so bitter as to make me an implacable foe to the fair sex. They thought I had been "cradled into magazines by wrong," and had learned in the Divorce Court what I taught in three-volume novels.[9]

The association of publishing with sexual exposure, added to women's more generalized ambivalence about fame, accounts for the intensity of the distress—quite unlike anything men experienced—that the Brontës, Gaskell, and Eliot felt about having their identities revealed. But there were other reasons to conceal name and gender. Reviews of books known or suspected to be by women were greeted with an exasperating condescension, like Thackeray's, that it was well worth trying to avoid. The assumption that women wrote from their own experience, moreover, was very often true of first novels, both by women and by men, so that prudence as well as timidity might warn a beginner against revealing her name.[10]

But although anonymous and pseudonymous publication were designed to

ward off personal scrutiny, they also invited it. Reviewers enjoyed speculating
about masked authors, and uncertainty about gender opened the way for particularly wounding insults.[11] The problem was not unique to women, intrusive
personal publicity being generally agreed to be one of the disagreeable hallmarks of the age. People who were well-known, or hoped to be, or corresponded with those who were, assumed that someone would want to publish
their correspondence, and many of them tried to prevent it. Harriet Martineau
demanded that her friends destroy letters from her, and Robert Browning
burned a vast correspondence. "I never keep very private letters, but destroy
them at once," Geraldine Jewsbury assured Jane Welsh Carlyle, her most intimate correspondent and the wife of a very famous husband, "having the fear of
a coroner's inquest before my eyes, and a great horror of all executors who can
pry into secrets from a sense of duty!"[12] Others' families protected their posthumous privacy with similar acts of destruction, and either prohibited biographies, wrote them themselves, or chose biographers they hoped to control or
trusted to be discreet. Women writers' double-edged concealment of their
names reflected in intensified form the ambivalence of the whole literary culture about the loss of privacy that publication entailed.

Rivals and reviewers liked to take for granted that women could not write as
well as men, and many women believed this too. Women's brains were too
weak, their emotions too uncontrolled, their reproductive systems inimical to
and easily damaged by mental exertion, and their experience of life and the
world necessarily, given the social constraints that bound them, inadequate.
Their undeniable successes in prose fiction only proved their limitations. The
eminent critic Richard Holt Hutton, for example, asserted in 1858 that wom-
en's imaginations cannot go beyond "the visible surface and form of human
existence"[13] — the domain of the novel — into the higher realms of poetry. Im-
pressionable and quick to feel, women were incapable of conceptual profun-
dity, abstract thought, or sustained, shaping creativity. Few women could entirely reject such discouraging views, which literary history apparently
confirmed. Many of them were passionately certain, however, that women's inferiority was at least partly the result of education.

Until well into the nineteenth century most girls of the middle and upper
classes were educated primarily at home, and some were hardly educated at all.
When the major Victorian women writers were growing up, schools for girls
offered a smattering of fairly elementary academic instruction and (in varying
degrees according to wealth and class) some "accomplishments": music, drawing, dancing, and other activities designed to make them attractive to suitors
and agreeable at home. Most schools were small, and a comfortable family atmosphere was an important attraction. The best of them taught French, Italian,
and sometimes even Latin, but they did not copy the curriculum, dominated by
the classical languages and a little mathematics, that was given to boys. A girl
from a reasonably cultivated family could learn as much at home. During the

1840s and 1850s some excellent, highly influential secondary schools for girls came into being, as well as a few nonresidential, non-degree-granting colleges. In the 1860s women were allowed to take examinations given by the University of London, and in 1869 the first university college for women and the first lectures for women began at Cambridge. These developments gradually altered the shape of the arguments about women's abilities, but they came too late to benefit the major Victorian writers. The Brontës, Eliot, and Gaskell attended schools that were reasonably satisfactory by the standards of their day, but Barrett Browning and Rossetti (whose mother had been a governess), as well as Oliphant and many others, were educated entirely at home, and most of those who attended schools did so for only a few years and often with little benefit. Elizabeth Sewell's mother wanted her daughters to be capable of independence and sent them to expensive, well-regarded boarding schools where Sewell was ill-taught and unhappy. Harriet Martineau, more fortunate, attended an excellent day school for boys that had been forced by declining numbers to admit girls, but the school's decline continued and after two years it closed; later she spent some time at a boarding school run by cultivated and intelligent women, her cousins and aunt.

In some respects girls were lucky. Boys' schools were often brutally unpleasant, with narrow curricula, teaching methods ranging from uninspired to sadistic, and uncontrolled bullying and sexual exploitation among the pupils. Some, such as Thomas Arnold's Rugby, were well run and drew students' grateful loyalty; but no woman writer's educationally deprived childhood matches for sheer sustained awfulness Trollope's account of his years at the best schools in England, where he was ostracized, bullied, and beaten, and learned (so he claimed) nothing at all.[14] The Greek and Latin to which schoolboys devoted almost all their time were no more useful to most of them (even those who, unlike Trollope, actually learned something) than girls' amateur dabbling in the arts; many boys would have been better off in practical terms studying modern languages, like girls. But the point was not utility. It was access to culture and power, to which the classical languages, and especially Greek with its exotic alphabet, held the magic key. Training in these languages was required for entrance to the universities, where genuine intellectual life and companionship were available to those who wanted them. Boys' studies, being considered more difficult, both demonstrated and developed their intellectual superiority to girls; and the ability to quote fragments of Greek and Latin that was all most of them retained from years of schooling reinforced class and gender identity by marking them definitively as gentlemen. They naturally wished to keep women out of the club, which was partly defined by precisely that exclusion; and women ambitious for literary accomplishment, just as naturally, yearned to get in.

Such women had mostly to educate themselves. A start might come from a few years at a good school, a well-educated mother, a governess, a brother's tutor willing to let the sister sit in on lessons, or a cultivated father (most often a clergyman) who taught a daughter along with her brother or because he had no son. Boys always came first: Charlotte Yonge's clergyman father eventually taught her Greek and mathematics, but he began teaching her Latin only when her brother, who was five years younger, was ready to study it too, and Elizabeth Barrett's ardent desire to learn Greek had to wait until a tutor arrived to prepare her younger brother for school. Older siblings often taught younger ones, usually neither willingly nor well. Girls in their teens, left to their own educational devices, made resolutions and reading lists, but without substantial encouragement or assistance few could keep their resolves. Time not needed for other pursuits was supposed to be given to sewing (called "work"), a sociable and frequently useful activity carried out in the midst of the family circle. Girls' reading, in contrast, was regarded in many households, especially in the early part of the century, as unsociable, useless, even dangerous: knowledge gleaned from books might be injurious to innocence, erudition would scare off suitors, and mental exertion was blamed for illness and forbidden to those in poor health. Reading and studying were often secretly indulged and attended by guilt. Charlotte Brontë was among the few who persisted, guiltless but unhappy, in formal schooling, but even she felt some guilt at preferring the pen to the needle. She and her sisters stayed as long as they could endure it at schools they intensely disliked in order to qualify themselves to make a living as teachers. For this they needed French and music, not Latin and Greek, so those were the subjects they set themselves to master. Branwell, who was designed but not destined for higher things, stayed home and studied the usual male subjects with his father; but he was none the better for it.

Of the major women writers, only Barrett Browning and Eliot reached (in fact they exceeded) the level of a highly educated man. They had formidable intellectual endowments and immense self-discipline as well as access to books and to men willing to instruct them. After Elizabeth Barrett's brother went to school and his tutor left she read Greek on her own, and after years of successful self-instruction she became the protegée of a blind middle-aged classical scholar who happened to turn up in the neighborhood. She learned Latin, French, Italian, and German, and in her twenties solaced an anxious period with lonely studies in Hebrew. She demonstrated her scholarly credentials by translating Aeschylus' *Prometheus Bound* and publishing a series of essays on some exceedingly obscure Greek Christian writers. Eliot attended a school that offered music, drawing, English, French, history, and arithmetic, and then taught herself Latin, found teachers for Italian and German, and learned Greek, postponing mastery of Hebrew to her late forties.[15] Both women read widely in many subjects, especially history, but their formal instruction and self-instruction, like almost all women's, centered on languages.

When she was in her thirties Barrett Browning decided that learning languages was a waste of time, but by then she had learned them and reaped the benefit. She had acquired exact and extensive firsthand knowledge, in English and other literatures, of the poetic tradition in which she intended to take a place. Her formidable learning deflected critical condescension, although it seemed unnatural, even monstrous, and gave rise to some preposterous exaggerations in the press: that when she was eight years old, for instance, she "read Homer in the original, holding her book in one hand and nursing her doll upon her other arm"; or that she and Browning corresponded in classical Greek.[16] Having established her intellectual equality with men she forgot, perhaps, how crucial her mastery of the classical languages had been to her success.

Women poets who lacked Barrett Browning's linguistic accomplishments rarely ventured beyond the relatively unpretentious forms of verse, lyric and narrative and especially the ballad, for which English alone might seem sufficient. Keats, after all, knew no Greek. But the voice of Tennyson, master lyricist of the age, was drenched in classical verse; Browning was always displaying odd bits of erudition and frequently drew on classical languages and literature; Arnold extolled and overtly imitated classical forms of poetry, and most of his critical manifestos assumed an audience that read and appreciated Greek. Christina Rossetti had the good fortune to grow up in an intensely literary household where Italian was frequently spoken and read and everyone had an intimate knowledge of the great Italian poets. She knew French, German, and a little Latin but did not attempt Greek, which her brothers studied at school and her sister learned at home; her acceptance of the linguistic limitations thought proper for girls is both a sign and a cause of her exclusion from "masculine" realms of poetry. Augusta Webster, the best of the poets whose reputations died with the century, was as learned in languages as Barrett Browning and published translations of Aeschylus' *Prometheus Bound* (as Barrett Browning had done) and Euripedes' *Medea*. Only Emily Brontë wrote powerful verse rooted wholly in English tradition, and her idiosyncratic poems received almost no attention. For poets the lack of a classical education was both a perceived and a genuine disadvantage.

For novelists it mattered much less, the novel not being part of the classical tradition. Thackeray had the usual upper-middle-class education, culminating in an incomplete and unproductive sojourn at Cambridge; but Dickens's intermittent schooling ended at fifteen, and Trollope had to teach himself not only French but also Latin when his useless school years were over. Thackeray drew on Fielding and the tradition of classical satire, but the powerful precursors for women novelists were French and female: Madame de Staël and George Sand. For novelists, unlike poets, a catch-as-catch-can education based on modern languages and backed by a good library may well have been the best of all.

Eliot's novels obliquely acknowledge this in their repeated mockery of classical learning, which is presented as arid and useless except as a key to male power. Maggie Tulliver's frustration at not being taught Latin is largely a matter of ambition and jealousy: she yearns to exercise her quick intelligence, and she wants to demonstrate her superiority to her brother. Romola's father taught her Greek so that she could assist his scholarly labors and help establish his fame, but she herself takes no interest in it, and the bequest of his library and his unfinished labor is a dead weight on her life. Dorothea Brooke in *Middlemarch* is simply mistaken in thinking that Greek and Hebrew hold the keys to happiness; her husband, like Romola's father, bewilders himself with envious ambition and sterile scholarship and tries to bequeath to her the deadly burden of his work. Fred Vincy hasn't learned much at Oxford, but he knows enough Greek to squelch his sister.

> "Tell me [Fred challenges her] whether it is slang or poetry to call an ox a *leg-plaiter*."
> "Of course you can call it poetry if you like."
> "Aha, Miss Rosy, you don't know Homer from slang. I shall invent a new game; I shall write bits of slang and poetry on slips, and give them to you to separate." (*Middlemarch*, 126)

Knowing Greek allows men to establish "poetry" as their exclusive possession and to set the rules of a game women can't win. In Eliot's novels, classical learning functions as a weapon either in the battle of male egos or to intimidate women; the weapon may not be worth much, but those who don't possess it are defenseless against it, and while Eliot scorns the battle, she never lets us forget that she herself is well armed.

It is striking, in fact, that increasing educational opportunities for girls roused women novelists to satirical coolness if not downright disapprobation. It is as if the ethos of women's fiction, which arose outside the realm of male high culture, was intrinsically hostile to women who wanted to move into that antithetical realm. The novelists understood that power and prestige, not knowledge, were really at issue. A learned young woman in a Victorian novel is almost certain to be selfish, unfeminine, and probably a fraud. One expects no better from Charlotte Yonge, who preached women's obligations to home, church, and father, although the punishments that befall women in her books who pride themselves on intelligence and learning may still strike us as extreme; the eponymous heroine of *The Clever Woman of the Family*, for instance, is not only humiliated by having her intellectual pretensions exploded but literally kills where she seeks to benefit. Yonge sympathizes with girls who crave a man's education, but not with those who flatter themselves that they have it, or would be selfish enough really to attain it. But the worldly and independent Mary Braddon is almost as cool as Yonge to "Poor Lucy," who "had been mercilessly well educated; she spoke half a dozen languages, knew all about the natural sciences, had read Gibbon, Niebuhr, and Arnold" (*Aurora Floyd*, 22). Mrs. Oliphant's Phoebe Jr. has studied German, attended lectures at a ladies' college, and read "Virgil at least, if not Sophocles" (*Phoebe, Junior*, 18); but she hides her learning, using it only to write brilliant speeches for her rich and stupid husband once she gets him into Parliament. And of all her heroines Eliot allows classical learning only to Romola, who is neither English nor modern and prefers not to use it.

The debates about female education, abilities, and roles in society went on throughout the century and provided gainful employment for many female pens. There was an apparently inexhaustible market for books and essays on childrearing and education and a growing demand for children's books suited to the changing times. Conduct literature for girls and women, generally of a conservative sort, was an established genre, the most famous Victorian examples being Sarah Ellis's exhortations to the women, wives, mothers, and daughters of England. Elizabeth Sewell's *Principles of Education* and Charlotte Yonge's *Womankind* complement their almost equally didactic fiction and teach the same lessons. "I have no hesitation in declaring my full belief in the inferiority of woman," Yonge asserts, "nor that she brought it upon herself."[17] Christina Rossetti also asserted women's inferiority, taking like Sewell and Yonge a religious ground. "The fact of the Priesthood being exclusively man's," she told Augusta Webster, "leaves me in no doubt that the highest functions are not in this world open to both sexes." In one of her tracts for girls Rossetti teaches "the limit of God's ordinance concerning our sex," but she adds that "one final consolation yet remains to careful and troubled hearts: in Christ there is neither male nor female, for we are all one."[18] Different writers, of course, located "the limits of God's ordinance" in different places. Some, from Anna Jameson and Harriet Martineau early in the period to Augusta Webster at its end, supported the feminist movement. Others, like Eliza Lynn Linton—best known as the author of a notorious attack on female emancipation as manifested in the "Girl of the Period"—entered the fray from whatever viewpoint was most salable at any given moment. Voices were raised on all sides.

Such questions bore both directly and by implication on writers' professional functions, and few women found easy answers. They generally deplored (usually from bitter experience) the scanty and haphazard education given to girls, whether or not they wanted them to have the same opportunities boys did. Many lamented the prejudices against female authors and the lack of satisfactory occupations for women who had to support themselves.[19] Almost all successful writers were ambivalent at best about feminism, even as their own examples helped create a wider view of female life. They were inclined to underestimate the obstacles they had surmounted and to assume that any women who deserved success could attain it. Harriet Martineau wrote in 1855:

> Often as I am appealed to speak, or otherwise assist in the promotion of the cause of Woman, my answer is always the same:—that women, like men, can obtain whatever they show themselves fit for. Let them be educated,—let their powers be cultivated to the extent for which the means are already provided, and all that is wanted or ought to be desired will follow of course. Whatever a woman proves herself able to do, society will be thankful to see her do,—just as if she were a man. . . . I judge by my own case.[20]

They all agreed that it was essential for women to be "womanly"—selfless, loving, and pure—and most were afraid that womanliness was incompatible with work directed outside the house or with agitation for a wider sphere.

Very few, in fact, were interested in opening up careers that could not be carried on at home, or at least in a home-like setting. *Aurora Leigh* offers passionate testimony to a woman's right and sacred obligation to do her own work, but the ideal situation toward which the poem moves is that of a married woman plying her pen within a reformed domestic sphere. And perhaps because being a writer required both a commitment to interiority and a frightening degree of publicity, poets and novelists tended to shun engagement in public affairs. Many were willing to sign a petition in favor of a bill that would allow married women control of their own earnings, but few cared much about the less personally urgent question of the vote. Harriet Martineau thought it absurd that she herself, a property-owning woman with a significant influence on public affairs, was disenfranchised, but the suffrage movement was not high on her agenda, and the two most important political women of the century, Queen Victoria and Florence Nightingale, did not support it at all. Caroline Norton fought for women's rights in regard to divorce and the custody of young children, but her own children, freedom, and money were at stake. The first woman writer of note to hold elective office was Augusta Webster, who worked actively for women's suffrage and in 1879 and 1885 was elected to the London School Board: the welfare of children and the lower classes, including their education, belonging like issues of custody in an extended feminine sphere.

For most women, motherhood was the central defining fact of gender difference, and it was a fact that could tell in different ways. Anna Jameson, who warmly encouraged a younger generation of feminist reformers, took it in a conservative direction:

> The natural and Christian principles of the moral equality and freedom of the two sexes being fully recognised, I insist that the ordering of domestic life is our sacred province indissolubly linked with the privileges, pleasures, and duties of maternity, and that the exclusive management of the executive affairs of the community at large belongs to men as the natural result of their exemption from the infirmities and duties which maternity entails on the female part of the human race.
>
> And by maternity I do not mean the actual state of motherhood—which is not necessary nor universal—but the maternal organisation, common to all women.[21]

Christina Rossetti, despite her belief in the inferiority of women, thought mothers deserved to vote:

> I do think if anything ever does sweep away the barrier of sex, and make the female not a giantess or a heroine but at once and full grown a hero and giant, it is

that mighty maternal love which makes little birds and little beasts as well as little women matches for very big adversaries.[22]

In an essay published before she began writing fiction, George Eliot attributes women's special literary contribution to maternal "sensations and emotions," as well as to "the fact of her comparative physical weakness."[23] The enshrinement of maternity was in some ways the least disabling formulation of sexual difference that was current in the period, since it emphasized female power. If the maternal ideal implied self-sacrifice, self-effacement, and domestic seclusion, it also included the power to create, nourish, guide, and teach.

Few of the leading women writers—Gaskell, Wood, Braddon, Oliphant, Webster, and Barrett Browning after the age of forty-three—were mothers, and while Jameson and Martineau took quasi-maternal responsibility for their nieces and Eliot was a devoted stepmother to Lewes's sons, none of these relationships involved caring for young children. Writing itself, however, could be defined in maternal terms, and engagement in public life was acceptable if it seemed to fulfill a maternal role. Queen Victoria was the exemplar of prolific maternity, her ambivalence about childbearing not being generally known. Florence Nightingale, although she was unmarried and childless and her great career was as an administrative reformer, was idealized as a nurse. The traditional models of feminine public engagement were the country squires' and clergymen's wives and daughters who brought soup, clothing, practical advice, a little elementary schooling, and simple spiritual instruction to their poor neighbors. Among the many disappointments of Dorothea Brooke's unfortunate first marriage is a local population that requires no such assistance, while Oliphant's benevolently domineering Miss Marjoribanks's prospects of marital felicity are completed by a delightfully needy village at her gate.

> It gave her the liveliest satisfaction to think of all the disorder and disarray of the Marchbank village. Her fingers itched to be at it—to set all the crooked things straight, and clean away the rubbish, and set everything, as she said, on a sound foundation. . . . The recollection of all the wretched hovels and miserable cottages exhilarated her heart. (*Miss Marjoribanks*, 488)

The hovels and cottages are extensions of the sphere of home, awaiting her maternalistic intervention.

By 1866, when *Miss Marjoribanks* was published, such opportunities were already declining. The new urban proletariat was less accessible, less easily assisted, and less grateful than the rural poor, as the heroines of Gaskell's *North and South* and Rhoda Broughton's *Not Wisely But Too Well* discover. But new kinds of philanthropy, more elaborately organized, arose instead, bringing groups of like-minded women together and extending maternal and domestic values across barriers of class, moral standing, and even species. Prostitutes and other "fallen women" were particular objects of concern; Catholics and high Anglicans like Georgina Fullerton and Christina Rossetti worked with re-

ligious sisterhoods that assisted poor and outcast women, while others organized political action such as the agitation to repeal the "lock laws," which
attempted to control venereal disease by forcing women whom the police
thought might be prostitutes to undergo medical examination. The antivivisection movement attracted others. And writing served similar functions.

That literature has a moral effect—for good or for ill—was generally agreed,
and in the high Victorian period no necessary conflict was seen between art
and instruction. George Eliot's entertaining stories and her explications
of moral law were woven together in satisfactory if not always seamless
wholes, and even at lower levels of art and intellect the nineteenth-century
novel was a schooling in morals and manners, especially for girls. Women were
said to rule by influence—on their children first of all, although also on their
husbands—and writers did the same on a wider scale. All novelists teach, Trollope insisted, whether they know it or not, and most of them knew it. "I have
ever thought of myself," said Trollope, "as a preacher of sermons." The first
serious review of sensation fiction, in 1863, complained that sensation novelists corrupt society by doing "the preacher's office . . . moulding the minds and
forming the habits and tasks of its generation"—but doing it all wrong.[24] Poetry was expected to perform its educational task by cultivating pure feelings
and high sentiments, an expectation some male poets, like Swinburne, zestfully
defied. Literature was thought to nourish the sympathies that bind people together, an essential function in an increasingly industrialized society that saw
social bonds decaying and selfishness enshrining itself in the doctrines of lais-
sez-faire.

Like philanthropists, women writers reached across the iron boundaries of
respectability, money, and class to declare sisterhood with sexually disgraced
women and arouse maternal and sisterly sympathy in their readers. Barrett
Browning's Marian Erle in *Aurora Leigh*, who emerges from the brutalizing
depths of poverty and bears an illegitimate child as the result of rape, is in spirit
a virgin mother, and Gaskell's Ruth, the pure-hearted victim of a callous se-
ducer, is also sanctified by motherhood. *Mary Barton* offers sympathy between
individuals of opposed social classes as the cure for class warfare and the rav-
ages of urban poverty: the rich man and the poor, the crudely materialistic
manufacturer and the embittered Chartist who saw his own child die of starvation and murdered the manufacturer's son, come together in their common
pain as bereaved fathers. *Mary Barton* is designed to give its middle-class readers an experience like that of its characters: to make them see the essentially
domestic virtues and feel the sufferings of people from whom in reality they
would be alienated by class and economic status. This may not strike us as
much of a solution to the horrors of unregulated industrialism, but to many
intelligent people at the time it seemed the only one available. It is a solution
that is uniquely in the power of the novelist and the poet; and as a kind of
superior philanthropy that educates and binds society together through the affections, offering in effect to solve the most intractable social problems by

translating them into the domestic sphere—the sphere to which Southey urged Charlotte Brontë to restrict herself—it is uniquely suited to women. Even in their most conservative forms, that is, the ideas about women's role and nature that made them afraid to write also enabled them to do so.

4. Poetry

Women fared less well writing poetry than fiction. Barrett Browning's reputation rose high in her lifetime but fell drastically after her death, although *Sonnets from the Portuguese* has had an enduring popularity with readers if not with critics. Emily Brontë's strange and compelling verse was almost unknown in the nineteenth century and is not much read today. Christina Rossetti has been much admired, but as an anomaly: perfect, perhaps, but small. And these three stand essentially alone. Felicia Hemans and Letitia Landon early in the century, and Adelaide Procter and Jean Ingelow later on, had considerable lyric gifts and were extremely popular, but they have been long and no doubt irrevocably forgotten. Augusta Webster, who wrote strong and interesting verse, has never been well known. There is no one else to match against the host either of women novelists or of male poets: the Brontës, Gaskell, Eliot, Oliphant, Yonge, Braddon, and others on the one hand, Tennyson, Browning, Arnold, Clough, Dante Gabriel Rossetti, Meredith, Morris, Swinburne, Hardy, and Hopkins, along with many lesser lights who appear in literary histories and anthologies, on the other.

There are many causes, no doubt. Fear of self-exposure may have inhibited use of the lyric first-person, especially in erotic contexts. The poet, says Augusta Webster,

> is taken as offering his readers the presentment of himself, his hopes, his loves, his sorrows, his guilts and remorses, his history and psychology generally. Some people so thoroughly believe this to be the proper view of the poet's position towards the public that they will despise a man as a hypocrite because, after having written and printed, "I am the bridegroom of Despair," or "No wine but the wine of death for me," or some such unsociable sentiment, he goes out to dinners and behaves like anybody else.[1]

The philanthropic and educative motives that justified women's fiction were less innoxious in verse: except in the most expert hands, palpable didacticism is injurious to poetic art, and poems that try to arouse humanitarian feeling seem irredeemably sentimental today. Poetry in its higher modes was not only part of the culture for which most women lacked the classical education that served as initiation and key; it was also embedded in a religious context that defined the poet in similarly exclusive terms as prophet, priest, or sage. And the Romantic movement, out of which Victorian poetry arose, was based on relationships between male poets and female nature that allowed no space for women to be poets.[2]

Men had many of the same problems women did. They too feared self-betrayal, although not with the same urgency, when they used the lyric "I." Almost all of them had lost the religious certitude that previously sustained prophetic or sacerdotal utterance, and the Romantic idea of nature, in which poets formed a new kind of priesthood, dwindled under the pressure of science, industrialization, and religious doubt into wistful nostalgia. But for women the difficulties were not just historical, social, or psychological; they were part of the inherited structure of English poetry, in which woman is not the seer but the object seen; not the imagination that shapes and is shaped by nature, but nature itself; not the poet who desires, but the object of his desire: not Byron, but Byron's beloved.

The first poem in Rossetti's first volume of verse, privately printed by her grandfather when she was in her teens, explores this highly problematic structure in terms of quest romance. In "The Dead City" the speaker—of unspecified gender but clearly, as the plot develops, not male—finds an empty city and a palace decked for feasting in which all the inhabitants have been turned to stone. This is the story of Sleeping Beauty, in which the speaker is taking the prince's part, but there is no one to awaken with a kiss. All the relationships among the inhabitants of the palace—man with maiden, mother with child—are complete already. In traditional poetic stories, questing figures are male, and the object of quest, desire, and vision is female. The woman who tries to be a questing poet finds no object for her desire, no sleeping prince. Instead, the speaker herself becomes the object of a gaze that is not amorous but hostile: as she looks at the stony figures she feels them looking at her, and she averts her eyes and flees. The city vanishes, the quest fails, because within traditional plots a woman cannot be a poetic visionary. "What was I that I should see / So much hidden mystery?"[3]

Similar plots in two early quest-narratives by Barrett Browning, "The Deserted Garden" and "The Lost Bower," end in similar failure. The garden remains deserted, the bower is found only to be lost again, because they contain no object for the speaker's desire—no one, in fact, at all. In poetic symbology gardens and bowers represent the site of female sexuality and the female body itself—so what could a female poet discover there? The woman poet finds herself in the position of both subject and object, having to play both roles in stories that require two characters; and Barrett Browning and Rossetti learn very early in their careers that the roles are not reversible and that one person cannot fill them both.

The most brilliant versions of such stories of impasse are those of Emily Brontë, generally set in the imaginary realm of Gondal that Emily and Anne created when Charlotte and Branwell created Angria. No prose narratives of Gondal survive, but the manuscripts of Emily's poems identify many of their speakers as Gondolian characters. In this Byronic world, passionate personages enact tales of desire, revenge, and remorse, politics and war, exile and imprisonment and ambiguous rescue. Boundaries are permeable and shifting both within Gondal and in the definition of its borders. Emily and Anne, even more than Charlotte, treated the characters they created as existing in some sense on the same plane of reality as themselves, Emily in 1841 recording the condition of the Brontës and the Gondalians in the same note. The boundaries of the self are also permeable: in 1845 Emily recorded an excursion she took with Anne during which "we were, Roland Macalgin, Henry Angora, Juliet Angusteena, Rosabella Esmaldan," and four other male and female characters, "escaping from the palace of instruction to join the Royalists who are hard driven at present by the victorious Republicans."[4] Gender, too, is ambiguous and fluid in Emily Brontë's poems, just as Emily and Anne "were" both men and women; it is often impossible to guess a character's gender, which sometimes appears to change between or within poems. Some of the most Byronically bold voices apparently belong to women; anyone, it seems, can be either Byron or Byron's beloved. The result is a struggle between male and female forces for imaginative dominance.

The speaker in "Ah! why, because the dazzling sun" (a poem not set explicitly in Gondal, but Gondalian in tone) is in bed after a happy night during which the "glorious eyes" of the stars "Were gazing down in mine," and "one sweet influence, near and far, / Thrilled through and proved us one." But this perfect mutuality of subject and object, in which each looks on each and each therefore *is* the other, is broken by the sunrise. The stars are plural and ungendered, but the sun is "he," and the speaker cannot repel his violent penetration of her bedroom windows and her closed eyelids. Like the prince who rescues Sleeping Beauty, the sun breaks the "spell" that bound her through the night and forces her to see the world in the coloration he gives it.

> Blood-red he rose, and arrow-straight
> His fierce beams struck my brow:
> The soul of Nature sprang elate,
> But mine sank sad and low!
>
> My lids closed down—yet through their veil
> I saw him blazing still;
> And bathe in gold the misty dale,
> And flash upon the hill.
>
> I turned me to the pillow then
> To call back Night, and see
> Your [the stars'] worlds of solemn light, again
> Throb with my heart and me!

But everything around her responds with joy, and despite her resistance the rhythms of her own voice respond joyfully too.

> It would not do—the pillow glowed
> And glowed both roof and floor,
> And birds sang loudly in the wood,
> And fresh winds shook the door.[5]

Her visionary power vanishes under the gaze that objectifies and transforms her as it transforms nature. Yielding to his power, she sees his visions, not her own.

Essentially the same story recurs as a Gondal episode in "Silent is the House—all are laid asleep," in which a man named Julian roams through his dungeons and stops to gloat over a beautiful prisoner, A. G. Rochelle, with whom he promptly falls in love. Different voices struggle for the position of speaker and central consciousness, but Julian triumphs at every level. He takes control of the narrative and the events within it, carries Rochelle off, wins her reluctant love, and stops her visions. In prison, she says, "A messenger of Hope comes every night to me" (67) with the promise of life beyond death.

> He comes with western winds, with evening's wandering airs,
> With that clear dusk of heaven that brings the thickest stars;
> Winds take a pensive tone, and stars a tender fire,
> And visions rise and change which kill me with desire—
> . . . .
> But first a hush of peace, a soundless calm descends;
> The struggle of distress and fierce impatience ends;
> Mute music soothes my breast—unuttered harmony
> That I could never dream till earth was lost to me.
>
> Then dawns the Invisible, the Unseen its truth reveals;
> My outward sense is gone, my inward essence feels—
> Its wings are almost free, its home, its harbour found;
> Measuring the gulf it stoops and dares the final bound! (69-84)

But under Julian's gaze and in response to his offer of rescue not only are her visions interrupted, but her visionary commitment itself falters. "Earth's hope was not so dead, heaven's home was not so dear," Julian reports triumphantly, "I read it in that flash of longing quelled by fear" (111-12). As in "Ah! why, because the dazzling sun" a male imagination forces a woman to see and be seen as part of an erotic, violent, highly colored, and ineluctably gendered Byronic world. But the opposition is not simple, for the Byronic world is also Gondal, which Brontë herself created; and the female imagination is defined as darkness and silence, mute music, unuttered harmony: peace rather than mad joy, heaven rather than nature, the spirit rather than the senses—in short, as something very much like death. Like Rossetti's and Barrett Browning's quest romances, these poems end in self-contradiction and impasse.

The end of *Jane Eyre*, in contrast, reverses the Sleeping Beauty story with full success. Magically summoned by Rochester's voice, Jane makes her way through a mysterious overgrown wood, as in the fairy tale, finds him helpless—blind and without a candle, doubly in the dark—and awakens him to life, love, and light. But poetry, with less space to develop and explain unfamiliar situations and a much more restricted tonal range, did not have the flexibility novelists did. Rossetti's *The Prince's Progress*, for instance, retells

the story of Sleeping Beauty not as the adventures of a female quester but as the
story of a dilatory prince and the princess who wearies of waiting and dies before he arrives: not a role reversal but a shift in point of view. The narrator
follows the pleasure-loving prince with cool disdain until he comes within sight
of the palace and plucks a rose: "His hand shook . . . And the rose dropped
dew" (443-44). The rose being the traditional poetic symbol of woman as
erotic object, this is an image of sexual violation and response, like Brontë's
sun piercing the speaker's eyelids. The prince, who knows how the story is supposed to end, looks forward to a life of "Easy pleasure" with "the dear Bride
won" (455-56). But a chorus of women scolds him:

> Too late for love, too late for joy,
>   Too late, too late!
> You loitered on the road too long,
>   You trifled at the gate:
> The enchanted dove upon her branch
>   Died without a mate;
> The enchanted princess in her tower
>   Slept, died, behind the grate;
> Her heart was starving all this while
>   You made it wait. (481-90)

He was not worth waiting for; but alternatives to smug princes and violent
suns were not easy to come by. *Jane Eyre* reverses gender roles by translating
the story into a complex narrative, with a rich tonal mixture of astringency and
passion, and redefining the protagonists in terms fit for prose; but within the
prevailing tonalities of Victorian poetry a questing princess liberating an enchanted prince conceived as a rose or a dove would be ridiculous.

For a poem's speaker or center of consciousness to conceive herself as the
passive object of someone else's quest can produce considerable erotic energy,
as Emily Brontë's poems show, but the eroticism is likely to have disturbingly
violent overtones. Such a speaker, furthermore, is necessarily aware of her
physical self as seen and desired—or not seen or not desired, as the case may
be—by a man. This violates not only social but also poetic decorum, and it
usually makes both poet and reader very uncomfortable. A male sonneteer
praises the beloved's beauty, never his own: his part is to desire, hers to be
beautiful. Each presupposes the other; but whereas poetic desire can maintain
itself without a response—it is defined, in fact, in terms of deferred fulfillment—beauty is the value bestowed by the lover's desire and cannot exist
without it. Brontë's speakers are forced to remain alive and become part of nature when male desire compels them; correspondingly, in the absence of her
lover Rossetti's princess loses the beauty that entitles women to a place in amatory verse, and so she dies.

Barrett Browning never entirely freed herself from this configuration of poetic desire—one of her last and best poems, "A Musical Instrument," suggests

that the source of poetry is the pain of a violated woman—but she experimented with forms in which the gender of the speaker might not matter: translations, ballads, didactic verse, verse drama, elegy. Her poetry came most fully to life when she brought to bear some of the freedom and flexibility provided by the novel: the opportunity to remake traditional plots and characters by placing them in modern settings and giving them substantial narrative development. *Sonnets from the Portuguese* inaugurated what was to become the most important generic innovation of the Victorian age: a quasi-autobiographical lyric sequence in a contemporary setting, telling a novelistic story and filled with novelistic detail, in which the poet works out her or his relation to poetic tradition. For men, such poems provided new subjects at a time when the old ones seemed to have been exhausted, and allowed for an ironic exploration of discords between poetic convention and contemporary life. Like men, women used such poems to build a bridge between poetry and the domestic world that novels, but not poems, were accustomed to explore; but they could not afford irony, since their first task was to show their right to a place in poetry, not their discordance with it. They were too unsure of their place within poetic tradition to be able to mock it, and they could not count on the sympathetic audience, sharing their values and attuned to nuances of expression, that irony requires. Irony, moreover, with its doubleness of meaning and emotional detachment, went against everything a woman writer was supposed to be.

Sonnets from the Portuguese begins by demonstrating the speaker's familiarity with classical poetry and her mastery of the sonnet form, establishing her right to speak in both traditions.

> I thought once how Theocritus had sung
> Of the sweet years, the dear and wished-for years,
> Who each one in a gracious hand appears
> To bear a gift for mortals, old or young:
> And, as I mused it in his antique tongue,
> I saw, in gradual vision through my tears,
> The sweet, sad years, the melancholy years,
> Those of my own life, who by turns had flung
> A shadow across me. Straightway I was 'ware,
> So weeping, how a mystic Shape did move
> Behind me, and drew me backward by the hair;
> And a voice said in mastery, while I strove,—
> "Guess now who holds thee?"—"Death," I said. But, there,
> The silver answer rang, "—Not Death, but Love."

Defining the female speaker as a figure fit to appear in a poem is a deadly serious task, and the absence of irony in *Sonnets from the Portuguese* and the amatory stream that flows from it has laid women's verse open to parody and scorn. The speaker is passive, solitary, tearful—like the poetic persona of Thackeray's Blanche Amory, who by entitling her volume "Mes Larmes" also starts off by establishing melancholy and a foreign language as her credentials. She is like Rossetti's princess, for whom years have passed in sorrow and youth has gone, a woman whose story would seem to be over. But she does not allow this to exclude her from poetry: for a lover does come to awaken her, and while he is a poet, she is a poet too.

There are problems with this truly remarkable assertion of creative equality. The novelistic details forbid our imagining the speaker in hazily glamorous terms, and she insists that she is neither young nor beautiful. It is embarrassing to see a Victorian woman in the humble posture of a courtly lover, and we wince at her cruel self-descriptions. But on the whole it works very well. By the time we reach the last sonnet, traditional images have been renewed and enriched in meaning.

> Belovèd, thou hast brought me many flowers
> Plucked in the garden, all the summer through
> And winter, and it seemed as if they grew
> In this close room, nor missed the sun and showers.
> So, in the like name of that love of ours,
> Take back these thoughts which here unfolded too,
> And which on warm and cold days I withdrew
> From my heart's ground. Indeed, those beds and bowers
> Be overgrown with bitter weeds and rue,
> And wait thy weeding; yet here's eglantine,
> Here's ivy! take them, as I used to do
> Thy flowers, and keep them where they shall not pine.
> Instruct thine eyes to keep their colors true,
> And tell thy soul their roots are left in mine.

In return for flowers from a real garden she gives the flowers of her verse (Thackeray's heavy-footed Miss Bunion is the author of "Passion Flowers") grown in the garden of her heart: that is, she gives flowers that spring from her desire in return for flowers that represent his. She is the garden the lover seeks to enter, like Rossetti's prince plucking the rose; but the flowers are both her love and her art, and while the lover's desire brought them into being and preserves their beauty — "Instruct thine eyes to keep their colors true" — she plucks them herself. In *Sonnets from the Portuguese*, Barrett Browning reshapes the conventions of amatory poetry to fit a contemporary, novelistic story, told from a woman's point of view.

Aurora Leigh brings poetry even more fully into the domain of fiction. It is a novel in verse, the exuberant, flamboyant, triumphantly excessive story of a woman poet who overcomes the various obstacles imposed by gender and wins independence, fame, and marriage. Aurora has the happy conviction that her work is the best in the world, since she expects poetry to outdo philanthropy and remake society on a new spiritual basis; and like her creator she proves in her own person that a woman can be a poet. Barrett Browning's example, like

Aurora's, was even more encouraging to aspiring writers than Charlotte Bron-të's or Jane Eyre's, since it combined literary success and personal happiness. (In her poem "A Woman's Answer," Adelaide Procter invokes *Aurora Leigh* as an object of love more worthy than a man.) But Barrett Browning's boldness and exuberance, her willingness to articulate sexual desire and assert ambition, were grounded in unusually fortunate circumstances. She published such works when she was respectably married, living abroad, and could afford not to worry about annoying her male relatives or affronting English decorum. As a wife and mother she would not be accused of publishing erotic daydreams or advertising for a lover. Marriage and maternity gave her both the freedom and the confidence to use the skill she had acquired through long years of literary apprenticeship. And her life, with its princess-like seclusion, long close brush with death, and romantic elopement from paternal tyranny, was a revision of romance that could be generalized to good purpose: her poems heralding the battle against slavery in America and the imminent reunification and rebirth of Italy drew passion and conviction from the fact that they mirrored her own experience of liberation and renewal. No other poet of the century had such experience, such freedom, or such vision. And yet Aurora's triumph, like Jane Eyre's, requires that her lover see only through her eyes and not see *her* at all: like Jane, she will not marry him until he is blind.

Barrett Browning's work was thought to show an anomalous and not en-tirely attractive combination of masculine and feminine qualities: masculine power of intellect, feminine flow of emotion. Emily Brontë's astonishing novel and her ferociously independent character were a direct affront to nineteenth-century notions of womanhood. Mrs. Gaskell, who had never met Emily, thought she must have been rough and odd, and even her sister Charlotte had doubts about her, portraying her in *Shirley* as a woman who wanted to be like a man and writing in an introduction to *Wuthering Heights*: "Whether it is right or advisable to create things like Heathcliff, I do not know: I scarcely think it is."[6] For an exemplary feminine life and a pure, perfect, perfectly fem-inine art, critics then and later turned to Christina Rossetti, whose imagination inhabited no Byronic worlds and who rarely tried to escape the position poetry assigned to women: a position to which she had been accustomed, if not rec-onciled, from childhood.

Like Barrett Browning and Brontë, Rossetti had a brother who was given opportunities much greater than her own. Like Branwell Brontë, Dante Gabriel Rossetti eventually destroyed himself with drugs and alcohol. Unlike Barrett Browning's and the Brontës' brothers, however, his weakness was not of a kind to bolster his sister's artistic self-esteem. He was older than she was, greatly gifted, a very successful poet and painter, and one of the centers around which a lively artistic world revolved. Both Dante Gabriel and the other brother, William Michael, were members of the Pre-Raphaelite Brotherhood, a group of young men, mostly painters, who came together in 1848, when Christina was seventeen, and drifted apart a few years later. They enjoyed the fun of being a secret society, shocking the public with unconventional paintings and theories that were soon to make a great impression on British art. William Michael recalled:

> We were really like brothers, continually together, and confiding to one another all experiences bearing upon questions of art and literature, and many affecting us as individuals. We dropped the term "Esquire" on letters, and substituted "P.R.B." . . . We had our thoughts, our unrestrained converse, our studies, aspirations, efforts, and actual doings. . . . Those were the days of youth; and each man in the company, even if he did not project great things of his own, revelled in poetry or sunned himself in art.[7]

This was the kind of shared artistic life and ambition, codified in mock-serious ritual and secrecy, that nourished the lives of young male poets but had no counterpart for women. Christina Rossetti gave the brotherhood poems for their magazine, *The Germ*; she achieved the first literary success of the movement with the publication of *Goblin Market and Other Poems* in 1862; she was, said Swinburne, "the Jael who led their host to victory"; but she was not one of them. Dante Gabriel proposed her as an honorary member, but the brethren wanted no sisters, and he withdrew the suggestion.

> When I proposed that my sister should join, I never meant that she should attend the meetings, to which I know it would be impossible to persuade her, as it would bring her to a pitch of nervousness. . . . I merely intended that she should entrust her productions to my reading; but must give up the idea, as I find she objects to this also, under the impression that it would seem like display, I believe, —a sort of thing she abhors.[8]

Exclusion is explained as withdrawal.

Rossetti was not part of what might be called the Pre-Raphaelite sisterhood either. She was the model for the first painting that Dante Gabriel exhibited with the initials P.R.B., *The Girlhood of Mary Virgin*, and she was briefly engaged to one of the brothers, the engagement ending about the same time the brotherhood did. But she had little in common with the women Dante Gabriel and his friends took as models, mistresses, and wives. Being one of them, moreover, would have meant not being one of the artists. Her mother and sister, to whom she was deeply attached, were not artists either, and the protagonist of her short novel *Maude* feels that by being a poet she is betraying her mother. Much of Rossetti's poetry stems from the sense of belonging nowhere: neither with the artists, nor with the women.

Often her speakers situate themselves on or beyond the border between waking and sleeping, life and death, speech and silence: at a liminal point, that is, where the silent woman of men's art becomes her own antithesis, the speaking subject. Many of her poems are conceived as responses to poems about women written by men. The first issue of *The Germ* has two apparently reciprocal poems on facing pages: Dante Gabriel's "My Sister's Sleep," which tells with unctuous delectation of the speaker's sister sleep of death, and Christina's "Dream Land," about a woman who travels to a deathlike land of dreams. One of her finest lyrics, "When I am dead, my dearest," eerily imagines being dead and thereby becoming the object of grief and art.

> When I am dead, my dearest,
>   Sing no sad songs for me;
> Plant thou no roses at my head,
>   Nor shady cypress tree.
> Be the green grass above me
>   With showers and dewdrops wet;
> And if thou wilt, remember,
>   And if thou wilt, forget. (1-8)

She won't see the flowers or hear the songs. The trappings of sweet poetic sorrow will not affect her, and the lover will scarcely matter anymore.

> I shall not see the shadows,
>   I shall not feel the rain;
> I shall not hear the nightingale
>   Sing on, as if in pain:
> And dreaming through the twilight
>   That doth not rise nor set,
> Haply I may remember,
>   And haply may forget. (9-16)

Beneath the sweet self-abnegating surface this is an acerbic reply to poems like Dante Gabriel's "My Sister's Sleep" that use dead women as their occasion. Rossetti in tacit reciprocity gives voice to the indifference of corpses, the grievances of ghosts, and the self-sufficiency of women whose sleep of death will end in a happy resurrection beyond all earthly loves.

Sometimes she identifies with a nature alienated from man: the rose no lover plucks, winter that won't tell its secret. In what is apparently the last poem she wrote her voice comes with brilliant living artistry as if from the heart of nature, the grave.

> Sleeping at last, the trouble and tumult over,
>   Sleeping at last, the struggle and horror past,
> Cold and white, out of sight of friend and of lover,
>   Sleeping at last.

No more a tired heart downcast or overcast,
No more pangs that wring or shifting fears that hover,
Sleeping at last in a dreamless sleep locked fast.

Fast asleep. Singing birds in their leafy cover
Cannot wake her, nor shake her the gusty blast.
Under the purple thyme and the purple clover
Sleeping at last.[9]

The dead woman is insentient, emotionless, unseen. This is both peace and imprisonment ("locked fast"), a last enchantment from which she will be awakened only by God.

Monna Innominata, an amatory sonnet sequence partly modeled on *Sonnets from the Portuguese*, explicitly speaks from the position of the traditional poetic object. Each sonnet is prefaced by quotations from Dante and Petrarch, and the speaker is defined as a kind of Beatrice or Laura. But *Monna Innominata* ends with the lover's defection, and so it concludes where *Sonnets from the Portuguese* began: .

Youth gone and beauty gone, what doth remain?
The longing of a heart pent up forlorn,
A silent heart whose silence loves and longs;
The silence of a heart which sang its songs
While youth and beauty made a summer morn,
Silence of love that cannot sing again. (14: 9-14)

A lover wakens Barrett Browning's speaker to poetic utterance, and the absence of a lover brings Rossetti's to silence. A woman abandoned by the desire to which her verse responded is no longer young, no longer beautiful, and so she no longer belongs in poetry.

Rossetti also shared the contemporary assumption that women are poems, not poets. Dante Gabriel describes a woman and a sonnet as interchangeably self-enclosed and self-admiring: the woman is "subtly of herself contemplative," the sonnet "of its own arduous fulness reverent." How does one tell them apart? Christina says in a sad little poem, "A Wish," "I wish I were a song once heard / But often pondered o'er." She describes Jean Ingelow in terms that make the same equation: she "appears as unaffected as her verses, though not their equal in regular beauty." Elizabeth Barrett was afraid that Robert Browning loved her poems, not herself—"I love your verses with all my heart, dear Miss Barrett," he wrote before he had ever seen her, "and I love you too."[10] Many of Rossetti's poems, unlike those of Barrett Browning and most other nineteenth-century women, are small, carefully molded, shapely and beautiful objects. But poems, like women, do not speak.

Rossetti's art is built on the paradox of speaking from the place of silence. Often her poems, like Emily Dickinson's, tease the reader with an enactment of secrecy, flaunting the fact that something is being withheld. She wrote about oblivion and became famous, and her art eloquently espoused self-suppression. But she had other voices too: dramatic impersonations of women who resent the limitations of femininity, celebrate female independence, take pride in illegitimate offspring, denounce unfaithful men. Dante Gabriel disliked what he called the "falsetto muscularity" of such voices, which he attributed to Barrett Browning's influence and declared "utterly foreign" to his sister's "primary impulses";[11] he liked her to talk only in the lyric tones he considered feminine and her own. She generally adhered to his standards, although not without protest, but she often expressed rebellious feelings in verse that seemed on the surface femininely tame. And she could imagine heroism like Godiva's emerging from her typical speaker's isolation, self-concealment, and sense of her own unloveliness. The princess in "A Royal Princess"—sad, lonely, "old and haggard in the face" (42)—resolves to offer her wealth and her love to the starving populace her father has oppressed: She will appear before the people "face to face" (101), "Once to speak before the world, rend bare my heart" (106), and then, probably, die.

In *Goblin Market*, her boldest and most surprising exploration of women's place in art, she simultaneously evades disapprobation and circumvents the problem of self-location by using third-person narrative rather than lyric, and by disguising the poem as a moral tale for children. It is the story of two sisters, Laura and Lizzie. Laura tastes the forbidden fruit with which the goblins lure maidens, and falls into a decline when she discovers that she can hear them no longer and obtain no more fruit. As in other nineteenth-century poems about encounters with mysterious beings from another world—Coleridge's "The Ancient Mariner," Keats's "*La Belle Dame Sans Merci*," Tennyson's "Tithonus" and "The Holy Grail"—this is an imaginative engagement that cuts the protagonist off from human life, as Southey warned Brontë would happen to her. It is also a sexual encounter: another of the goblins' victims "for joys brides hope to have / Fell sick and died" (314-15); and as in a cautionary tale for girls about seduction and betrayal, once Laura has given in to the goblins—eaten their fruit—their desire for her ends. But *Goblin Market* makes a new kind of story from the old plots. Laura is saved by Lizzie, who goes to the goblins to get Laura the fruit she can no longer obtain for herself; trying to force her to eat, they smear her with their fruits' juices, which she carries home for Laura, who licks them off and is cured of her craving. Among many ways of reading this richly multivalent poem, we can see it as a revision of the world of male poetry, and especially that of the Pre-Raphaelites, from a woman's point of view.[12]

Laura is in effect a "fallen woman." A prostitute's life, the speaker in Dante Gabriel's "Jenny" says, is like "a rose shut in a book / In which pure women may not look." But in fact that book was a central text for female philanthropy, which often focused on the plight of prostitutes; and when Lizzie determines to find the goblin fruit and save her sister she begins "for the first time in her life . . . to listen and look" (327-28). Rossetti herself looked in the forbidden book by working at a home for fallen women, and she wrote several remarkably uncensorious poems about women who have been seduced and abandoned. She defended one such poem against Dante Gabriel's disapproval:

> Whilst I endorse your opinion of the unavoidable and indeed much-to-be-desired unreality of women's work on many social matters, I yet incline to include within female range such an attempt as this: where the certainly possible circumstances are merely indicated, as it were, in skeleton. . . . Moreover the sketch only gives the girl's own deductions, feelings . . . and whilst it may truly be urged that unless white could be black and Heaven Hell my experience (thank God) precludes me from hers, I yet don't see why "the Poet mind" should be less able to construct her from its own inner consciousness than a hundred other unknown quantities.[13]

Lizzie's venture is a declaration of the poet's imaginative freedom.

It is also a raid into enemy territory. "Brother with queer brother" (94), the goblins and their fruit show themselves to Laura with a sensuous richness and amoral charm that suggest the art of the Pre-Raphaelite Brotherhood, and when Laura's responsive desire is awakened she looks like the long-necked, long-haired women in Pre-Raphaelite paintings. But Lizzie sees the goblins as nasty creatures, "Grunting and snarling" (393) instead of "wagging, purring" (391) as they did for Laura. The goblins' efforts to coerce her desire is a kind of attempted rape, as in Brontë's "Ah! why, because the dazzling sun," but it fails: she won't give them a lock of her hair, or open her mouth, or eat their food, or become what they want her to be.

Resistance succeeds here while it fails in Brontë's poems because Lizzie counters the goblins' story of sexual seduction and sensuous delight not with an unearthly, deathlike vision but with an equally lively but entirely different kind of story. As in a folktale, she tricks the goblins into giving her what she wants without paying their price and runs home impelled by joy and filled with "inward laughter" (463). She is also a Christian heroine, imitating Christ. "Eat me, drink me, love me" (471), she cries to her sister, her sacramental gift simultaneously demonstrating that the goblin fruit is bitter and calling forth her sister's redemptively penitent love. She brings the "fiery antidote" (559) to the forbidden fruit, and like Christ she *is* the antidote. "Hug me, kiss me, suck my juices" (468), Lizzie cries, and Laura "kissed and kissed her with a hungry mouth" (492); these lines may trouble modern readers, aware of erotic possibilities that Victorian readers apparently did not think about, but the conflation of spiritual and erotic imagery follows the example of seventeenth-century poets like Crashaw and Donne. The counterpoise to the Pre-Raphaelite vision is created by combining a folktale vision of female heroism, the great age of English religious verse, and the imitation of Christ.

Within this larger context, *Goblin Market*, like *The Prince's Progress*, is a transformation of fairy tale and amatory lyric. The sisters live alone in a cozy little house, their sleep protected as if by enchantment: "Wind sang to them lullaby, / Lumbering owls forebore to fly, / Not a bat flapped" (193-95). Verbal ambiguity suggests that they are imprisoned, "Locked together in one nest"

(198), like sleeping princesses waiting for princes to awaken them. Laura fades and pines like the waiting princess in *The Prince's Progress*. But there are no princes, only goblins, and she is saved by discovering in time what the princess learns too late: that what she pined for is not worth it. The bitterness of the juices Lizzie brings her cures her longing; she is saved not because her prince comes but because she learns not to want him. At the end of the poem the sisters are married and Laura tells and retells the story as a ritual to bind their children together. The moral she draws is not that girls should avoid goblins — the sisters seem to remember them, in fact, with some pleasure — but that "there is no friend like a sister" (562). Sleeping Beauty, that is, tells her own story, and the rescuing prince is her sister. The encounter with the goblin world, like Rossetti's encounter with Pre-Raphaelitism, generates a new kind of poetry, and the energy, freedom, easy control, and fluent irregular meter reflect Rossetti's triumphant appropriation of Pre-Raphaelite materials, like Lizzie's of the goblins' fruit, for her own purposes.

Unlike most of Rossetti's lyrics, *Goblin Market* is a thoroughgoing revision of poetic tradition rather than a response to it, and for such a project narrative is essential. A lyric has meaning only as a moment in an implied narrative, and so a new lyric situation requires in effect a new narrative; but lyric — being relatively short, and ill-designed to tell stories except by allusion and indirection — can rarely create this alone. Barrett Browning's most innovative and successful lyric work is *Sonnets from the Portuguese*, in which each individual poem takes its meaning from its position in a highly original narrative. Some sentiments, furthermore, like those in *Goblin Market*, were too bold to be expressed without a story to render them not only comprehensible but acceptable. Adelaide Procter's "A Legend of Bregenz," for instance, tells about a woman from the Tyrol who lives for many years as a servant with a family in Switzerland and then rides off on a white horse, warns her native city of an impending attack by the Swiss, and becomes a famous Tyrolean heroine. An apparently affectionate and contented domestic woman, in other words, achieves adventure and fame by betraying the family and community in which she lives. Stripped to its bare bones, this is the familiar nightmarish version of female ambition. Procter needs a narrative that distances the heroine by nationality and social class, sets the incident three centuries back, and defines the story as "legend" rather than anything that might actually happen in contemporary life, to turn ambition into acceptable action.

Even the best Victorian poets, however, rarely do narrative well. They are apt to fall into stilted locutions that retard the action, awkward archaisms that make dialogue sound neither elevated nor natural, and an unattractively stiff simplicity. *Sonnets from the Portuguese* and *Monna Innominata* establish formal diction, slow movement, and an archaizing solemnity, especially the use of the second person singular, as the hallmarks of female amatory verse even with a narrative frame. The most readable Victorian narratives, like some of Browning's and Clough's, cut ironically against the grain of poetic diction, but women could rarely afford irony. The ballad, which women often used, encouraged not only archaic diction but improbable plots and a sentimental tone. And narrative encouraged the diffuseness that is the special curse of minor poets. The two great successes are *Goblin Market*, which uses short irregular lines, deliberate quaintness, and motifs from street-song and children's literature to create a language that is neither stiff nor falsely sweet; and *Aurora Leigh*, which imitates the varied cadences of heightened speech with considerable power despite some awkward or ludicrous moments. But *Goblin Market* and *Aurora Leigh* are too idiosyncratic, too far outside the ordinary parameters of nineteenth-century poetry, to be repeatable, and their association with genres of low prestige—children's literature, the novel—apparently acquiesces in the notion of women's poetry as separate and inferior.

One of the odder features of women's poetry, particularly common in Victorian England and America, is the presence of animals and children. When a woman looked for something to take the same relation to her within a poem that female figures take for male poets, the equation often reads: a male poet is to a woman as a female poet is to a child or an animal. Tennyson in *In Memoriam* compares his loss to that of a girl whose lover has died, and calls the girl a "meek, unconscious dove" (vi). Barrett Browning, in contrast, writes about real doves ("My Doves"), which like Tennyson's young woman are less intellectual and closer to God and nature than the poet is. Her cocker spaniel appears in "Flush, My Dog" and "Flush or Faunus" exuding womanly sympathy and watching tenderly at a bedside. Rossetti's animals, like the women portrayed by Pre-Raphaelite men, are erotically appealing and yet mysterious, inhuman, and somewhat repulsive: the lover whom Rossetti affectionately compares to a blind buzzard and a mole in "A Sketch," the sexy, self-satisfied crocodile in "My Dream," and the seductive goblins of *Goblin Market*: "One had a cat's face, / One whisked a tail, / One tramped at a rat's pace, / One crawled like a snail, / One like a wombat prowled obtuse and furry" (71-75).

Children in women's poems serve all the nonerotic functions of women in poems by men. They are beautiful, innocent, made only for love, and seem most poetical when they are strange, alien, and silent: dying, that is, or dead. Often, like fallen or outcast women, they are victims of a heartless society, and their apparent helplessness, like Godiva's nakedness, is their defense. As Barrett Browning says in "The Cry of the Children," "the child's sob in the silence curses deeper / Than the strong man in his wrath" (159-60). A mother's lament for a dead child is the feminine equivalent of a man's lament for a dead beloved, and maternal visions of angelic children or angels that carry them off to heaven are like men's desolating encounters with beautiful nonhuman women. Purity and uncensorious love make children agents of salvation to prostitutes and unmarried mothers, just as pure women are redemptive objects of worship for men. In Adelaide Procter's "The Requital," a "little Child Angel" (3) wanders through a stormy night, "With trailing pinions, / And weary feet" (5-6), looking for shelter. At first no one hears her appeals: like a woman in a Romantic poem she seems to be part of nature (her wings beat like rain on the windows) and her cry is incorporated into a poetic dream. But at last a poor prostitute hears her, takes her in, and is rewarded with the angel's kiss of death.

Children can also have a more ambiguous moral function. Poetic lovers traditionally value their beloved more than all the world's goods, and when the speaker in Rossetti's "Cousin Kate" taunts the rival who stole her aristocratic lover she triumphantly displays her possession of the lover's illegitimate child and of that child's love:

> My fair-haired son, my shame, my pride,
>   Cling closer, closer yet:
> Your father would give lands for one
>   To wear his coronet. (45-48)

Love for a child can even, like erotic love in Renaissance poetry, be renounced as an overvaluation of earthly things. The dying infant in Barrett Browning's "Isobel's Child" complains that his mother begrudges him the bliss of heaven, and in Jean Ingelow's "The Mariner's Cave" maternal love prevents a woman from looking up to heaven until her child is taken there by the child Jesus.

Children, animals, and angels have done a lot to discredit women poets. Like goblins, they don't seem to belong in serious poetry—only the barest handful of children appear in the canon before the Romantic period (and even then mostly in highly stylized poems by Blake and Wordsworth), and animals and angels are not common either—and they usually come swathed in an atmosphere of sentimentality that post-Victorian readers find peculiarly offensive. As with narrative, no adequate diction was available in which to present them. Still, these poems can be more varied and interesting—convey more complicated attitudes—than the usual quick revulsion would allow. And they offered a kind of solution, if not a very good one, to women's difficulty in situating themselves within poems.

Since women had appeared in poetry almost exclusively as amatory objects, it was generally assumed that when they wrote poems themselves love should be their theme, and the first women poets to attain popularity in the century evidently agreed. Felicia Hemans and Letitia Landon became famous in the vacancy left in the 1820s and '30s by the early deaths of the younger Romantic generation, but they always insisted that love, not fame, is woman's only source of happiness and that the two are incompatible. In a typical paradox, they sang their way to the fame they denigrated to the chords of lost or longed-for love. Their lives appeared to prove the point, since both were famous, both were unfortunate in love, and both were apparently unhappy. Hemans's husband went off to Italy before the birth of their fifth child and never returned, and Landon died mysteriously of poison soon after her marriage. "[T]he infusion of sorrow," said the American poet Lydia Sigourney, perfected Hemans's "high harmonies": "How else could she have learned such sympathy with those who mourn? — or become a soothing song-bird to the sad of heart? Her lot of loneliness was an affliction, which every passing year made more palpable and painful."[14] Every subject, however unlikely, could resolve into the same refrain: Hemans's "Woman on the Field of Battle," for example, expresses little surprise at the sight of a beautiful dead woman — "Woman hath been / Ever, where brave men die, / Unshrinking seen" (34-36) — but asserts that while men fight for glory or excitement or weariness of life, women die only for love.

Hemans's poetry is fluent, high-minded, sweet, and sorrowful, covering a wide range of times, places, and subjects. She read and translated from several languages, liked chivalric and martial themes almost as much as sentimental ones, and made frequent use of foreign settings. Like Landon she produced many narratives and incidents dramatically recounted, and was too prolific to make the best use of her talent. Landon was even more fond of exotic scenes and stories, concentrated more exclusively on romantic love, and tended to portray more violent passions. Barrett Browning, coming just after, enlarged the scope, scale, and intellectual seriousness of women's poetic terrain, writing substantial works of many kinds on subjects other than love.

Rossetti, Procter, and Ingelow, however, who first attracted attention around the time of Barrett Browning's death in 1861, kept within narrower bounds. They were more overtly and strictly religious than their female predecessors, and very much more so than almost all of their male contemporaries. Much of Rossetti's poetry is devotional and renunciative, and Procter's and Ingelow's inculcates simple piety and conventional morality. Unmarried, all three led scandal-free lives and allowed no fuss about their fame. They were all very successful, however; Rossetti was highly esteemed, and Procter and Ingelow had exceptionally large sales: in 1877, thirteen years after her death, Procter outsold every living writer but Tennyson, and Ingelow's works sold over 200,000 copies in America alone before her death in 1897.[15] The taint of Byronism never touched them, and to their contemporaries they exemplified the pure ideal of poetic womanhood.

When Adelaide Procter became a pseudonymous contributor to Dickens's journal, *Household Words*, the staff fabricated an identity for her that shows what women poets were expected to be. "We settled somehow, to our complete satisfaction," Dickens explained in an introduction to her collected poems, "that she was a governess in a family; that she went to Italy in that capacity, and returned; and that she had long been in the same family." They assumed, that is, that she was poor, single, dependent, and emotionally deprived. In fact, Dickens discovered, she was comfortably situated as the daughter of his old friend, the poet Barry Cornwall, and was an energetic feminist as well as a convert to Catholicism. Dickens found her active life unpleasing but was charmed by her death, which he attributes to her unseemly exertions.

> Now, it was the visitation of the sick that had possession of her . . . now, it was the
> raising up of those who had wandered and got trodden under foot; now, it was

the wider employment of her own sex in the general business of life; now, it was all these things at once. . . . Under such a hurry of the spirits, and such incessant occupation, the strongest constitution will commonly go down.

Soon she took to her bed. "All the restlessness gone then, and all the sweet patience of her natural disposition purified by the resignation of her soul, she lay upon her bed" for over a year until "with a bright and happy smile, look[ing] upward" she "departed."[16]

Illness that wastes the flesh and leads to an edifying death was felt to be suitable for poetesses. Thackeray's Miss Bunion comically violates the stereotype by having a hearty appetite and large feet. William Michael Rossetti reports that, his sister's health being delicate from the age of fifteen, "She was compelled, even if not naturally disposed, to regard this world as 'a valley of the shadow of death,' and to make near acquaintance with promises, and also with threatenings, applicable to a different world." The duration although not the seriousness of Elizabeth Barrett's illnesses was exaggerated by admiring readers, as was her ethereality. Poetesses were also expected to be creatures of emotion: William Michael Rossetti says that Christina's "life had two motive powers, — religion and affection: hardly a third. And even the religion was far more a thing of the heart than of the mind."[17] Their susceptibility to emotion, it was assumed, eroded their bodily strength.

Their poems, like themselves, were expected to be modest, unself-conscious, unpremeditated, and sincere. Rossetti's "habits of composition," said William Michael, despite all the evidence in her finely wrought poems of her careful craft, "were entirely of the casual and spontaneous kind." Ingelow's biographer reports that "She began her singing like a bird . . . because she could not help it."[18] Procter's most famous poem was "A Lost Chord" (set to music by Sir Arthur Sullivan), in which the speaker tells how her "fingers wandered idly / Over the noisy keys" (3-4) of an organ and struck by chance a splendid chord that reconciled pain and sorrow, the discords and perplexities of life. She was not the creator but the instrument's instrument: the chord "came from the soul of the Organ, / And entered into mine" (21-22). The image of the poet as musical instrument is a Romantic commonplace, but as usual a commonplace disclaimer of power reads like a literal expression of helplessness when a woman expresses it. A more elaborate version of the same idea appeared a few years later in Robert Browning's "Abt Vogler": the difference is that Browning's organist takes full credit for the evanescent music — "All through my keys that gave their sounds to a wish of my soul" (41) — not a single chord, moreover, but a long extemporization. Abt Vogler is a serious musician, Procter's speaker an idling amateur.

The ideal woman poet of mid-Victorian England would be Eliot's Dinah Morris: modest, selfless, loving, spontaneous, and unself-conscious, ascribing her works and words to the inspiration of God. Eliot, of course, never imagined that she herself could live or write that way, but the ideal seemed more attainable for poets. It was realized by Frances Ridley Havergal, author of hymns set to music by Gounod and other composers and of widely reprinted devotional works. Like Dinah, Havergal attended to the souls of everyone she met, including servants in houses she visited and strangers she met abroad. She regarded her writing as a direct transaction with God.

> I have a curiously vivid sense, not merely of my verse faculty in general being *given* me, but of every separate poem or hymn, nay every line, being *given*. I never write the simplest thing now without prayer for help. . . . It is peculiarly pleasant thus to take every thought, every verse as a direct gift; and it is not a matter of effort, it is purely involuntary.

Effectiveness mattered more than art: "Very often, strangers write and tell me that my lines comfort or help them, even when I know there is not a spark of poetry in them. Now *I* cannot tell what will comfort others, so I ask God to let me write what will do so."[19] The memoir of Havergal written by her sister is a kind of legend of a poet-saint and had, like her hymns, a wide circulation.

The ideal of spontaneity encouraged women to write lyrics and other apparently simple, unpretentious forms. Jean Ingelow's poems are often quite long, but they are usually fairly straightforward narratives. Her verse is fluent and energetic, frequently in anapestic measures; the diction despite some irritating archaisms is unpretentious and clear; and the world she depicts is English, pastoral, and innocent. Dim murmurs of the social and intellectual ferment of the times sometimes waft by, but they are easily dispelled. The characteristic Ingelow poem has two people in it, one of whom—a man—goes out into the world (there is a mild recurrent wistfulness about the pleasures of travel) while the other, usually but not always a woman, stays home. Sometimes one or the other is a poet. The meaning of this basic plot in terms of woman's place in poetry is made clear in "The Star's Monument: In the Concluding Part of a Discourse on Fame," in which a poet tells the woman he loves a long story about a poet who made a monument for a lost (female) star; regretting the star's lost fame, that is, he achieved his own fame by memorializing her. The woman in the frame narrative is identified with the star and with nature, and after telling the story the poet awaits her response.

> Adieu, he said, and paused, while she sat mute
>   In the soft shadow of the apple-tree;
> The skylark's song rang like a joyous flute,
>   The brook went prattling past her restlessly:
> She let their tongues be her tongue's substitute:
>   It was the wind that sighed, it was not she:
> And what the lark, the brook, the wind, had said,
> We cannot tell, for none interpreted. (60)

The poet leaves, embittered by her apparent unresponsiveness—"men," he says, "were made to roam" (53)—while the woman, like nature, remains mysterious, speechless, and unknown to fame.

When Ingelow's protagonist is a woman, however, expectations drop drastically and the tone turns comic. In "Gladys and Her Island (On the Advantages of the Poetical Temperament)" an orphan girl makes a brief and happy visit to a visionary island on her one day of freedom from drudgery in a school. Gladys neither achieves nor expects love or fame, and she does not complain about her lot or criticize the world. "[S]ince we are not grand," says the narrator in the concluding "Moral," "and as for cleverness, / That may be or may not be,—it is well / For us to be as happy as we can!" (828-30). As with Barrett Browning's and Rossetti's narrative presentations of women who are or represent poets, there is only one main character instead of Ingelow's usual pair, and instead of a potential lover Gladys meets a fey child who guides her to the island. Ingelow's poems are mostly, like Gladys, cheerful and undemanding; she is very much aware of the limitations set by gender on her verse but, unlike Barrett Browning, Brontë, and Rossetti, she rarely struggles against them.

Augusta Webster, in contrast to Procter and Ingelow, is forceful and erudite. Her specialties are poetic drama and dramatic monologue, the antitheses of feminine unpretentiousness and lyric spontaneity. She translated Aeschylus and Euripides and won her greatest acclaim with *The Sentence* (1887), a blank-verse play about Caligula that William Michael Rossetti declared "the supreme thing amid the work of *all* British poetesses." Christina Rossetti also admired *The Sentence* and considered Webster "by far the most formidable" woman poet she knew of.[20] Her work, like Barrett Browning's, was perceived as combining masculine and feminine qualities, and like Barrett Browning she was married and had one child. Her education had been subordinated in the usual way to a younger brother's—she learned Greek in order to help him—and largely self-acquired, but she had more opportunities than her predecessors did. She went to school for a while when she was young, and when her family moved to Cambridge in 1851 she had access to books and attended classes at the Cambridge School of Art, acquired French in Paris and Geneva and then Italian and Spanish. A skilled public speaker, she actively supported feminist causes, including full university education and votes for women, and in 1879 and 1885 was elected to the London School Board with large majorities.[21]

She began publishing with ballads and romances in apparent imitation of Barrett Browning's early works, and also with explorations of women's traditional location within nature, identifying with a dandelion, a flock of birds, and a serpent imprisoned in a chest at the bottom of a lake. But her best poems are long dramatic monologues in the style of Robert Browning, exploring character and motive and often showing the taste for macabre cruelty that led her to write her best play about the nastiest of the Roman emperors. Some of her characters are perfectly nice modern English people, but others include a man who locks his rival in a room with a dead body, a pathologically jealous ghost in the Catacombs, Judas Iscariot, Pontius Pilate, Circe, and Medea after she has killed her children.[22] In a different vein, she left an uncompleted sonnet sequence called "Mother and Daughter," which like George Eliot's "Brother and Sister" extends the emotional range of the sonnet sequence beyond its traditional amatory concerns.

Webster's dramatic monologues, which she uses like Barrett Browning and Rossetti to defy social and especially sexual conventions, allow her to tell new kinds of stories and express aberrant points of view. She gives a voice not just to women who had been idealized and silent, or to those whose generous passions led them astray, but also to the mysterious, morally ambiguous or evil figures who haunt Romantic and Pre-Raphaelite art but seldom find expression in women's verse. Her self-admiring speakers add to male portrayals of such figures a fierce contempt for men. Circe despises all the men she's turned to swine and gloats over her own beauty — "oh lips that tempt / my very self to kisses." Circe cannot literally kiss her own lips, however, except in a mirror, and her frustration images the impasse of the woman poet who cannot be both subject and object of desire. But in "A Castaway" a rich prostitute — a modern Circe — gloatingly regards her mirrored image:

> Aye let me feed upon my beauty thus,
> be glad in it like painters when they see
> at last the face they dreamed but could not find
> look from their canvass on them, triumph in it,
> the dearest thing I have.

She is both painter and painting, both visionary and dream; complete herself, she needs lovers only for money. She hates men. Rejecting the tawdry glamorization with which artists depict women like herself, and also their smug condemnation, she boldly declares her sisterhood "with any drab / who sells herself as I, although she crouch / In fetid garrets . . . our traffic's one." She refuses the usual dehumanizing oversimplifications: she's "no fiend, no slimy thing out of the pools," and not "a sort of fractious angel misconceived" either.[23] Her self-sufficiency is buttressed by feminist social analysis as she traces the conditions (not enough husbands, jobs, education, or knowledge of the world) that drive women to her trade. Self-consciousness, self-exposure, and woman's double place as subject and as object in art are reinterpreted by Webster in light of an emergent feminist ideology, and she vastly enlarges the range of voices through which women poets can speak. She exploits without subterfuge or apology the assault on poetic tradition that her predecessors began. But that tradition has had its revenge: despite their excellence, her poems remain almost entirely unknown.

5. The Range of
Prose Fiction

❧ ❧ ❧

Some of the most popular women novelists wrote books that were intended, like popular women's poetry, for the moral guidance and spiritual inspiration of their readers. Religious novelists accepted the subordination of women as ordained by God, but their faith gave them a firm ground (if not an actual pulpit) from which to do their own preaching. It also gave them the assurance that a woman's life did not need romance or marriage to give it meaning, thereby enabling them to vary conventional plots and explore kinds of lives usually scorned or ignored in fiction. Charlotte M. Yonge's favorite heroines—Ethel May in *The Daisy Chain*, Geraldine Underwood in *The Pillars of the House*—do not marry, but they live happily ever after nonetheless. Elizabeth Sewell wrote fiction designed "to show that life could be happy, and its events of importance, apart from marriage."[1] In a different mode, Lady Georgiana Fullerton's melodramatic *Ellen Middleton*, a novel of blackmail, mystery, and domestic violence, turns themes of doubleness and exposure into a demonstration of the spiritual value of confession.

Like Ingelow and Procter, their poetic counterparts, these women lived exemplary lives, although like Procter they were considerably more energetic and participated more in worldly business than innocent readers might imagine. Neither Yonge nor Sewell married, but Yonge's literary and editorial activities and Sewell's work in literature and education added up to substantial careers. Fullerton, like Procter, converted to Catholicism, and after the death of her only child she devoted herself to spiritual and charitable works and an extreme austerity of life; but she was also an organizer and administrator, her power enhanced by her secure position in the aristocracy. They all feared the corruptions of fame and used their earnings for altruistic purposes, Sewell to support her family and schools, Yonge for the church and missions, Fullerton for charity. Charlotte Elizabeth Tonna, who like Havergal believed her work to be divinely inspired, had a livelier career, having lived in the wilds of Canada and Ireland while married to her abusive first husband; she too became a busy professional, her creative and editorial labors singlemindedly devoted to religious purposes.

At the other extreme were the romantic and sensation novelists for whom writing was a worldly career, who shocked and titillated readers while nominally adhering to conventional morality, and who violated feminine decorum with impunity in their behavior as well as their books. Mrs. Henry Wood, author of the fantastically popular *East Lynne* and other melodramatic novels, worked without scandal as writer, editor, and magazine proprietor to support her large family. She punished her heroine's misdeeds with exemplary severity: the errant wife in *East Lynne* loses her beauty in an accident, returns unrecognized to be governess to her own children, and suffers the agony of witnessing her husband's new marriage and her son's death. But Mary Elizabeth Braddon became an actress to support her mother and herself, was launched as a writer by a man who may or may not have been her lover, and then settled down with John Maxwell, a publisher with five children whose mad wife was in an asylum. She had six children with Maxwell and married him years later when his wife died. When she had achieved fame with what she referred to as her "bigamy novels," *Lady Audley's Secret* and *Aurora Floyd,* Maxwell tried to regularize their domestic situation—their own version of bigamy—by announcing their "marriage" in the press, thereby inciting his brother-in-law to announce the existence of Maxwell's wife with equivalent publicity. Her fame became ill fame, her characters' problems her own.

Braddon edited several magazines and made her fortune by producing what the market demanded. "The Balzac-morbid-anatomy school is my especial delight," she told an editor, but she was willing to provide what he wanted instead: "a sensational fiction."

> I will give the kaleidoscope (which I cannot spell) another turn, and will do my very best with the old bits of glass and pins and rubbish.
>   There they all are—the young lady who has married a burglar, and who does not want to introduce him to her friends; the duke . . . ; the two brothers who are perpetually taken for one another; the twin-sisters ditto, ditto; the high-bred and conscientious banker, who has made away with everybody's title-deeds. Any novel combination of the well-known figures is completely at your service, workmanship careful, delivery prompt.[2]

Themes from Eliot, Brontë, and Gaskell are reborn in such works, which as Braddon's list suggests explore the mysteries of identity and the doubleness of the self. Self-consciousness in Braddon's novels is explicitly the consciousness of a concealed and usually illicit sexuality. The audiences earlier heroines seek and fear crystallize into detectives or blackmailers, and fear of exposure is thematized in an essential element of Braddon's plots that does not appear on her list: blackmail, usually for sexual transgressions. Aurora Floyd, for instance, is a rich, sexy, boldly unconventional woman who marries a handsome groom and then makes a more suitable marriage under the impression that her first husband is dead; when he returns to blackmail her he is murdered and suspicion falls on Aurora. The true murderer is detected, however, and Aurora and the remaining husband ride out the scandal and live happily ever after. Exposure, it seems, is not so terrible after all.

In both her life and her work Braddon wrote with bold, broad strokes what other women feared. She began by literally exposing herself on the stage; unlike Jane Eyre, she did not object to living with a man whose mad wife made marriage impossible; and her bustling, fertile extralegal union produced scandal of a sort that Eliot, aloof and severe, never suffered. Reviewers' sneers at her character annoyed her, and her eventual marriage shocked her servants, who had assumed that she and Maxwell were married already, into leaving, which was both humiliating and inconvenient. But she kept on her way undeterred and ended up rich, happy, and respectable, free to write books she took seriously instead of potboilers, and treated with respect as a friend and artist even by Henry James. Like Aurora Floyd she broke the laws of decorum and marriage and was found out, and in the end it didn't matter.

Braddon's friend Ouida (Marie Louise de la Ramée) was to the romantic novel what Braddon was to sensation fiction. Both had their first great successes in the 1860s, made a lot of money, and were extremely prolific, although Ouida's more than forty books were no match for Braddon's enormous output. Critics laughed at her stories, but everyone read them, and late in her career Max Beerbohm with an air of pleasant paradox celebrated her "Titanic force," her amazing vitality, her professionally constructed plots, and her wide-ranging evocations of romance:

> Her pen is more inexhaustibly prolific than the pen of any other writer; it gathers new strength of its every dip into the ink-pot. . . . Her every page is a riot of unpolished epigrams and unpolished poetry of vision, with a hundred discursions and redundancies. . . . No writer was ever more finely endowed than Ouida with the love and knowledge of all kinds of beauty in art and nature. . . . Ouida's descriptions of boudoirs in palaces are no more vulgar nor less beautiful than her descriptions of lakes and mountains.[3]

It is impossible to praise Ouida's books without laughing at them, just as Braddon joked about her own plots; and yet for both writers there was a perilous link between the apparent absurdities of their highly unrealistic novels and their own hard-working professional lives. Her father like Braddon's having ceased to provide for the family, Ouida moved to London with her mother and grandmother before she was twenty and almost immediately began to support them by writing. Her extremely entertaining tales of intrigue and adventure among rich, highborn, and fabulously glamorous people made her rich herself and provided her with Worth gowns, horses, expensive flowers, and other accoutrements of her fictions. She could not buy an aristocratic lineage, but she did what she could by changing her name from Ramé to de la Ramée. Settling in Florence, she fell in love with an Italian marchese whom she lost after ten years to his longtime mistress, a married Englishwoman. Her extravagance and addiction to grand gestures reduced her to penury, until at last she had no money to bury her mother or buy food. True to the end to her self-creation, she tore up checks from her friends and fed the food they sent her to her dogs. She died impoverished, crazy, and alone.

Ouida did what the young George Eliot had reprehended in Scott and feared as a consequence of writing. She didn't just match in her stories the experiences of her life, as Braddon did; she tried to inhabit the world of her own imagination, and her success in doing so destroyed her. She had been a happy child who dramatized stories with cardboard knights and ladies and studied hard in order to become a rich and famous writer and have a passionate love affair, and the woman accomplished what the child had planned. It is as if Charlotte Brontë had decided to spend her adult life in Angria. And in fact Ouida's world has a distinctly Angrian air. Her proud, suave, bold aristocrats would be quite at home among the Angrian lords and ladies; and in the last will and testament of an Angrian lady, a document carefully prepared by the young Charlotte Brontë as a miniature imitation of the real thing, one finds a detailed catalog of the sort of luxurious objects in which Ouida takes delight. Like Brontë, Ouida strongly defended the rights of imagination; and she insisted that her imaginary world corresponded more or less literally to reality:

> what I object to is the limitation of realism in fiction to what is commonplace, tedious, and bald—is the habit . . . of insisting that the potato is real and that the passion flower is not. . . . I have known very handsome people, I have known very fine characters, I have also known some very wicked ones, and I have also known many circumstances so romantic that were they described in fiction, they would be ridiculed as exaggerated and impossible.[4]

She criticized and satirized high society as well as celebrated it, and she movingly represented the sufferings of the poor; but she never fully emerged from her early dream.

Her own books should have taught her better. The real marchese who divided his attentions between two women seems to be an avatar of the fictional Bertie Cecil, the aristocratic hero of a book she had written before meeting the marchese: *Under Two Flags*, which sold millions of copies and was reborn in the twentieth century as a classic comic and a film. Before the story really gets going Bertie relieves his tedium with a married woman and a kept mistress, and his unabashed duplicity foreshadows the irresolute marchese. When men of high rank such as Bulwer Lytton and Lord Curzon fastidiously drew back from Ouida she might have recalled the unreciprocated love of the camp follower Cigarette for Bertie when he is serving as a private soldier in the French Foreign Legion. Cigarette is clever, brave, proud, and honorable; like Ouida she loves animals; she spurs the soldiers to heroism; and she is an artist whose dances for the entertainment of the troops delight all but the fastidious Bertie.

Like *Mary Barton* and *Adam Bede*, *Under Two Flags* contains a trial, a journey, and a last-minute rescue, but the outcome is not the same. When Bertie is condemned to death for striking an officer, Cigarette borrows a horse from an

Arab chieftain, gallops across the desert with a pardon, and is killed when she throws herself in front of Bertie at the moment the firing squad shoots.[5] Bertie himself, however, recovers his position in society and marries a highborn lady who would never expose herself in public or engage in errant heroism; it was in defense of her reputation, in fact, that Bertie struck the officer. Cigarette's sacrificial death only saves him from completing his self-sacrifice for another, more conventional, woman. There is a warning for the woman artist here, but Ouida did not heed it.

Most novelists, of course, fell somewhere between Sewell and Yonge on the one hand and Braddon and Ouida on the other. Frances Trollope, for instance, wrote all sorts of books, including novels of social protest, to keep her family going. Eliza Lynn Linton combined opportunism and conviction in her equally hardworking career, always trying to figure out what would sell and producing among other incompatible works both "The Girl of the Period," an antifeminist satire, and *Joshua Davidson*, a thoroughgoing assault from a more or less communist perspective on the whole social, economic, and religious system of Britain. Felicia Skene, another of the novelists whose work was dedicated to pious ends and who wrote fiction in order to earn money for charity, fiercely depicted the dark side of Victorian life as her philanthropic work had revealed it to her. In the preface to her novel *Hidden Depths*, in which the heroine discovers and tries to ameliorate the sufferings of girls whom her brother and (she eventually discovers) her fiancé have seduced and abandoned, she justifies her writing by its social truth and denies any indulgence of her own or her readers' imaginations:

> This book is not a work of fiction, in the ordinary acceptation of the term. If it were, it would be worse than useless; for the hidden depths, of which it reveals a glimpse, are no fit subject for a romance, nor ought they to be opened up to the light of day for purposes of mere amusement. But truth must always have a certain power, in whatever shape it may appear; and though all did not occur precisely as here narrated, it is nevertheless actual truth which speaks in these records. (Preface)

The novel exposes the gender and class inequities of the sexual double standard, the horrors of prostitutes' lives and the inhumanity of the institutions that try to reform them, and also the dire results of the religious rationalism that tried young men's faith in the great universities.

In another key entirely, Anne Thackeray Ritchie's youthful *The Story of Elizabeth*, written in a lively, breathless, abrupt style with considerable wit and irony, portrays the life of religious fundamentalists in France as seen by an ignorant, passionate English girl and contains a rather bold depiction of a mother's sexual rivalry with her daughter, a theme the author's father had treated too. Rhoda Broughton, inspired by Anne Thackeray, made sexier books out of similar material, which she padded and stretched to fill three volumes: her strong, sturdy, passionate heroines fall helplessly in love with sexy cads but manage to keep their virtue physically intact. They may not get the men they want, who aren't worth having, and some of them sacrifice their lives for others, but they are clear-sighted and good-humored, and their disdain for the stupid, mean-minded, conventional people around them is always endorsed by the author. Broughton's books were mildly scandalous, but she established a social position for herself in Cambridge with the sturdy self-reliance that makes her heroines so appealing. Skene, Ritchie, and Broughton may stand as representative of the broad middle range of Victorian women's writing.

The best of the novelists outside of the canon is Margaret Oliphant, whose literary labors through a long and arduous life supported herself, her children, and various other relatives, including at times her brothers, one of whom was a hopeless alcoholic who squandered his opportunities like Branwell Brontë but did not die young. After her husband's early death she had entire financial responsibility for a household that varied in size but was always expensive, since she lived on a generous scale and sent her two sons and a nephew to Eton. She published well over a hundred books, including novels and stories (mostly domestic fiction but also some very good tales of the supernatural), biographies, books of travel, literary history, and a history of the publishing house of Blackwood, as well as stories, essays, and reviews in periodicals that included many influential anonymous reviews in *Blackwood's*. "I had always a lightly flowing stream of magazine articles, &c, and refused no work that was offered to me. . . ."[6] Stimulated by recurrent crises when it seemed that money would run out entirely, exhilarated when it didn't, she "loved the easy swing of life, without taking much thought for the morrow" (117), and she never stopped writing. When her much-loved daughter died at the age of ten in 1864 Oliphant was in Italy, a widow with two younger children and two unfinished novels being serialized in magazines; with the break of a month, the novels continued.

Not surprisingly, most of her books, like Braddon's and Ouida's and Broughton's, show marks of haste: careless writing, padding, repetition, badly constructed plots with elements brazenly lifted from other novelists, and eruptions of silly melodrama in otherwise lifelike and engaging stories. She doesn't take plot very seriously; the conventionally happy ending of *The Perpetual Curate* (one of the books she was writing when her daughter died), for instance, is mocked by the hero's strong-minded aunt: "'Poetic justice!' she said, with a furious sneer. . . . 'I don't approve of a man ending off neatly like a novel in this sort of ridiculous way'" (537). But she has a supple and elegant style, an acerbic wit, a bracing coolness about human nature, and a remarkable ability to create lifelike characters. Her skill in displaying complexities of feeling and motive makes limited, ordinary, selfish, or foolish people exceptionally interesting, and minor characters are often the best things in her books. She dissects the frustrations, disappointments, vanity, pleasures, and heroism of ordinary people leading uneventful lives: spinsters who enjoy their independence while they fear that they're missing the heart of life, wives who make the best of decent but self-centered husbands, young people afflicted with exasperating relatives. Love stories are dished up with just enough acerbity to make them palatable. And the subtle shades of domestic tyranny, the intricate adjustments of marriage, and the half-conscious self-deceptions that keep life going are wonderfully depicted.

By publishing carelessly conceived and hastily executed work, Oliphant visibly disavowed ambition and played into the belief that women cannot rise to a masculine grasp of an artistic whole. "The poor soul had a simply *feminine* conception of literature," Henry James pronounced with fastidious condescension: "such slipshod, imperfect, halting, faltering, peeping, down-at-heel work."[7] She herself, however, thought her work marred not by a woman's weakness but by a mother's strength. Motherhood, in which Jameson, Eliot, and Rossetti found the source of woman's special power, was the central fact of Oliphant's life; and while it may have empowered her as a woman she felt that it enfeebled her as a writer. Her *Autobiography* mulls over the conflicting claims of motherhood and literature, convinced that each has hurt the other. The book is shaped by the deaths of her five children, and she was haunted by fears that her writing had harmed them. Her second and third babies died in infancy, and Mary Howitt (herself a writer and editor)

> frightened me very much, I remember, by telling me of many babies whom she had lost through some defective valve in the heart, which she said was somehow connected with too much mental work on the part of the mother,—a foolish thing, I should think, yet the same thing occurred twice to myself. It alarmed and saddened me terribly. (40)

That a mother's brain-work injures her child's heart, literally and figuratively, is standard nineteenth-century lore. But Oliphant also blamed herself for not seeming to work hard enough. She had quenched "a little stirring of ambition" with the conventional thought "that to bring up the boys for the service of God was better than to write a fine novel" (16); but later she thought sadly that if she had been more ambitious she might have written better and earned more, while her sons "might have learned habits of work which now seem beyond recall" (16). For if the novels were unsatisfactory, the boys did not turn out well either. Betraying the promise of their Eton years, their Oxford careers were undistinguished or worse. Cyril, the elder, drifted aimlessly to an early death: "He went out of the world, leaving a love-song or two behind him and the little volume of 'De Musset,' of which much was so well done, and yet some so badly done, and nothing more to show for his life" (153). Cecco, the younger son, redeemed himself by application to study and devotion to his mother, but ill health thwarted his attempts to make a career and he too died young. She wondered miserably if she had set a bad example by making her own unremitting hard work look easy and inconsequential (117, 152). Like other women writers of the century, from Jane Austen on, she wrote in the midst of family life, where she could always be interrupted, or when everyone else was asleep, making no display of her labor; but what was proper behavior in a woman was a deadly model for young men.

Her best book, her *Autobiography*, mimics in its formal structure the hesitations and shifting purposes of her working life. A series of fragments written between the early 1860s and 1892, selected and rearranged after her death by her cousin in accordance with the chronology of events and with many of the most poignant or acerbic passages excised, its lack of a coherent narrative line links it with other women's autobiographies of the period, many of which were published posthumously and given their final shape by others.[8] Until very recently critics have thought her autobiography unworthy of comparison to the autobiographies by men, stiffened by purposeful plots and a firm sense of self, that have set the standard for the genre. And yet the book not only is deeply moving but also—both uncut and arranged in order of composition, and in the edited version that was first published—feels satisfyingly complete. Like Jameson's *Diary of an Ennuyée* it seems ideally feminine: perfectly spontaneous, artlessly responsive to the emotions it conveys, a brilliant enactment of the characteristics attributed to women writers, with every strength magnified and every fault become a virtue. And yet, of course, Oliphant was a thorough professional and knew exactly what she was doing.

The fluidity of structure is augmented in the original edition, and the balance decisively changed, by the fact that the autobiography itself is followed by a selection of letters, with commentary, that is substantially longer than the autobiography itself and, since a large proportion of the letters are to her publishers, foregrounds her professional career. The book she herself wrote, however, looks mostly inward, to private emotions and domestic events, and is shaped and suffused by that most feminine of themes, the deaths of children; but with a tough-mindedness—the faults of the dead are not hidden, although they are touched with delicate reticence—that wards off sentimentality, while the emotional richness averts the coldness of tone that may sometimes repel us in her novels. Long passages of anguished outpouring and self-analysis— almost, at times, prayer—were excised by her editors, presumably because they were too personal and revealed too much about the dead; but even in the truncated version the sense of pain is delicately pervasive, while memories of disconnected little scenes and episodes glow with warmth and life. For instance, she recalls traveling in Italy:

> I think with pleasure of the pleasant tumult of that arrival,—the delight of rest, the happy sleepy children all got to bed, the little party of women, all of us about the same age, all with the sense of holiday, a little outburst of freedom, no man interfering, keeping us to rule or formality. (107)

Male rule and formality are kept out of this sentence too, and out of the *Autobiography* as a whole.

The text itself has a fluid, unfixable existence. The two versions now in print are taken from fragments written at different times; and since Oliphant assumed that her heirs would cut and edit them, if they published them at all, no finally definitive version can even be imagined. The same is true of experience as she narrates it. The past is transfigured by memory, and by memories of remembering, so that emotional truth is located, if anywhere, in some impossible space that includes a sequence of moments but *is* none of them. "The immense relief of getting over a crisis," she recalls, for example, "gave a kind of reflected enjoyment to the trouble between" (136), and both the relief and the trouble are transformed again by the moment of writing. Events that might have happened but did not, or that cannot happen, shimmer among events that really occurred. For instance:

> I wonder sometimes if what has been ever dies! Should not I find them all round the old whist-table, and my Cecco, with his bright face and the great blue vein that showed on his temple, proud to be helping to amuse the old people, if I were but bold enough to push into the deserted house and look for them now? I have so often felt, with a bewildered dizziness, as if that might be. (125)

An air of magic and mystery plays, delicately but persistently, even over commonplace events: "At Genoa we were somehow strangely fortunate" (68). And as the number of her dead increases, they hover, almost palpable, around her.

The flow and counterflow of feeling, memory, and imagination structure the book and take the place of plot. Retrospective narrative is embedded in a sequence of present moments with an immediacy that gives the effect of extreme spontaneity. We are often shown the writer in the act of writing. For instance:

> I have been reading the life of Mr. Symonds, and it makes me almost laugh (though little laughing is in my heart) to think of the strange difference between this prosaic little narrative, all about the facts of a life so simple as mine, and his elaborate self-discussions . . . . But it is vain for me to go on in this strain. I have fallen back into my own way of self-comment, — and that is such a different thing. (99-100)

Oliphant speaks of her "perfectly artless art" (104) even as she watches herself writing, and watches herself watching.

Anthony Trollope, whose autobiography was published while Oliphant was writing hers, is Oliphant's male counterpart, and the contrast between them is instructive. He too was not quite of the first rank as a novelist; worked at writing as a trade; tried to turn out what the market demanded; and was aware that he might be thought to have written too much. Like Oliphant too, he wrote in the time spared from the main business of life, consisting in his case of a position in the post office and an addiction to fox hunting as well as a family. His books, like hers, deal with ordinary people and mixed, obscure motives, and her most popular series, the *Chronicles of Carlingford*, tries shamelessly to exploit the popularity of his Barsetshire novels. They are well matched despite their differences: the superior construction of his novels is balanced by her finer command of language, his brilliant use of politics as a subject by hers of the supernatural, his intenser conviction of his characters' reality by her perhaps sharper insight and more subtle analysis. But in their autobiographies the similarities are erased by differences that all relate to gender.

Trollope begins:

> In writing these pages, which, for the want of a better name, I shall be fain to call the autobiography of so insignificant a person as myself, it will not be so much my intention to speak of the little details of my private life, as of what I, and perhaps others round me, have done in literature; of my failures and successes such as they have been, and their causes; and of the opening which a literary career offers to men and women for the earning of their bread.[9]

Self-belittlement is common to both, but whereas Oliphant remakes the form to fit her own perceived unfitness for it, Trollope remarks his insufficiency and then goes ahead in the usual way. He writes a linear narrative which is almost entirely about his public career, apologizing in advance for the intrusion of the kind of personal elements that are the substance of Oliphant's book.

> And yet the garrulity of old age, and the aptitude of a man's mind to recur to the passages of his own life, will, I know, tempt me to say something of myself; — nor, without doing so, should I know how to throw my matter into any recognised and intelligible form. (1)

He tells us about the miseries of his childhood but almost nothing about his wife and children beyond the fact that they exist. In his own view, his adult life formed a harmonious and satisfying whole, and his narrative moves smoothly along while it explains, as autobiographies traditionally do, how he became the self-integrated narrator who is telling the story. Although he makes no grand claims for either his book or his life, he regards himself as an interesting model of a type of successful literary man; not, like Oliphant, an anomaly and a failure. His career is not a puzzle but an instructive example. He does not pretend to genius, but he is proud of his workmanlike habits of composition and reports the rewards, financial and otherwise, with engaging candor. "There is perhaps no career of life so charming as that of a successful man of letters" (209).

By recounting what he conceives to be a representative career and not just a personal history Trollope is following the central tradition of Victorian autobiography. John Henry Newman's *Apologia Pro Vita Sua* defends Roman Catholicism along with his own probity, and John Stuart Mill's *Autobiography* is conceived as the history of an educational experiment and the development of a utilitarian philosopher. The older confessional mode of spiritual autobiography follows a highly stylized pattern of spiritual development. But Oliphant does not feel herself representative of anything; dissatisfied with herself both as a mother and as a writer, having lived an unplanned life with no theory or institution to support it, still uncertain how she could have done things better, she cannot offer her career as exemplary of anything but muddle and loss. And yet she feels that she did accomplish a great deal—enough, at any rate, to make her story worth writing and likely to be read. The problems of a woman trapped by the contradictory demands of family and career seemed to her too unusual, too odd and sad—she was not a feminist—to be of general interest. She could neither find a traditional pattern by which to organize her experience nor imagine a new one; but this apparent failure provides the organizing principle of her book.

Writing an autobiography is a definitive act of exposure even for those who eschew personal confession. Trollope, lacking a woman's sensitivity to the multifarious dangers of self-display, seems not to have anticipated that describing his businesslike habits of composition would damage his reputation as an artist; but Oliphant's sense of her life as an inextricable mingling of public and private, familial and professional, was accompanied by a very complicated sense of audience. Like Dinah Morris and other heroines, she preserves her integrity by keeping herself for most of the time unconscious of spectators, although her own self-consciousness is always very strong. Most often she seems to be writing for herself: to express painful feeling, for the bitter-sweet pleasures of memory, or in an effort toward self-understanding. For a while, she says, she was writing for her sons, and thought Cecco would not publish the book (he "did not like publicity, and would have thought his mother's story of her life sacred" [87]). Trollope wrote for his son, too, but from the beginning he expected publication. Later she thinks of it being published to make money for her nieces and wonders if her sons, now dead, will be a spectral audience (95). When she imagines the book actually being published she shifts to less personal anecdotes and her confidence falters: "I feel all this to be so vulgar, so common, so unnecessary, as if I were making pennyworths of myself" (95)—writing as a kind of prostitution. But she is always her own first reader, allowing no hint of vanity to pass without comment, and with a ruthless ear for self-aggrandizement and self-pity.

She compares herself, for instance, to George Eliot and George Sand:

> These two bigger women did things which I have never felt the least temptation to do—but how very much more enjoyment they seem to have got out of their life, how much more praise and homage and honour! I would not buy their fame, with their disadvantages, but I do feel very small, very obscure, beside them, rather a failure all round, never securing any strong affection, and throughout my life, though I have had all the usual experiences of a woman, never impressing anybody—what a droll little complaint!—why should I? I acknowledge frankly that there is nothing in me—a fat, little, commonplace woman, rather tongue-tied—to impress any one; and yet there is a sort of whimsical injury in it which makes me sorry for myself. (17)

Here is the kind of sentence—apparently artless and unpremeditated, loose in construction yet never out of control, conveying subtle shifts and turns of feeling and fine gradations of tone—that years of practice had perfected. Physical self-consciousness ("fat, little, commonplace") is matched by an endlessly self-correcting moral self-awareness in a performance as seductive and yet free of vanity as Dinah Morris's preaching.

Oliphant never resolves the dilemma of her life. Part of her freedom from rule and formality in the autobiography is her freedom not to choose. She accepts the doubleness, even duplicity, that conduct-books reprehended and Eliot feared. She feels sorry for herself because no one ever took care of her, but she rejoices in the memory of independence and the power to take care of others. She denigrates her work, but feels insufficiently recognized and rewarded. She is glad that she never roared in society as a literary lion, but resents not being treated like one. She never bargained for money ("I took what was given me and was very grateful" [102]), but knows she should have been paid more. And she never settled the balance, although she kept trying, between the two main facts of her life: that she was a mother and had had "all the usual experiences of a woman," and that she was a professional writer.

Conflict between love and literature is the theme of the book, and provides closure:

> When [Cecco] was absent [in the last years of his life] he wrote to me every day. I never went out but he was there to give me his arm. I seem to feel it now—the dear, thin, but firm arm. In the last four years after Cyril was taken from us, we were nearer and nearer. I can hear myself saying "Cecco and I." It was the constant phrase. But all through he was getting weaker: and I knew it, and tried not to know.
> And now here I am all alone.
> I cannot write any more. (154)

The speaker of Rossetti's *Monna Innominata* lapses into silence in the final sonnet because with youth, beauty, and her lover gone, she can no longer sing. Oliphant's book ends in the silence occasioned by the loss of another kind of love. When she has only writing, she does not even have that. Duplicity kept her going: "I knew it, and tried not to know." Like Rossetti and many other Victorian women, Oliphant did her best work under the pressure of an irresolvable conflict between femaleness and writing, between a unitary ideal and the fact of doubleness, and at the end of the *Autobiography* she too speaks from a place dedicated to silence. Along with the desolation that suffuses the book, however, we always feel what made her write and makes us read: the energy generated by paradox, and the irrepressible pleasure of writing.

🍏 🍏 🍏 *Part Three*

6. The Female Sage

❧ ❧ ❧

Literary culture was most resistant to female infiltration in the arena of high-prestige nonfictional prose. Polemical and critical works by Thomas Carlyle, John Ruskin, John Henry Newman, John Stuart Mill, Matthew Arnold, Walter Pater, and some others became icons of high culture, literary monuments in their own right; and here "masculine" powers of mind—soundness and breadth of conception, originality and coherence of thought, force of argument, and the spiritual vision, moral fervor, and compelling utterance that in earlier ages belonged to prophets, sages, and great poets—held, it seemed, undisputed sway. Although these writers more often than not set themselves in histrionic opposition to the society they wanted to chasten and make new, they spoke from a position of assured cultural centrality and their voices resonate with the rhythms, allusions, and authority of high culture.

As John Gross points out in *The Rise and Fall of the Man of Letters* (a book which includes no Victorian *woman* of letters except George Eliot), Victorian literature was closely linked to public life.[1] Writers served in Parliament and as prime minister, and journals central to cultural life were political organs. Intellectual activity was still relatively unprofessionalized and unspecialized, so that every man of letters, it seemed, felt free to pontificate on every subject. Scientific works became part of the general culture, and literary men wrote seriously about science. Intellectual and public affairs were carried on by networks of interlocking groups, bound up with the centers of political and cultural power, that rarely included women.

And yet much of the distinctive flavor of the Victorian prose that has entered the literary canon—its flexibility, its unsettling, insinuating power, its peculiar charm—comes from elements conventionally coded as feminine. Its practitioners were not always clearly aligned with conventional masculinity: suspicions were aroused by the annulment of Ruskin's unconsummated marriage, Newman's celibacy and his influence over young men, Mill's support of women's rights. Only Carlyle, the first and most ferocious of the Victorian sages, seems (at least during his lifetime) to have been secure from feminine associations. Matthew Arnold's appeals for "sweetness and light" and detachment from public affairs gave a feminine cast to both classicism and "culture." The writings of Walter Pater, whose enervated rhythms and richly colored glorifications of aesthetic experience seemed strange and perverse to sturdy right-thinking Englishmen, brought the homoerotic strain of classical Greek culture perilously close to the surface. But the suffused homoeroticism of Pater's writings belonged to a school and university ethos in which women hardly existed even as objects of desire.[2] Except for Mill, none of the Victorian sages welcomed women into their intellectual worlds; and while Mill credited Harriet Taylor (who became his wife) as his collaborator in much of his work, the actual publications were in his name alone and his testimony to her intelligence has been derided and disbelieved.

The fact that formal education was dominated by the classics was convenient, however, for women who wrote about other subjects. New disciplines were developing in which academic specialization had hardly begun, and the self-taught could participate in intellectual discourse and earn money by servicing the public appetite for instruction. Harriet Martineau expounding political economy, Agnes and Elizabeth Strickland in history, Anna Jameson in art history, Mary Somerville in science, and many others in other fields of intellectual endeavor succeeded without any formal training in their subjects. Female intellectuals rarely indulged in the self-dramatizing rhetoric of the great Victorian prose masters or created vivid, authoritative personae for themselves; they were not expected to be original or creative; but they were allowed ancillary roles in moral or pedagogical enterprises, and some achieved more than that. Feminists carved out their own territory: Barbara Leigh Smith Bodichon, for instance, who argued vigorously for women's need and right to work, or Frances Power Cobbe, who wrote about religion, women's rights, antivivisection, and other topics.

Many women in effect reaffirmed their marginal status by writing about women's affairs, and even the most venturesome usually kept to territory where men were not likely to get in their way. Agnes and Elizabeth Strickland published many historical studies of royal figures, mostly female (under Agnes's name alone, Elizabeth refusing to put hers in print). Their books were based on extensive original research and filled with details of private and domestic matters, including manners and costume, that enthralled large audiences while arousing critics' disdain. But they insisted on the seriousness of their project. In the preface to *Lives of the Queens of England*, published in twelve volumes from 1840 to 1848, they explain:

> We have related the parentage of every queen, described her education, traced the influence of family connections and national habits on her conduct, both public and private, and given a concise outline of the domestic, as well as the general history of her times, and its effects on her character, and we have done so with singleness of heart, unbiassed . . . . A queen is no ordinary woman, to be condemned on hearsay evidence; she is the type of the heavenly bride in the beautiful 45th Psalm: — "Whatsoever things are lovely, whatsoever things are holy, whatsoever things are pure, and of good report" in the female character, ought to be found in her. A queen-regnant occupies a still higher position, — she is God's vicegerent upon earth."[3]

The Stricklands present their royal heroines as, in effect, the female counter-parts of the heroes (all, of course, male), who for Carlyle embody the highest human ideals and the motive force of history. They often point to instances where women's political activity has been underrated by male historians, and are in advance of their times in emphasizing the historical significance of private and domestic life. But since they attribute women's importance in history to womanly virtue they do not, in the end, seriously challenge the principle of gender exclusiveness in conventional history.

Early in her career Anna Jameson wrote books somewhat on the lines of the Stricklands': about women loved by poets, Shakespeare's heroines, and (in 1831, almost a decade before the Stricklands' *Queens of England*) female sovereigns. Her scholarship in these books is less thoroughgoing than the Stricklands', but it is considerably more serious than the work on "Criminal Queens" with which Trollope's fictional hack, Lady Carbury, made her mark later in the century. *The Loves of the Poets* covers classical, troubadour, Italian, German, French, and English writers and is a work of considerable learning. Jameson was careful to disarm criticism, however, with prefaces that define in very modest terms her subject, her work, and herself.

> These little sketches (they can pretend to no higher title) are submitted to the public with a feeling of timidity almost painful.
> They are absolutely without any other pretension than that of exhibiting . . . many anecdotes of biography and criticism, and many beautiful poetical portraits . . . all tending to illustrate a subject in itself full of interest,—the influence which the beauty and virtue of women have exercised over the characters and writings of men of genius. But little praise or reputation attends the mere compiler.

She defines an appropriate audience:

> It is for women I write; the fair, pure-hearted, delicate-minded, and unclassical reader will recollect that I do not presume to speak of these poets critically, being neither critic nor scholar; but merely with a reference to my subject, and with reference to my sex.[4]

Despite such protestations, however, her early books and many of her later ones are in fact studies of female power, and although her views of women's nature remained conservative she became a strong supporter of younger feminists and of women's need and right to work.

Her greatest interest, however, was in the fine arts. Like the Stricklands, Jameson had a gift for research and was very hardworking (having left her husband in Canada, she supported herself and several relations), and she became a learned and popular expositor of art, iconography, and the history of art, subjects in which a large nonelite public was beginning to seek instruction. She continued to write about women, as in *Legends of the Madonna*, and about such matters as the appropriate domestic atmosphere for pictures of the Holy Family. As her expertise and confidence grew, the apologetic tone of her earlier works disappeared. And yet while Jameson and John Ruskin (who was a quarter of a century younger than she, but precocious) were together largely responsible for forming Victorian taste and values in regard to painting, she was no more considered on a plane with Ruskin than the Stricklands were with Macaulay or Carlyle. Ruskin was read as a latter-day prophet, she as a compiler of useful information.

Like Ruskin, Jameson makes decisive moral, social, and aesthetic judgments, but her unpretentious, unprophetic manner was taken at face value. Ruskin occasionally drew on her books for factual information, but he kept her firmly in her place. He and Jameson happened to be staying at the same hotel in Venice, he records in his autobiography, and in the evenings they and two male friends of Ruskin's walked through the city together. The three men argued about everything they saw, "extremely embarrassing" Mrs. Jameson by their disputes.

> Mrs Jameson was absolutely without knowledge or instinct of painting (and had no sharpness of insight even for anything else); but she was candid and industrious, with a pleasant disposition to make the best of all she saw, and to say, compliantly, that a picture was good, if anybody had ever said so before.[5]

Ruskin reads her conciliatory manner as deficiency of judgment. But if she had assumed the denunciatory tones of a Victorian sage he would no doubt have been harsher still—and probably less willing to walk with her.

For some women, entrance to high culture came naturally and decorously as an inheritance from their fathers. Jameson's father was a moderately successful artist, and one of her first publications was a text to accompany works he had been unable to sell. Professions inherited from strong and successful parents, however, can be onerous for children of both sexes, and the Victorians' immediate literary inheritance, Romanticism, was particularly unfit for daughters. Sara Coleridge, one of the most gifted female writers of nonfictional prose, was disprized and neglected by her father, Samuel Taylor Coleridge, and discouraged from writing by Wordsworth and Southey because of her sex. As a result of her parents' estrangement she grew up mostly in the household of Southey, whose views on women writers were most notoriously expressed in his letter to Charlotte Brontë. Helped, however, by her mother—whose character and abilities were disparaged by her husband, his friends, and literary chroniclers then and later—she scraped together an education that she turned first to the service of her brother, by translating a Latin work to help pay for his university education, and eventually into a long labor of filial piety. She married her first cousin (like Aurora Leigh, thereby keeping her father's name) and eventually devoted herself to the immense task of ordering, editing, publishing, explaining, and defending the disorganized mass of uncompleted manuscripts that her father left unpublished when he died. She began this project in collaboration with her husband, who published the first installment under his name alone, and after his death she continued it. She had previously published, besides translations, a long poem and didactic works for children, but her serious intellectual projects, especially in theology, developed in her editorial, ancillary role.

Shortly before her death Sara Coleridge began to record her life history, but she could find neither plot nor meaning in it. "On reviewing my earlier childhood, I find the predominant reflection"—with these words, in the middle of a sentence, her autobiography ends.[6] The modern reader is likely to reflect predominantly on her distress at the small place she held in her father's attention and her evident if unacknowledged resentment of her brothers and of the Lake poets under whose eye she grew up. She records the poets' taste in girls' clothing: Wordsworth thought white dresses spoiled the harmony of a landscape, but Coleridge considered them expressive of women's delicacy and purity, "not merely," his daughter says tartly, "a component part of a general picture" (21). Her childhood was dominated, that is, by poets who thought girls inferior to boys except as figures of purity or parts of a landscape.

"What *was* I?" Sara Coleridge asks; and she answers in terms of her appearance, her health, and—finally, and at greatest length—her "nervous sensitiveness" and "morbid imaginativeness" (24). She was terrified by the (paternal) ghost in *Hamlet* and by Southey's ballads; Southey laughed at her fears, but her father was sympathetic and helpful. Imagination, like the ill health and addiction to opium that marked her kinship with her father even while helping to keep them apart, linked her with Romantic poets, but not in Romantic joy. It made her a writer, but in her father's service. Her own daughter's continuation of the memoir she could not herself complete shows Sara Coleridge reflected in the writings of men—"the admirable strength and subtlety of her reasoning faculty shown in her writings and conversation," one man says, "were less to me than the beauty and simplicity and feminine tenderness of her face" (29)—more than as a writer herself. Sara Coleridge, her daughter asserts, "hardly considered herself to be a woman 'of letters'" (50); which, considering that she had been relentlessly instructed by all her poet-fathers that to be a woman of letters is to be unwomanly, is not surprising.

Perhaps the most liberating and invigorating access to a literary life for women was travel, the opposite of the inheritance binding Sara Coleridge to her family: movement, literally, away from home into the wider world. Although it presupposed a degree of freedom that most women did not have, some girls' fantasies of adventure did achieve fulfillment in travel, which in turn could lead to writing on many topics, from art to society to religion. Jameson's first book, *Diary of an Ennuyée*, fictionalized her travels as a governess within the convention of romantic travelogue established by Byron and Madame de Staël, taking the occasion the convention provided both to express Byronic moods and sentiments and to comment on literature and art. In later books she drew extensively and less Byronically on excursions to Canada, Italy,

Germany, and elsewhere. For women who chafed at the restrictions of domesticity and propriety, travel was a wonderful relief, and some who were chronically feeble at home toughened up marvelously when they hit the road.

Travel was perhaps the only aspect of a woman's personal experience which could normally be presented as a matter of general interest, regardless of gender, while also bestowing authority to speak on a variety of subjects. Frances Trollope, Harriet Martineau, and Fanny Kemble wrote books about America in which personal experience is the peg on which social analysis hangs. Martineau's *Eastern Life* is a bold analysis of Christianity in the guise of a travelogue. Elizabeth Rigby (later Lady Eastlake), one of the first women to write extensively for prestigious journals, author of the most notorious attack on *Jane Eyre* as well as of a great deal of criticism of art—she completed the last volume of *Sacred and Legendary Art*, which Jameson left unfinished when she died—began her career with a story based on her studies in Germany during a long family visit there and followed it up with essays on German life and literature. More surprisingly, in 1838, when she was in her late twenties, she set off alone to visit her sister in Russia; her letters describing her adventures made a successful book, and the experience gave her another useful area of expertise. In the last quarter of the century several women published accounts of even more exotic travels, in Africa, Asia, and the American West; but in earlier years sojourns closer to home sufficed to launch or enliven a literary career.

The most prominent female writer of nonfictional prose was Harriet Martineau, whose fame was of the same unprecedented magnitude as Barrett Browning's, Charlotte Brontë's, and George Eliot's. She burst upon public attention with a series of tales illustrating principles of political economy and went on to produce books, essays, pamphlets, and newspaper editorials about politics, history, education, domestic economy, mesmerism, childrearing, the condition of women, and other subjects; reports of her travels and observations in America and the Holy Land and a tourists' guide to the Lake District; stories for children, a fictionalized life of the Haitian revolutionary leader Toussaint L'Ouverture, and a novel that imitates Jane Austen; a translation and condensation of Auguste Comte's *Positive Philosophy*; a correspondence espousing heterodox ideas about religion; an autobiography; and many obituaries, including her own. Everything that happened to her was transmuted into discourse; when illness confined her for five eventless years to a sickroom, she wrote a book about that.

Martineau was regarded by her contemporaries as the model, for good or ill, of an androgynous intellectual. Barrett Browning described her as "the most manlike woman in the three kingdoms—in the best sense of man—a woman gifted with admirable fortitude, as well as exercised in high logic."[7] Her clearly organized, logically constructed, and rationally argued writings normally tackle subjects usually reserved for men: political economy first and foremost, a subject that Mrs. Gaskell in the preface to *Mary Barton*, which deals with the problems of industrial society, strategically if disingenuously disavows any knowledge of. But her first tentative and inconspicuous publication was an essay on female writers about practical divinity; the expositions of political economy that made her famous were couched as little stories; and later she wrote about childrearing, home nursing, and other feminine concerns and became an outspoken defender of women's rights. She was consulted by cabinet ministers, urged to support political causes, feted and flattered, and felt herself to be at the center of great affairs; but she insisted on being treated as a lady, not a celebrity. She was proud of her businesslike habits of work, but she declined (after much hesitation) what she saw as a masculine position as an editor, and with editors and publishers she refused to drive a hard bargain and, like Oliphant, would sometimes not bargain at all. She prided herself on both her professional accomplishments and her womanliness: her preference for a private life, skill at sewing, mastery of household arts, strong familial affections, and instinct to nurture and love. The house she built in the Lake District looms as large in her *Autobiography* as her brilliant London career.

In the *Autobiography* Martineau, like Jameson's Joan of Arc or Barrett Browning's Beth, is both hero and heroine of romance. When her family loses its money, a lover who had kept silent while he thought her rich comes to the rescue in the best tradition of romantic fiction; but the engagement ends in his madness and early death, and Martineau, animated by necessity and enjoying her escape from the restrictions of genteel domesticity and of marriage, gladly rescues herself. Too deaf to become a governess like the heroine of a woman's novel, she goes to London like an ambitious young man in a *bildungsroman*; but her mother comes too, and at the pinnacle of fame and influence she submits to her mother's destructive authority. Later, champion of truth, justice, and oppressed peoples on two continents, she courageously encounters danger; but illness imprisons her like a poetess or fairy princess. No prince is expected or comes, however, and after finding her own cure in spite of her doctors, she lives happily ever after in a house built by her own money, under her own supervision, performing the functions of both master and mistress among loving nieces and maids.

But filling both roles herself seems to have meant that something—someone—was missing; and Martineau's triumphantly self-sufficient career is founded in incompleteness and deprivation. This is located in the first instance in her body. Autobiographies by men rarely convey much sense of the writer as a physical object, but in Martineau's we are constantly aware of bodily insufficiency and pain. Her *Autobiography* begins with early memories of painful or terrifying sense impressions, balanced by sensory deprivation: she had no sense of smell and little of taste, and deafness cut short her early joy in music and made social intercourse awkward and exhausting. From earliest childhood she suffered from severe gastric illness, and later from a large uterine or abdominal tumor, and when she became a professional writer she immediately began to overwork herself to the point of physical collapse.

She associated her bodily tribulations with imagination and ambition. Her deafness, she thought, was "seriously aggravated by nervous excitement, at the age when I lived in reverie and vanities of the imagination."[8] When she was about seven years old a child she knew well had a leg amputated and became "the talk of the whole city" (1: 34) for her courage and composure, providing Martineau with an irresistible model of fame:

> It turned my imagination far too much on bodily suffering, and on the peculiar glory attending fortitude in that direction. I am sure that my nervous system was seriously injured, and especially that my subsequent deafness was partly occasioned by the exciting and vain-glorious dreams that I indulged in for many years after my friend E. lost her leg. All manner of deaths at the stake and on the scaffold, I went through in imagination, in the low sense in which St. Theresa craved martyrdom; and night after night, I lay bathed in cold perspiration till I sank into the sleep of exhaustion. (1: 34)

As for Geraldine in Yonge's *The Pillars of the House*, whose amputated foot is the price of being a painter, imagination is a self-indulgence paid for with the sacrifice of part of the body: E's leg, Martineau's hearing. Like Eliot, Martineau (at least retrospectively) associates imaginative activity with vanity, an insatiable desire for praise and the esteem of others; and like Brontë, she indulges it in solitude and secrecy. But Martineau's guilt is marked on her body: in deafness, "cold perspiration," exhaustion.

Not surprisingly, Martineau minimized the role of imagination in her adult work. Like Charlotte Brontë's Lucy Snowe, who is terrorized by the workings of her imagination, she tries to present herself as businesslike and unromantic. She worked efficiently and methodically, and her style is straightforward and matter-of-fact, eschewing the stylistic play, prophetic grandeur, and exuberant self-creation practiced by male contemporaries. She declared of herself in her obituary:

> Her original power was nothing more than was due to earnestness and intellectual clearness within a certain range. With small imaginative and suggestive powers, and therefore nothing approaching to genius, she could see clearly what she did see, and give a clear expression to what she had to say.[9]

This is not just self-denigration; she had escaped, she felt, from the tyranny of a tainted imagination.

And yet she was sure that imagination is the highest human faculty and the most beneficial to humanity, and for her deficiency in it she blamed her cold and censorious mother. Romantic mythology links imaginative development with nurturing by maternal nature, and Martineau makes bitterly explicit the sense of deprivation and loss felt by daughters who could neither emulate their mothers successfully as women nor be favored by them like sons trained for independence. In *Household Education*, her excellent and widely read treatise on childrearing, she explains that deeply imaginative children (those devoted, as she had been, to reading and religion) must be "on terms of perfect confidence with the mother" (286) for their nascent powers to grow. Her own mother's refusal to give her the affection and understanding she craved, she thought, had impaired her imagination and made her unable to express her feelings. As one of the younger children, and apparently the least favored, in a large family, she had neither the affection a daughter might expect nor the experience of superiority that compensated some girls for the disadvantages of gender. In her *Autobiography* she recalls her childhood as a nightmare of fear, shame, self-hatred, and "a haunting, wretched, useless remorse" (1: 22) that fed on itself: "I was ashamed of my habit of misery" (1: 33).

She found refuge in intellect. She was taught arithmetic, Latin (not Greek), French, and Italian, and read widely from a very early age in history, philosophy, theology, and literature. Her father being a manufacturer at a time of great economic uncertainty, her parents tried to educate their daughters as well as their sons to be able to support themselves. Having first had her elder sister and brothers as more or less unsatisfactory instructors, according to the custom of the time, she was sent at the age of eleven to a day school for boys that had been forced by declining attendance to admit girls. She found her two years' schooling there "delectable" (1: 47). "In an intellectual life I found then, as I have found since, refuge from moral suffering, and"—in the language of Romantic descriptions of nature and poetic imagination—"an always unexhausted spring of moral strength and enjoyment" (1: 50). In the category of intellect she included poetry. From the age of seven, she reports, she fell asleep repeating passages from *Paradise Lost*. "I think this must have been my first experience of moral relief through intellectual resource" (1: 32-33): relief in part, presumably, from the fantasies of martyrdom that began at the same age and also occurred in bed.

Whereas other women who grew up to be writers in the first half of the nineteenth century were nourished on Byron's Promethean rebellion, Martineau sustained herself with *Paradise Lost*, in which Satan and Eve, the grandest Byronic hero in English literature and the first woman, are punished for ambition;[10] and she learned very early to associate writing with ambition and vanity. When she was very young she made tabulations of scriptural texts and expressed the hope that they might be printed; but an older sister "twitted me with my conceit in fancying that I could be an authoress. . . . The ambition seems to have disappeared from that time; and when I did attempt to write, it was at the suggestion of another [her brother James, who suggested that she write something to cheer herself up when he went away to school], and against my own judgement and inclination" (1: 90). Like Eliot, she attributed responsibility for her writing to a man, and the project is like Eliot's first recorded plan for a book, a chart of ecclesiastical history from the birth of Christ to the Reformation. These schematic and tedious projects make no call on imagination and leave the author invisible.

In her *Autobiography* Martineau asserts with irritating persistence her de-
testation of flattery and indifference to fame. She saw her whole career in terms
of derision followed by praise. Even her management of her land, when she
settled in the Lake District, fell into this pattern: "At first, we were abundantly
ridiculed, and severely condemned" (2: 34) by the neighborhood, but her wisdom (as always) was soon acknowledged. She attributed the tumor that drove
her out of London to her mother's jealousy of the social position fame had won
her (1: 442), and savored fame with the clearest conscience when it felt like
martyrdom. The "more brutal" the reviews of her work, she found, "the more
animating," and "personal mortifications" put her "in a happy state of mind"
(1: 447). Still, the pain was real. "Do I improve in courage about learning the
consequences of what I do?" she asked herself in her journal. "I commit myself
boldly, but I suffer a good deal. But I do not think I go back."[11]

"On five occasions," she says, "I have found myself obliged to write and
publish what I entirely believed would be ruinous to my reputation and pros-
perity" (1: 151). She always emerged unharmed, indeed triumphant; but each
episode was a test of courage like Lady Godiva's. The first was caused by a tale
in the *Illustrations of Political Economy* demonstrating the Malthusian doctrine that population must be kept down to avoid starvation, and thereby implicitly advocating birth control. The *Quarterly Review* sneered at her "unfeminine and mischievous doctrines":

> We should be loth to bring a blush unnecessarily upon the cheek of any woman;
> but may we venture to ask this maiden sage the meaning of the following
> passage: —
>   "A parent has a considerable influence over the subsistence-fund of his family,
> and *an absolute control over the numbers to be supported by that fund.*"
>   . . . A *woman* who thinks child-bearing a *crime against society*! An *unmarried
> woman* who declaims against *marriage*!! A *young woman* who deprecates charity
> and a provision for the *poor*!!![12]

Martineau protests her innocence. "I was aware that some evil associations
had gathered about [Malthus's doctrine], — though I did not know what they
were" (1: 151-52).

On later occasions, however, she was deliberately provocative: in her testi-
monials to the medical effectiveness of mesmerism, attacks on slavery in America, and the publication of rationalist views of religion. Her public announcement that mesmerism had cured her — an announcement she felt necessary both
for truth's sake and so that others could profit in the same way — occasioned
the most painful insults. She could not array herself against the medical-scien-
tific establishment with impunity: her brother-in-law, who had been her physician, published details about her uterine tumor, and again journalists sneered.
But she asserted that those who use their fame to serve humanity recover "the
genuine privacy of soul, which they believed forfeited for ever, while the con-

sciousness of the gaze of the world was upon them,"[13] and she found in Godiva a figure that purified ambition.

Martineau invites us to see both her political commitment and her literary
career as the reflex of her early misery. As a child, she says, "I had a devouring
passion for justice; — justice, first to my own precious self, and then to other
oppressed people" (1: 14). The first "other"'s with whom she learned to sympathize were servants, who in the Martineau household were not allowed to
speak for themselves any more than she was, and her sense of injustice, then
and later, was closely bound up with the suppression of speech. Her coura-
geous support of the early abolitionist movement during her travels in America
was concerned as much with freedom of speech as with slavery. "Her stimulus
. . . from first to last," she said of herself in her own obituary, "was simply the
need of utterance."[14] Her writing was compulsive and cathartic: she forced
herself to work every day, hardly ever allowing herself a holiday, and described
the delights of composition with words like "joy" that are not generally associated with expository prose. She valued the process of writing more than the
product; it let her control her imagination, and it provided the catharsis she
needed after the bitter silence of her childhood.

Her joy in writing, however, is seldom communicated to the reader. Her style
is often graceless and formulaic, her tone hectoring, her manner humorless and
self-important. Sara Coleridge's brother Hartley described her as "a *mono-ma-
niac* about *every*thing,"[15] and indeed she is easy to laugh at. She wrote from a
point of view, moreover, that exacerbated her failure to charm. The social science she expounded was arid and schematic and often seemed cruelly at odds
with humane values; the great Victorian works of social protest in all literary
genres either ignore or passionately condemn it. Accepting the principles of political economy, which claimed to represent scientific rationality in opposition
to sentiment and prejudice, she argued against interference in the workings of
the free market, although she eventually recognized the need for some govern-
ment regulation of working conditions and some forms of communal action by
workers. She opposed philanthropy that left the basic conditions of poverty
unchanged, and supported the New Poor Law that Carlyle and Dickens condemned for its cruelty, of which Oliver Twist was the most famous victim. Martineau was more radical than Carlyle or Dickens, and unlike theirs her sympathy was always with the oppressed — slaves, servants, children, women, the
poor. But her radicalism, being more rational and schematic and obdurately
unsentimental, seemed less humane — and unfeminine.

As Victorian England's most famous female intellectual, Harriet Martineau
was both an inspiration and a warning. Although she had no apparent literary
genius, fortunate connections, or graces of person or manner, her masterful intellect, very hard work, unwavering social and intellectual conscience, and
great courage brought her independence, influence, and fame. But she was
more likely to be admired than imitated. Her political and religious radicalism
horrified many people and exposed her to public attacks and — worse — ridicule

and innuendo. She insisted that the domestic life she created for herself was fully satisfying and called herself the happiest single woman in England; but her *Autobiography* is suffused with a sense of inadequacy as a woman. When she turned her relentless faculty of analysis on the object nearest to hand, herself, the object often seemed unattractive and the self-consciousness repellent. Her success demonstrated both the possibilities and the penalties for engaging in intellectual discourse beyond the feminine sphere.

7. Religion

❦ ❦ ❦

The center of Victorian discourse, in which all questions were implicated and to which all roads led, was religion. There were lively public debates and a lot of private excitement and anguish. Central issues included the Evangelical, Anglo-Catholic, or Ritualist movements within the Church of England, the undermining of the literal authority of the Bible by science and the Higher Criticism, the increasing acceptance of dissenters, Roman Catholics, Jews, and freethinkers in public life, and the question of religion's role in the development of public education. The existence of an established church meant that religious questions were necessarily political ones; and political ones—such as, most notably, the antislavery campaigns and almost everything concerning England's ill-starred rule in Ireland—were saturated with religious significance. The disconnection of the urban proletariat from the Church of England heightened middle-class fears of revolution and democracy and provided a vast field for missionary enterprise, as did the expansion of empire. The much-feared, much-lamented decline of religious faith throughout the century gave poetry a characteristic note of sadness and self-doubt; the quintessential Victorian poem, *In Memoriam*, published at mid-century, records a painful if ultimately successful effort to affirm belief in personal immortality and the existence of a benevolent deity in the face of intellectual forces apparently demonstrating the contrary. And the drama of religious excitement, doubt, and change was played out in individual lives: many women writers changed their religious beliefs, usually in early adulthood and often with dire personal consequences.

In most official ways the ferment of activity excluded women. Except for the bumptiously unrespectable Salvation Army, church hierarchies were exclusively male. Religious teachers reminded women of their duties to fathers and husbands, while Eve's error and the Pauline strictures against female speech were invoked to keep women in subjection. "Let your women keep silence in the churches: for it is not permitted unto them to speak" (I Corinthians xiv: 34); "I suffer not a woman to teach, nor to usurp authority over the man, but to be in silence" (I Timothy ii: 12). Women called on the "prophetess" Deborah who "judged Israel" (Judges iv: 4) and a few other Old Testament heroines to justify speech on sacred and public subjects, but this did not weigh very heavily against St. Paul's explicit prohibitions. Women were expected to embody the Christian virtues of love, purity, self-abnegation, and self-sacrifice, and to instill a Christian atmosphere at home. Religion strongly reinforced the fears of vanity and ambition that beset women who aspired to write. But it also (many Victorians believed) enhanced the status of women by valorizing feminine qualities for which neither classical culture nor the world of business and power had any place. It lent its imposing authority to the doctrine of separate spheres that restricted women's access to the world, but it also gave them a kind of moral authority, limited but real, that writers found particularly useful.

Women writers often, in fact, performed teaching and preaching functions analogous to those of the clergy—as Elaine Showalter says, many of them would have liked to be clergymen[1]—and Victorian clergymen had a lot in common with women. They were expected to inhabit a purer atmosphere and observe higher standards of morality than other men, and to avoid many masculine arenas of business and pleasure. Fox hunting, for instance, was as dubious a pastime for a clergyman, in many circles, as for a woman; and like women they engaged in charitable and educational activities and visited the ill and the poor. "The character of a clergyman," remarks Mrs. Oliphant when one of her clerical heroes is suspected of sexual misconduct, is "almost as susceptible as that of a woman" (*The Perpetual Curate*, 255-56). The young clergymen—or, as they called themselves, priests—of the Ritualist movement, with their penchant for sacerdotal self-adornment, church decoration, and incense, their real or suspected leanings toward an ideal of clerical celibacy, and their eager female followings, were mocked and feared as effeminate. In religion even more than in literature, however, the feminization of a male activity did not mean that women were welcome to join in—on the contrary. The classical education that was the usual preliminary to taking orders in the Church of England helped keep the lines of cultural authority firmly drawn, as did the sacred tradition of male priesthood: John Ruskin warned girls not to "profanely touch" the male precincts of theology.[2] And when Anglican sisterhoods and their Evangelical counterparts, the orders of deaconesses, were established, most clergymen wanted them limited to philanthropic rather than sacred functions and kept in strict subordination to the male hierarchy.[3]

But religion could also authorize resistance to patriarchal authority, including husbands' and fathers'. Religious conviction gives the heroine of Anne Brontë's *The Tenant of Wildfell Hall*, for instance, warrant to flee her bullying, profligate husband and support herself and their child in secret by painting pictures, despite his legally enforceable authority to confiscate her earnings and keep her and the child at home.[4] The ferment of controversy, furthermore, created space for maneuver. Women could draw strength from the traditional Protestant reliance on private judgment and the primacy of Scripture to justify changing their religious allegiance in the face of familial opposition, and the profusion of religious organizations offered many directions to move in, from Roman Catholicism and Anglican sisterhoods on the one hand, to unitarianism, spiritualism, or free thought on the other.

Religion also provided opportunities to act in the world and to write. Church-sponsored philanthropic work could give access not only to useful activity outside of the home but also to knowledge and experience of life—that is, subject matter—that would otherwise have been closed to women. Religious publishing ventures always needed contributors and editors who would work for little or no pay and offered literary careers in the guise of service. There were similar opportunities at both ends of the Church of England spectrum: both the extreme Evangelical Charlotte Elizabeth Tonna and the High Church Charlotte M. Yonge edited journals that served their own party. Yonge's novels were an important part of the Oxford Movement's propaganda efforts, read and approved by its leader, John Keble; her father would not have allowed her to publish otherwise.

An avowedly religious purpose justified literary self-display. Mrs. Tonna (who published as "Charlotte Elizabeth" to avoid using the surname of her first husband, from whom she was separated), "after some struggle against a plan so humbling to literary pride," decided to limit her first "little books and tracts" to a style that a five-year-old could comprehend.[5] And yet she published during her lifetime an autobiography containing highly colored dramatic accounts of youthful sins of imagination, adventures at sea and in Canada and strife-torn Ireland, encounters with sly priests and deluded nuns who seem to have wandered in from a Gothic novel, and other exciting events, as well as of her views and endeavors in literature, politics, and religion. The story follows a pattern of spiritual autobiography established by St. Augustine and is offered as an example of the workings of Providence and grace. Just as Jesus Christ "shone out upon" her at the moment of conversion, so she is "standing before" the reader—exposing herself to view—"in the character of one who . . . had found in Christ Jesus a refuge from the storm of God's anger" (41). Similarly but in a quieter key, Elizabeth Missing Sewell justified her autobiographical project on the grounds that her life showed God's Providence at work. Sara Coleridge's daughter, adding an organizing principle to the story for which Coleridge herself could offer none and at the same time justifying its publication, explained that her mother's life was "a practical evidence of the truth of that Religion, which made her what she was."[6] Harriet Martineau, writing her *Autobiography* within the framework of beliefs she had rejected, turns the conversion plot into one of deconversion and proves the truth of her apostasy in the usual terms of pious narrative: by the tenor of her later life and her calm acceptance of death.

By offering the assurance that in God's eyes everything in every life is spiritually significant—"It seems as if I could see the meaning of almost every joy and every sorrow," Sewell says[7]—religion could make ordinary, uneventful lives not only transcendently important but fit for literature. Girls and women were blamed, and blamed themselves, for devaluing domestic reality by indulging in imaginative activity; and yet the sanctification of the everyday was the essential contribution of religion to Victorian women's fiction, and—for good or ill—of fiction to its readers. The apparent triviality of well-to-do women's lives, especially the unmarried or childless, was a source of torment for many women. Before she broke free from her family and found her vocation, Florence Nightingale bitterly complained:

> a woman cannot live in the light of intellect. Society forbids it. Those conventional frivolities, which are called her "duties," forbid it. Her "domestic duties," high-sounding words, which, for the most part, are but bad habits (which she has not the courage to enfranchise herself from, the strength to break through) forbid it. What are these duties (or bad habits)?—Answering a multitude of letters which lead to nothing, from her so-called friends—keeping her up to the level of the world that she may furnish her quota of amusement at the breakfast-table; driving out her company in the carriage. And all these things are exacted from her by her family which, if she is good and affectionate, will have more influence with her than the world.[8]

(She omits the particular bane of most intellectual girls, sewing.) Women's novels often dealt with just such lives—we recognize the scene, if not the tone, from Austen—and for less ambitious women than Nightingale, religion could give them meaning.

In Yonge's books religion endows seemingly insignificant actions with crucial—literally, life and death—importance. In *The Pillars of the House* three people drown because a girl sings a song when she knows she shouldn't, and the heroines of *Heartsease* learn to treat "little matters" (1: 234) with the utmost seriousness and "to see in little trials the daily cross" (1: 264). Theodora in *Heartsease* destroys her beloved brother by asking him to go to the races, and her primary duty is defined as affectionate obedience to her rich parents, who hardly need her. She learns "to view the weariness and enforced uselessness of her life . . . in the light of salutary chastisement and discipline" (2: 145). For Yonge, religion justifies the novelist's vocation by affirming the importance of uneventful, restricted lives.

In Oliphant's novels, on the other hand, women living lives of enforced uselessness are sometimes satirized, sometimes pitied, and people who fuss about religious formalities are objects of satire. Oliphant had faith in a benevolent and attentive God, but not in the assumptions that supported fiction's implicit self-justifications and its happy endings. In one of her best novels, *Miss Marjoribanks*, she mocks the heroic seriousness with which her protagonist performs her duties as housekeeper and hostess for her father, a widower with no particular desire for her services or company. Lacking other outlets for her benevolence and administrative genius, Lucilla Marjoribanks applies her relentless attention to choosing drawing-room furnishings that match her complexion, organizing evening parties, or masterminding a parliamentary campaign for a dull-witted, unenterprising candidate. Part of Lucilla's absurdity is her assumption that divine Providence concerns itself with such matters. When after a brief period of difficulty the happy ending arrives, in the form of a husband who will do whatever she tells him and a small estate to manage, she is not surprised.

"It is a special Providence," said Lucilla to herself, with her usual piety. . . . Lucilla . . . felt no difficulty in discerning the leadings of Providence, and she could
not but appreciate the readiness with which her desires were attended to, and the
prompt clearing-up of her difficulties. There are people whose inclinations Providence does not seem to superintend with such painstaking watchfulness; but
then, no doubt, that must be their own fault. (483)

Satire on Evangelical egotism is common in Victorian fiction, but Oliphant's
contempt for Lucilla's harmless self-importance suggests serious doubt about
novel writing itself. For if the little things that make up women's lives do not
clearly matter to God, why should books about them matter? And why should
the books have neat, happy endings?

Religious faith was particularly likely to justify novelists' work when it was
combined with social purpose. Like Martineau and Saint Theresa, Charlotte
Elizabeth wished as a child to be a martyr. Her fervor was deflected into literature, however, beginning with "the pernicious study of nursery tales" (*Personal Recollections*, 3). After her conversion to fervid Evangelicism she recalled
her early excesses of imagination with a horror like Eliot's and Martineau's.
Satan had been leading her, she thought, to become a novelist: "To God be all
the glory that I am not now pandering with this pen to the most grovelling or
the most impious of man's perverted feelings!" (3). Immediately after her conversion she wrote her first story, a tract, on what proved to be divine impulsion, for a letter immediately arrived requesting such a work. Later, urged to
try speaking in tongues and otherwise put herself forward in a religious context, she was stopped by the Pauline prohibition. "I was quite sure that if such
an important change was to take place in the character of the dispensation, and
women to become public teachers of men, I should find some express warrant
for it" (108). She consulted her Bible, and found no such warrant. But her fiery
and influential novels exposing the oppression of industrial workers, like her
tracts and her autobiography, were exempt from interdiction.

Other women whose faith grounded their social protest novels include
Skene, Sewell, and Gaskell. Religion gave them not only a justification for writing but also an authority to pit against male power and the cold rationality of
political economy. In *Mary Barton*, Gaskell finds the solution to the miseries
consequent on industrialization in the Christian love her novel teaches: that
owners and workers must "acknowledge the Spirit of Christ as the regulating
law between both parties" (46). And social protest novels could turn Christian
ideals against Christian institutions. Eliza Lynn Linton, a prolific and successful novelist, essayist, and reviewer, achieved her greatest success with *The True
History of Joshua Davidson*, in which an idealistic carpenter tries to take
Christianity literally—although he does not believe in the literal truth of the
Bible—and relive the life of Jesus in modern terms. Jesus, he says, was "poor,
unlearned, a plebeian, and a socialist, at war with the gentlemen and ladies of
my society, the enemy of forms, of creeds" (62). Davidson is a communist, ded-

icated to destroying the class system (or as he calls it, "caste"), "the vice at the root of all our creeds and institutions" (83). The book's denunciatory verve and energy probably spring from Linton's deep reservoir of anger against her prosperous clergyman father, and she obviously enjoys turning the piety expected from women writers into an attack on society and religion. Still, Christianity supplies her moral ground.

Women writers who changed their religious affiliation generally, like Linton, moved to extreme positions. Charlotte Elizabeth, rather to her own surprise, became a millenarian. Georgiana Fullerton and Adelaide Procter converted to Roman Catholicism, as did Mary Howitt at the end of a long voyage, by way of Unitarianism and spiritualism, from her austere beginnings in the Society of Friends. Harriet Martineau, George Eliot, and Frances Power Cobbe, like Linton, moved toward free thought or agnosticism, and Annie Besant traveled from the Church of England through free thought to the wilder shores of Theosophy. Those who stayed with the faith they had been brought up in were likely to be near the extremes too: Rossetti and Yonge as high Anglicans, Gaskell as a Unitarian. Barrett Browning thought sectarian disputes un-Christian and trivial and was attracted by the visionary writings of Swedenborg and by spiritualism, which confined its theology to proving the immortality of the soul and offered equal opportunity to women, Americans, servants, and other outsiders.

Women found most chance for action in denominations that emphasized the experience of conversion and individual access to the spirit world or the divine. Early in the century Quaker women were active in the ministry, and until 1803 the main body of Methodists allowed women, like Eliot's Dinah Morris, to preach. The first stages of Harriet Martineau's intellectual development were nourished and rewarded by the Unitarianism in which she was raised. Mary Howitt grew up in an extremely repressive Quaker household of "submissive women" who never opposed her father, while her young brother "had his will in all things"; but in 1837 she heard a woman preach at the Yearly Meeting of the Society of Friends ("a good-looking woman, in garments sufficiently flowing to give effect to her figure and gestures, raising her arm and pouring forth a really eloquent, but to my mind unChristian sermon"), and she and her husband worked together in the Quaker tradition of social action, founding *Howitt's Journal* "to urge the labouring classes, by means of temperance, self-education, and moral conduct, to be their own benefactors."[9] Catherine Booth and her husband founded the Salvation Army, which welcomed the outcast and indigent, brought an indecorous vivacity to public worship, and gave equal access to women throughout its ranks. Catherine Booth began preaching in public in 1860. "Making allowance for the novelty of the thing," she wrote, "we cannot discover anything either unnatural or immodest in a Christian woman, becomingly attired, appearing on a platform or in a pulpit."[10]

At other extremes, Annie Besant lectured at free thought meetings, and Roman Catholicism and some Anglo-Catholic practices offered transgressive opportunities for private speech: Protestants observed with horror that in the confessional a woman could speak alone with a man—perhaps even a young man—about matters best not spoken of at all.[11] Fullerton's conversion to Catholicism was preceded by her most popular novel, *Ellen Middleton*, which centers on the Protestant heroine's desperate need for ritual confession. The rabidly anti-Catholic heroine of Charlotte Brontë's *Villette* seeks relief from self-tormenting solitude in the confessional of a Catholic church. Nightingale, Jameson, and other writers also admired Catholic and Anglo-Catholic sisterhoods, especially charitable and nursing orders, which provided useful work, experience of life, and a female community. Rossetti's sister left home to join an Anglican sisterhood, and the poet herself was affiliated with one that did charitable work with fallen women, an experience she drew on for some of her poems: *Goblin Market* is among other things an apotheosis of Christian sisterhood. Rossetti's Anglo-Catholic faith, like Yonge's, provided plots for heroines, while the self-suppression it imposed on women takes aesthetic form in the intensity and finish of her art. And despite Rossetti's and Yonge's renunciations of ambition, their didactic and devotional works reached very large audiences.

Barrett Browning, more boldly, used Christianity to authorize her entry into poetry at the highest level. In *The Seraphim* she challenged classical culture by telling the story of the crucifixion as a revision of Aeschylus' *Prometheus Bound*; Aeschylus was a greater poet than she could ever be, but she had a greater subject. Then she challenged the Christian poetic tradition by bringing to bear an aspect of religious experience that she as a woman knew more about than Milton: *A Drama of Exile* is a sequel to *Paradise Lost* that centers on Eve's self-sacrifice, suffering, and love. The skill and status she had gathered from such works provided the basis for her exuberant, original poems about the modern world.

For most women, however, religion was not just a way to enter literature, but a stopping place. Hymn writing was open to women, as it had been in the eighteenth century, and could enable them to reach large audiences, but devotional poetry of every sort had sunk into a minor if popular mode. Christina Rossetti wrote very powerful religious poems that had many admirers in the nineteenth century and are now being reclaimed by criticism, but they seemed to fall outside the mainstream of high culture and until very recently were considered minor if excellent work when considered at all. This is not just a matter of gender: as a convert to Catholicism and a Jesuit, Gerard Manley Hopkins, the other great devotional poet of the century and an admirer of Rossetti's work, was in a similarly marginal position, and his innovative verse was unappreciated and mostly unpublished in his lifetime. Still, gender expectations worked against women. Their poetic expressions of faith, by replicating the childlike submissiveness that was expected of them anyway, are apt to seem somewhat flat, since they lack the tension between the strength and independence men are presumed to possess and the devotional poet's humility before

God. What is metaphorical and striking for men is merely literal for women, as in George Herbert's assertion that "Who sweeps a room as for Thy sake / Makes that and the action fine."[12] And on the other hand, the aversion to self-display that religion encouraged in women precluded Hopkins's self-dramatizing panache.

The most widely admired of Rossetti's religious poems is "Up-Hill," a four-stanza lyric that draws on traditional allegories of life as a journey toward death. Being composed entirely of dialogue between two genderless and unindividualized speakers, neither of whom can be identified with the poet, it evades problems of gender; and its potency arises from chill understatement.

> Does the road wind up-hill all the way?
>   Yes, to the very end.
> Will the day's journey take the whole long day?
>   From morn to night, my friend.
>
> But is there for the night a resting-place?
>   A roof for where the slow dark hours begin.
> May not the darkness hide it from my face?
>   You cannot miss that inn.
>
> Shall I meet other wayfarers at night?
>   Those who have gone before.
> Then must I knock, or call when just in sight?
>   They will not keep you standing at that door.
>
> Shall I find comfort, travel-sore and weak?
>   Of labour you shall find the sum.
> Will there be beds for me and all who seek?
>   Yea, beds for all who come.

In its unpretentiousness of form and tone and absence of any dramatized poet-speaker, as in its brilliant manipulations of rhythm and redeployment of traditional motifs, "Up-Hill" is akin to another Rossetti masterpiece, *Goblin Market*. Rossetti's poetry of religious anguish is arguably as great and terrible as Hopkins's, but its simple demeanor, like that of *Goblin Market*, has given it a lower place in a canon tuned to male voices.

No women poets, moreover, not even Barrett Browning, used poetry as men did to work through the intellectual issues of Victorian faith and doubt. Victorians generally considered the anguish and excitement of doubt a male prerogative. The poems of Tennyson, Clough, and Arnold were haunted by nostalgia for a deity who seemed to have withdrawn his presence from men but not from women. The speaker of *In Memoriam* is rebuked by a girl: "Sweet-hearted, you, whose light-blue eyes / Are tender over drowning flies, / You tell me, doubt is Devil-born" (xcvi). Women were expected to sustain belief with an all-embracing, even foolishly inclusive, love—and in fact many women writers' feelings drew them, if not to tears over flies, at least to antivivisectionism. In their fiction doubt is restricted to men or more rarely, as in Yonge's *Hopes and Fears*, to unfeminine intellectual women, and is depicted only to be condemned. Women poets rarely deal with doubt at all; Ingelow, exceptionally, does so in "Honors," but only through a dialogue between male voices in which faith easily wins. Social expectations were buttressed by artistic needs: women could not afford to question the faith that gave them poetic authority.

And yet the greatest drama of many women's lives was played out in the arena of religion. Many—perhaps even most—highly imaginative Victorian women seem to have had profound religious experiences in childhood and adolescence: characteristically, yearning for martyrdom, conviction of sin, and an ardent desire to renounce the vanity and ambition with which the idea of martyrdom was inextricably combined. The drama of faith was heightened by the attention paid to religious observance in most families, and by the absence of other distractions. On Sundays, for instance, profane reading was generally banned—which explains why so many people knew *Paradise Lost* almost by heart[13]—and there were few acceptable outlets for the stirrings of adolescent sexuality. Religion offered girls an object for ardor, an opportunity for heroic aspiration, and a framework for testing their capacity for self-development, self-discipline, and self-control.[14]

Sometimes the piety of fervent girlhood continued into later life, but often there was a reaction against it, and then a new act of the play began. Women's faith was protected by their exclusion from the universities, which were breeding grounds of doubt for young men, and unlike university fellows or clergymen they did not have to put their belief in the Church of England to a single critical test by subscribing to the Thirty-Nine Articles. But if they were protected from dangerous books and companions, they could still compare what they read in the Bible to the doctrine they were taught in church or observe that doctrinal correctness and moral conduct did not always coincide. They could notice inconsistencies in the Bible, or question the morality of the Judeo-Christian God as revealed in the Old Testament narratives, Christian doctrine, or the fact of human suffering. To the humanitarian spirit of the age the idea of eternal damnation was abhorrent, and Martineau and others disapproved of a system that enforced morality by rewards and punishments.[15] The spirit of rationalism, corrosive to the literal faith most girls were brought up in, could reach almost anywhere; and since the Evangelical impulse to bear witness to faith often survived the change to unbelief, deconversions were generally the occasion of severe family conflict and often of public condemnation—the martyrdom of unbelief—as well.

For writers the most auspicious of the prevailing winds of doubt was the movement in biblical interpretation known as the Higher Criticism, which read the Bible not as a direct revelation from God but as a myth that had developed in history and could be interpreted by the same methods as, say, the Homeric epics, of which the tradition of single authorship was also in dispute. Matthew Arnold in "Dover Beach" lamented with memorable plangency a world to which the erosion of faith had left "neither joy, nor love, nor light, / Nor certitude, nor peace, nor help for pain" (33-34); but by redefining religion as myth, or poetry, he hoped to save its essence. To most pious people the Higher Criticism seemed just another rationalist attack on faith; but to others the idea that religion is the product of the human imagination offered the exhilarating hope both of reinterpreting the Judeo-Christian myths and of making new ones. What the human mind had once invented, it could perhaps invent again; and if myths reflected the historical moment of their creation, better cultural conditions might create better myths. Perhaps, even, women might create them. Harriet Martineau's *Eastern Life*, for instance, is biblical criticism in the guise of a travelogue that "exhibits," she said, "the history and generation of the four great faiths—the Egyptian, the Jewish, the Christian, and the Mohammedan—as they appear when their birthplaces are visited in succession." Admiring Jesus while treating Christianity as one historically conditioned and still-developing faith among several rather than a uniquely privileged revelation, Martineau deplores the "mythological fable" that still "encrust[s]" Christianity and—the human race being in its infancy and the contribution of Western thought to the imaginative structures created by the East yet unmade—holds out the hope of better things to come.[16]

Eastern Life is one of Martineau's most daring books, refused by one publisher, banned in some homes, an affront to many believers. Anna Jameson's art-historical studies of Christian iconography, in contrast, are decorously reverent, although the fact that most of the works she studied were foreign and Catholic allowed her a good deal of freedom; but she too envisioned a better future, and with a feminist edge. In *Legends of the Madonna* she starts from the nineteenth-century commonplace that "With Christianity, new ideas of the moral and religious responsibility of woman entered the world." Martineau dismisses myths of the Madonna as unfortunate survivals of "old allegories of Egypt—the old images of miraculous birth, and the annunciation of it from heaven." But Jameson is delighted to find primitive and pagan goddesses foreshadowing the "pure, dignified, tender image of the Madonna" and "the coming moral regeneration, and complete and harmonious development of the whole human race, by the establishment, on a higher basis, of what has been called 'the feminine element' in society."[17]

Jameson imagines a female divinity rising out of the male-defined images of the past:

In the perpetual iteration of that beautiful image of THE WOMAN highly blessed—*there*, where others saw only pictures or statues, I have seen this great hope standing like a spirit beside the visible form: in the fervent worship once universally given to that gracious presence, I have beheld an acknowledgment of a higher as well as gentler power than that of the strong hand and the might that makes the right,—and in every earnest votary one who, as he knelt, was in this sense pious beyond the reach of his own thought, and "devout beyond the meaning of his will."

Jameson judges works of art that depict Mary by how closely they approximate "this great hope." Her ideal Madonna has the sweetness of idealized Victorian maternity — Jameson particularly admires paintings in which "the quiet domestic duties and affections" are "elevated and hallowed by religious associations, and adorned by all the graces of Art" — but she also has the power that the maternal function, in the view of Eliot, Rossetti, and others, gives to women. Mary is "intellectual, tender, simple, and heroic," with "the gifts of the poetess and prophetess" as well.[18]

This combination of qualities is easier to assert as a mythic ideal than to embody in a single figure, as novelists discovered. Perhaps the most exuberant and absurd celebration of a woman-oriented religion rising from the ashes of old beliefs is Geraldine Jewsbury's *Zoë*, published in 1845, which was the first of many very popular Victorian novels about the contemporary crisis of faith. Zoë is a beautiful freethinker who believes that "the maternal instinct is only one passion amongst the many with which a woman is endowed" (3: 45). A brilliant young Jesuit, Everhard, loses his faith as a result of his love for her, leaves his order, tries to find meaning in life through helping the poor, becomes notorious for philosophic books that he learns to write in Germany (home of the Higher Criticism), and dies still worshipping her.

Zoë does not deliberately undermine Everhard's faith nor, being married, allow herself quite to return his love; rather, "The strength and reality of his love for Zoë, made him thus acutely sensible of the falseness and worthlessness of all that had so long influenced him" (2: 219).

> There is in all strong affection, a purity, an intense reality, that exalts the individual in whom it burns, to a point of excellence he could never have attained by any other path. Love, rightly conceived in its highest manifestations, ceases to be a mere passion; it becomes a worship, a religion; it regenerates the whole soul; till a man has found an object to love, his faculties are not developed . . . he may have the capability of becoming great and noble, but he *is* neither, until the divine fire is kindled within, burning up all worldliness, selfishness, and the dross of sensuality. . . . The laws of mere conventional morality cannot be applied to a manifestation of the passion like that of which we speak. To love rightly, is the highest morality of which mankind is capable; no man can make an approach to true greatness till he can love — till he has loved.
>
> True love and high morality are the same. (2: 260-61)

But Zoë ends up with nothing to do but run a household. The question of what woman worships when men worship her was not easy to answer, as other writers discovered too.

Charlotte Brontë, who shocked the literary world a few years after *Zoë* with

Jane Eyre, was a clergyman's daughter and became a clergyman's wife. Christian faith sustained her, and in the world of her novels divine Providence rules. But like Jewsbury, she wants to wrench Christianity out of its male-centeredness; and whereas *Zoë* exalts woman as an object of both veneration and desire, *Jane Eyre* exalts female desire itself. Before Jane can fulfill the trajectory of her desire by marrying Rochester, she has to extricate herself from St. John Rivers's insistence that she devote her life to helping him fulfill his dream of missionary work in India, and her resistance receives divine sanction when she hears Rochester's voice calling her from miles away: an erotic version of the inner voice, the personal vision, that Protestantism allowed to every individual. Jane does not deny the validity of St. John's visionary vocation, his "calling" — indeed, the book ends by exalting it — but she counters it with a vision, a vocation, of her own. He is called by Christ, she by her lover.

Brontë's next novel, *Shirley*, takes both St. John's orthodoxy and Jane's rebellion against it to greater extremes, balancing a satirical indictment of irreligious, woman-hating clergymen with a poetical reimagining of the primary Judeo-Christian myth of woman. Shirley envisions a divinely nurturant Eve:

> I see her prostrate on the great steps of her altar, praying for a fair night for mariners at sea, for travellers in deserts, for lambs on moors, and unfledged birds in woods . . . I see her! (314)

This is the maternal nature goddess of Romantic poetry imbued with consciousness and power but still subordinate to a male divinity and still the mother of sons, the Titans. But if nature has no mythic daughters she has a modern one: Shirley tells her friend Caroline that she prefers worshipping "my mother Eve, in these days called Nature" (316) to attending church.

Shirley and Caroline then go to the church, where they are challenged by a workingman with the central misogynist Pauline text: "Let the woman learn in silence, with all subjection. I suffer not a woman to teach, nor to usurp authority over the man; but to be in silence. For Adam was first formed, then Eve." (I Timothy ii: 11-13) (322). Caroline replies with a good-humored parody of the Higher Criticism's readings of the Bible as a human, humanly transmitted, text.

> Hem! I—I account for [St. Paul's words] in this way: he wrote that chapter for a particular congregation of Christians, under peculiar circumstances; and besides, I dare say, if I could read the original Greek, I should find that many of the words have been wrongly translated, perhaps misapprehended altogether. It would be possible, I doubt not, with a little ingenuity, to give the passage quite a contrary turn; to make it say, "Let the woman speak out whenever she sees fit to make an objection"; — "it is permitted to a woman to teach and to exercise authority as much as may be. Man, meantime, cannot do better than hold his peace," and so on. (323)

Caroline's playful reinterpretation of the Pauline injunction supplements Shirley's visionary revision of the account in Genesis that is used to support that injunction. And later in the novel we get another version of Shirley's new myth, in the form of a French exercise she had written in her school days about Eva, an orphan reared by primal Nature who grows up to become Humanity and wed Genius, a kind of male muse. The complex transmittal of this essay mimics that of sacred texts as traced by the Higher Critics: its origin in fictional time is prior to the moment of narration and we never see the French original, which Shirley's tutor-lover recites from memory in English.

But the novel cannot answer the question with which Shirley's essay concludes: "Who shall, of these things, write the chronicle?" (460). *Shirley* itself does not bear out the vision of woman powerful and triumphant: Shirley marries and is mastered by the tutor, who has announced himself as Adam, lord of animals, flowers, trees (433), and presumably also of Eve; and after the story proper has ended Caroline's husband destroys a scene of magically beautiful nature to make way for the progress of industry. The marriages that comprise the happy ending mark the end of mythic possibility. More significantly, the essay, like Shirley's vision of Mother Eve, is composed in a high-flown, unreal style that is tonally out of key with this or any Victorian novel. The book itself points toward an ideal it cannot encompass. It talks about remaking myth, but it has neither a voice nor a plot that can do so. Able to counter the creations of the masculine imagination with satirical rereading, it can only gesture toward an alternative. In Brontë's last novel, *Villette*, Lucy Snowe sometimes worships a maternal goddess of imagination; but the moments of happiness imagination offers cannot stand against the deprivations that Providence ordains. This is hardly surprising; even the inimitable Zoë, widowed, ends up taking care of her household and children, and George Eliot's heroines, in books that tackle the same problem, do no better.

The evangelical fervor that made the young George Eliot distrust novels and disavow ambition reversed course when she was in her early twenties. After she refused to attend church and her father refused for several weeks to speak to her, she explained her position in a letter hardly likely to conciliate him.

> I regard [the Jewish and Christian Scriptures] as histories consisting of mingled truth and fiction, and while I admire and cherish much of what I believe to have been the moral teaching of Jesus himself, I consider the system of doctrines built upon the facts of his life and drawn as to its materials from Jewish notions to be most dishonourable to God and most pernicious in its influence on individual and social happiness. . . . I could not without vile hypocrisy and a miserable truckling to the smile of the world . . . profess to join in worship which I wholly disapprove. This and *this alone* I will not do even for your sake—anything else however painful I would cheerfully brave to give you a moment's joy.

"The prospect of contempt and rejection," she continues, "shall not make me swerve from my determination so much as a hair's breadth."[19] Unbelief like belief offered prospects of martyrdom, as Martineau and others also discovered, although Eliot and her father eventually agreed to disagree in silence and no martyrdom ensued. Eliot took her agnosticism as seriously as she had taken belief, and the making and remaking of myth is a topic to which her novels repeatedly recur.

She had translated two of the most important works of German biblical criticism, Strauss's *Life of Jesus* and Feuerbach's *The Essence of Christianity*, before she began to write fiction. Strauss analyzes the New Testament story in historical terms, starting with the assumption that miracles do not happen, and while she found his tone displeasingly irreverent she accepted his premises. Feuerbach, on the other hand, radically reinterprets the meaning of Christian myth. Strauss's Jesus is a human being, but for Feuerbach humanity, the human community, is or will become God. Feuerbach's developmental theology contains no patriarchal structure, no fall of man, and therefore no errant Eve. He exalts sexual love and marriage—the stuff of fiction, and of women's lives—in nonhierarchical terms. "The distinction between *I* and *thou*, the fundamental condition of all personality, of all consciousness, is only real, living, ardent, when felt as the distinction between man and woman."[20] And he sees the function of religion, finally, as giving "to common things an uncommon significance, *to life, as such, a religious import*." "Therefore," his book concludes, "let bread be sacred for us, let wine be sacred, and also let water be sacred! Amen" (278). "With the ideas of Feuerbach," Eliot said, "I everywhere agree."[21] The Feuerbachian affirmation of the sacredness of human life and the need to rise to the highest love, "consciousness of the species as a species, the idea of humanity as a whole" (269), validates, for Eliot, her work. For what better than prose fiction can serve these ends?

In *Adam Bede* Eliot shows how a society creates myth from its own experience of life, and how religious rituals and symbols naturally arise. The characters are seen by the narrator as mythic figures, and they unconsciously see each other so. For Dinah, the people in the Bible are as real and ordinary as her friends and neighbors (528-29), and her God is the unconscious projection of her own unstinting love. "The truly religious man unhesitatingly assigns his own feelings to God," says Feuerbach; "God is to him a heart susceptible to all that is human" (55). Dinah is herself an object of worship and awe—an angel—to simple souls, who discover divine love through their experience of hers. And while Dinah unknowingly creates God, the author of *Adam Bede* deliberately creates a new myth of fall and redemption.

In later novels Eliot explores the relation of women to the mythic systems of classical and Christian culture in successively wider contexts and with increasing deliberation on the author's part and consciousness on the characters'. In *The Mill on the Floss* Maggie makes her way through primitive fetishism, classical culture, and Catholic asceticism. And in *Romola*, which is set in fifteenth-century Italy at the confluence of the classical revival and a Catholicism in the throes of moral renovation, the heroine both embodies and judges the highest forms, the mythic heart, of both classical and Christian ideals. She is caught up first by the newly rediscovered classical tradition as represented by her father's barren scholarship and her husband's pagan beauty, shallowness of character, and amoral charm. Although this tradition is exclusively male and she is glad, finally, to be free of it, she is herself the living representative of its essential power: she is Ariadne, Antigone, Aurora, Minerva, or a primal divinity, like Shirley's Eve. She inspires in the man she marries "that loving awe in the presence of noble womanhood, which is perhaps something like the worship paid of old to a great nature-goddess, who was not all-knowing, but whose life and power were something deeper and more primordial than knowledge" (145). But his pagan awe does not make him a faithful or honorable husband.

With Christianity Romola fares somewhat better. Savonarola's tormented spiritual grandeur strikes a responsive chord in her, although she rejects his followers' sterile fanaticism and foolish reformist zeal, and under his influence she becomes a sort of Florence Nightingale of Florence. And whereas to pagan eyes she is a pagan goddess, to innocent and ignorant Christians she is the Madonna. The Florentines she succors, including her husband's mistress, worship her, and she achieves legendary status when in a delirium of self-abandon she floats off in a small boat to a plague-stricken village where she rouses a timorous priest to his duty, tends the sick, and leaves as mysteriously as she arrived. "Many legends were afterward told in that valley about the blessed Lady who came over the sea, but they were legends by which all who heard might know that in times gone by a woman had done beautiful loving deeds there, rescuing those who were ready to perish" (649). The novel shows how women came literally to be worshiped: how legends of the Madonna like those Jameson recounted were formed.

Like heroines' journeys in the early novels of Brontë, Gaskell, and Eliot herself, Romola's journey to the nameless village represents at one level the experience of writing. It is an imaginative movement into another realm of existence, dreamlike and apparently directionless, and at its culmination the heroine becomes an object for the general gaze while being selflessly engaged in saving others. The episode appears to have been closely bound up with the genesis of the book, like the final encounter of Dinah and Hetty in *Adam Bede*: it belonged, Eliot said, to her "earliest vision of the story."[22] The connection with writing is underlined by an earlier, aborted flight from Florence that recalls both Maggie running away to be queen of the Gypsies and St. Theresa setting forth as a child to become a martyr and being turned back by her uncle, a story Eliot uses in the Prelude to *Middlemarch* as a symbol of frustrated ambition. In this first attempt at flight Romola intends to seek the help of a famous woman scholar and write a book, but she is stopped by a monk who, reminding her of her obligation to her disease-stricken city, fills the role of Theresa's uncle or of Southey instructing Charlotte Brontë to exchange literary ambition for domestic responsibility. When Romola does eventually set forth, she casts herself adrift in a small boat and is borne to her unknown destination without knowledge or volition. She appears in the little village carrying an infant she has found along the way; not Hetty's badge of shame, however, but (Jewish and male, a little Jesus) the sign of her divinity.

Romola is Jameson's Madonna: heroic and tender, intellectual and maternal. But the Madonna as what Jameson calls "poetess and prophetess"—the woman who speaks—is less the heroine than the author herself, whom Lewes was in the habit of addressing as "Madonna," and whose sense of herself as a "prophetess" appears in her remark that in *Romola* "great, great facts have struggled to find a voice through me, and have only been able to speak brokenly."[23] To the jealous eyes of Eliza Lynn Linton, Eliot "was always the goddess on her pedestal . . . never for one instant did she forget her self-created Self—never did she throw aside the trappings or the airs of the benign Sibyl."[24] *Romola* gives prolonged and brilliant scrutiny to the prophetic character as represented by the great preacher Savonarola, in whom high and base motives, ideal devotion and self-aggrandizement, inextricably mix and contend. As Romola says, in words the novelist could have applied to her own artistic endeavors, Savonarola "sought his own glory indeed, but sought it by labouring for the very highest end—the moral welfare of man—not by vague exhortations, but by striving to turn beliefs into energies that would work in all the details of life" (664). Eliot seems to associate herself with Savonarola and his penitential practices when she tells a friend: "You are right in saying that Romola is ideal—I feel it acutely in the reproof my own soul is constantly getting from the image it has made. My own books scourge me."[25]

In the end, what Eliot cannot do is imagine a world for an ideal woman to live in. After her apotheosis, Romola returns to Florence and domesticity. All the men with whom she had any connection are dead and she is her own mistress, free to do what she wants; and what she does is devote herself to making a home for her aunt and her dead husband's mistress and children. When we last see her she is trying, with little apparent likelihood of success, to teach an ambitious boy the lesson of self-forgetful service to humanity. Having created a heroine with great and educated powers, placed her not in prosaic modern England but in exotic Renaissance Italy, cleared away every source of opposition or limiting authority, obviated the usual happy ending in marriage, and along the way provided a mythic apotheosis, Eliot can think of nothing for Romola to do except teach and nurture children.

Like *Shirley*'s visionary flights, moreover, Eliot's prophetic revision of divine myth is couched in a style that goes against the grain of prose fiction. The divine image of woman fits the texture of a nineteenth-century novel no better than it fits nineteenth-century life. It is not that the book takes itself too solemnly. Romola even in apotheosis can be laughed at, a little—she is reported to be "as tall as the cypresses" by the boy who first sees her in the plague-stricken village (646). But the Florentine setting comes all too evidently from study rather than experience and is more instructive than amusing. The dialogue, like Shirley's essay about Eve, often sounds like a literal translation from a foreign tongue, and the most obtrusively learned scholar in this book, which upholds the spirit of love against barren erudition, is the author herself. Like Dinah's preaching, it seems, the making of myth cannot be wholly deliberate; like Dinah herself in the last part of the book, *Romola* reveals its self-division by its self-consciousness and undercuts its claims to prophecy.

When Victorian women writers tried to bestow moments and aspects of divine heroism on their female protagonists, they had a good deal of difficulty, not surprisingly, in doing so in an attractive and convincing way. Gaskell's Margaret Hale in *North and South* and Eliot's Dorothea Brooke in *Middlemarch* (not to mention Romola) are on the whole appealing, complexly human characters, but their elegantly unadorned, unconscious beauty, queenlike grandeur, noble simplicity, and childlike sweetness would be more palatable with a leaven of authorial irony. Margaret's "face is as bright and strong" as an angel's (188) not only to a poor dying girl but to the narrator, and Dorothea has a similar effect on characters and narrator alike. Their qualities are not only improbably combined but also too grand for the world they live in. "The next Christ," said Florence Nightingale, "will perhaps be a female Christ. But do we see one woman who looks like a female Christ? or even like 'the messenger before' her 'face,' to go before her and prepare the hearts and minds for her?"[26] A nameless, half-mythical, plague-stricken village in fifteenth-century Italy was a more likely setting for "her" than modern England; and not even Romola can stay very long in such a village.

Male Victorian writers' revivals or revisions of old myths, like Tennyson's *Idylls of the King*, were often couched in unreal and inadequate language, and on the whole they felt little compulsion to make new myths or find new divinities. They had an excellent poetic subject in nostalgia for the old ones; and for them existing myths of woman—as angel or temptress, Mary or Eve—were still potent and useful. But women could hardly be nostalgic for a literary past that excluded them, and the myths that endured were not easily turned to their purposes. The story of Eve, which remained a culturally coercive force even as literal belief in the biblical narratives faded, was still used against them: even Barrett Browning's *A Drama of Exile* focuses on suffering, sacrifice, and guilt. Available images of Mary were too foreign and Catholic, as well as too wholly maternal, for most Englishwomen to use. In both *Shirley* and *Romola* the power to remake myth and re-envision the divine remains a powerfully stated but unrealized ideal, and other novelists had even less success.

Sometimes religious revisionism led in more practical fashion to feminist politics and a literary career dedicated to social reform. For Frances Power Cobbe what began as an Evangelical conversion experience in her seventeenth year quickly reversed direction, and she found herself doubting God's justice, the veracity of the Bible, the immortality of the soul, and even the existence of God. For four miserable years she struggled against her doubts, then devoted herself with deliberate equanimity to reading and study, and eventually emerged as a theist believing in the two crucial tenets of Victorian faith, personal immortality and a wholly beneficent God. She struggled in silence and secrecy, so as not to distress her parents, but she had adequate intellectual resources to draw on. Her father was a country squire with a large property in Ireland, and despite a few years at an expensive but ineffective boarding school she had received excellent instruction at home and could find the books she wanted. She kept her secret until after her mother's death, mothers being typically thought too tender to endure the knowledge of their children's lapses from faith, and when she told her father he was so shocked that he would not speak to her and sent her away for nearly a year to live with an unsympathetic brother. After a while, however, like George Eliot and her father in the same circumstances, they settled down together in a tacit, uneasy truce.

The first book in what Cobbe fairly described as "a long and moderately successful literary life"[27] was *Essay on the Theory of Intuitive Morals* (1855), based on her reading of Kant and attacked in the religious press as unfeminine and un-Christian (114). It was published anonymously so as not to annoy her father, but her gender became known. "Our dislike is increased," Cobbe quotes the *Christian Observer* as exclaiming, "when we are told it is a female (!) who has propounded so unfeminine and stoical a theory . . . and has contradicted openly the true sayings of the living God!" (114). Her father died a few years later, and thereafter she supported herself as a journalist, publishing books on religion, philosophy, and society without worrying about offending her relatives, and became a leader in political and philanthropic activities. She found journalism "a delightful profession," woman's equivalent of the church, especially during the seven years when she wrote more than a thousand short essays for a newspaper, the *Echo*.

> To be in touch with the most striking events of the whole world, and enjoy the privilege of giving your opinion on them to 50,000 or 100,000 readers within a few hours, this struck me . . . as something for which many prophets and preachers of old would have given a house full of silver and gold. And I was to be *paid* for . . . it! (429)

But she laughed at the self-importance men bring to the office of prophecy. "It was *my pulpit*, with permission to make in it (what other pulpits lack so sadly!) such jokes as pleased me" (436). Geraldine Jewsbury said of *Zoë*, which was attacked in the press as immoral, "*I* had thought I had been writing a *Sermon*";[28] much of Cobbe's sermonizing, like *Zoë*, was a freewheeling attack on men's sacred institutions.

The doctrines Cobbe preached were held together by intertwining threads of humanitarianism, feminism, and dislike for the kind of male authority exemplified by preachers too solemn for jokes. She supported the movements for female suffrage and higher education, but her feminism concentrated on the women who suffered most. She particularly disliked men who should have helped but did not: clerics who preached abstruse theology rather than practical morals, men who mismanaged the charitable institutions that women were not yet allowed to direct, scientists who experimented on animals, and the doctors she blamed for her years of invalidism (resulting from a badly treated sprained ankle) and more generally for discouraging women from active and healthy lives. She moved genially through the world to which her intellectual achievements and social connections provided access (her relatives included an archbishop and members of parliament), and she worked successfully with men on numerous committees. But her central commitment was to women, both as objects of philanthropy and social action and in a rich network of friendships.

Her political and religious heterodoxies were based, furthermore, on traditionally feminine virtues. We are, she said, "Human Beings of the Mother Sex,"[29] and she abhorred any suggestion that feminism implied laxity in sexual conduct or devaluation of household duties. Like Martineau before her and Besant after, Cobbe assumed that society was on the verge of a vast transformation in which religion would be purged of its superstitious dross and women would develop their full capacities. And like most Victorian women reformers, she believed that human progress is marked by the spread of sympathy and love. The antivivisection campaign, of which she was an indefatigable leader, was thus a centrally significant cause, a head-on confrontation between opposing gendered visions of social and moral progress: between ideals of nurture and love, and those of intellect and power. She hated the thought of giving pain—which was why, she said, she never wrote reviews (439)[30]—and the doctrine of eternal punishment appalled her. She was happy only when she could feel that God was perfectly kind and good.

This was in accord with the main development of Victorian religious ideas. The replacement of dogmatic faith by a diffusive benevolence, as in the immensely popular works of Dickens, affirmed feminine values, which was one reason why more women than men seem to have been able to rest comfortably within a vaguely formulated orthodoxy. Victorian religion increasingly centered in the feelings of the girl in *In Memoriam* who is tender over drowning flies—feelings affirmed by *In Memoriam* itself, which insists that in a divinely ordered universe not even a moth would suffer in vain. But while *In Memoriam* (which Cobbe frequently quotes) gave essential comfort in a time of confusion and doubt, women who took Tennysonian heterodoxy too literally often paid a heavy price. Once freed from concern for her parents' sensibilities, Cobbe cared little about the condemnation or ridicule that sometimes came her way. But that was partly because of the confidence that came from her social position, despite her relative poverty and unladylike career, and still more because her private life gave no opening for scandal. Annie Besant, like George Eliot, was in this respect less fortunate.

Most of Besant's career—born in 1847, she died in 1933—lies beyond the chronological scope of this study, but by 1880 she had become notorious as a propagandist for free thought who had been prosecuted under the obscenity laws as joint publisher of a pamphlet on birth control. In 1877, having won her case, she wrote and published a new pamphlet on the same subject that sold 175,000 copies in less than two decades. Her life up to 1880 recapitulates in a startlingly literal and extreme way the drama of earlier Victorian women's religious careers. As a girl she did not just dream of martyrdom; she tested her fortitude with self-flagellation. She turned against Christianity, with much anguish of spirit, when she was unable to reconcile her baby's painful illness with the idea of a benevolent God. Her entry into public speech came as a kind of divine calling in reverse; alienated from both her clergyman husband and her religion, she first found her voice in an impromptu address delivered from her husband's pulpit—a real pulpit, not Cobbe's metaphorical one—in his locked and empty church. A public lecturer as well as a writer, she literally exposed herself to insult: at some of her early appearances, people threw stones.

Besant preached not just reform and a Christianity stripped to its humanitarian essence, but radicalism and atheism. Like Martineau she got into trouble by dealing with what was known as the population question, a tremendously important issue both because limiting the number of children they produced was the only practical way for married women to control their economic situation and protect their health, and because of the religious and social taboos its advocacy—even mentioning the topic—violated. But whereas Martineau was sneered at for ignorance, Besant was accused of deliberately advocating unchaste behavior. She was actually arrested, and (with Charles Bradlaugh, her co-defendent) conducted her own defense in a court of law. And she achieved a genuinely painful martyrdom: she thought that her much-loved mother's death was hastened by "grief at my change of faith and consequent social ostracism,"[31] and she lost custody of her daughter because the judge declared her unfit, as an avowed atheist, to be a mother. She was sure that the real cause of the custody judgment against her was the pamphlet on birth control.

Besant followed the rationalist, humanitarian revolt against Christian doctrine fearlessly to its apparent end. And then, seeking a higher theory of life, a more vital ideal of service, and a female community, she was converted to Theosophy by its founder, a flamboyant charlatan called Madame Blavatsky who taught a doctrine based on reincarnation, occult phenomena, the wisdom of the East, and divinely appointed leaders. The political trajectory of Besant's rejection of oppressive power, which began as a rebellion against God and the church, eventually carried her to India and a role of leadership in the Indian revolt against British rule. Theosophy, like Martineau's allegiance to mesmerism and Cobbe's antivivisectionism, challenged the new oppressiveness of Victorian science. For as science challenged religion's position at the center of culture, women were pushed further to the periphery.

8. Science

❧ ❧ ❧

Victorian scientific and literary circles overlapped, intellectually and socially, and some of the leading men of letters were professional scientists. There were many amateurs of science, too, some of them—George Henry Lewes, for instance—highly competent, and meetings of the British Association for the Advancement of Science were social events which ladies attended as spectators. The great debates about geology and biological evolution were conducted in terms anyone could understand, with scientists addressing general audiences and nonscientists confidently joining the fray. The study of human culture came under the sway of the natural sciences, and science, broadly conceived, seemed threatening to displace religion as a way to explain and evaluate human history, human behavior, and even morality and ethics. The new worldview undermined the religious and cultural authority that kept women subordinate, but at the same time it called into question values that had empowered women writers, and it established new kinds of masculine domination.

In the early nineteenth century Christian orthodoxy assumed that God had created the world and all existing forms of life, in their current forms, about 6,000 years earlier. But geology gave evidence that the earth had existed for millions of years and had undergone drastic changes; that during this vastly elongated geological history different forms of life, including the human race, arose and flourished at different times; and that many species had arisen only to be extinguished. The place of man (the gendered collective term is appropriate) at the center of creation came into question, and the evidence of extinct species undermined traditional belief in a deity whose benevolence is made manifest in the Creation and a divine Providence that cares even for the fall of a sparrow—the deity, that is, by which values associated with women were supported. The theory of biological evolution made its decisive (although not its first) appearance in Darwin's *The Origin of Species* in 1859 and was popularly abbreviated to the idea that human beings evolved from apes; as a feminist in Gilbert and Sullivan's *Princess Ida* puts it, "a Darwinian Man, though well-behaved, / At best is only a monkey shaved."[1]

If man was a late arrival on earth, and not created directly by God, could the fall from Eden—or Christ's incarnation and death to redeem that fall—really have occurred? Eventually mainstream theology adopted less literal readings of Genesis to avoid such difficulties, but for a while science seemed to be offering an all-or-nothing challenge to religion. The challenge was sharpened by scientists who asserted that moral truth depended on scientific laws: Thomas Henry Huxley provocatively entitled a collection of essays *Lay Sermons*. It was assumed that "science" could speak in a unified, unitary voice, as Huxley purported to do on its behalf; that it should expound laws bearing on morality, behavior, education, and the organization of society; and moreover (with a pervasive confusion between descriptive and normative meanings of "law") that it should make those laws prevail.

Martineau and Eliot, the two most eminent women intellectuals, paid particular attention to a French lawgiver, Auguste Comte, who claimed to have invented the science of sociology. No one takes Comte seriously now; but Martineau translated and condensed his writings on "positive philosophy," or positivism; G. H. Lewes called him "the greatest thinker of modern times" and published a volume expounding his works; and John Stuart Mill ranked him with Descartes and Leibnitz.[2] Comte was the grandest and most preposterous of the polymathic autodidacts—among them Martineau, Eliot, and Lewes— who adorned the intellectual stage of the nineteenth century. He set forth in systematic fashion all branches of knowledge and the laws that govern them, in hierarchical order, from the mathematical and physical through the biological and social sciences. He traced three stages of development both in history and in individuals: the theological, the metaphysical, and the positive, the last being the best. Martineau and Eliot accepted Comte's ideas only temporarily and with many reservations, but they welcomed positivism as an explanation of their own lives in which the loss of religious belief became part of the whole world's progress toward an as yet unrealized good. Both Martineau's childhood and adolescence in the *Autobiography* and Maggie's in the quasi-autobiographical *The Mill on the Floss* are described in Comtean terms; Maggie as a little girl torturing her doll, for instance, is an example of fetishism, the earliest division of the theological stage. Positivism made girls' childish superstitions and adolescent follies comprehensible, important, and worth writing about, as representing the developmental history of the race.

Positivism seemed to combine masculine and feminine values, uniting (as Lewes explains) logic and sentiment, subordinating science and intellect to emotion and the heart, and acknowledging "the deep and paramount importance of our Moral Nature." "Science," says Lewes in a formulation with which Martineau and Eliot, like Cobbe and Besant, would have agreed, "is a futile, frivolous pursuit, unworthy of greater respect than a game of chess, unless it subserve some grand religious aim,—unless its issue be in some enlarged conception of man's life and destiny."[3] But positivism, which encompassed almost everything, could not accommodate intellectual women. History showed Comte that women had always been inferior to men in intellect and power, and would presumably always be so. In his later writings (which Martineau did not translate and Lewes and Mill did not admire) he gave increasing, and increasingly fantastic, homage to their spiritual nature—men of the future, he thought, would worship Woman, but what women would worship he did not presume to know: a position not unlike Eliot's at the end of *Romola*. But he would not allow them to sully their purity or dilute their influence by exercising power or leaving the shelter of home.

The more sober worldview of British philosophy and science did give some women a sense of opportunity and freedom. John Stuart Mill made the godless universe morally habitable and argued for the emancipation of women. Martineau was glad to be released from the intellectual constraints and moral obliquity of religious experience, and Eliot regarded the new emptiness as a space for intellect to expand in and moral vision to fill. But for writers whose vocations were founded in faith—novelists who worked to illuminate the spiritual import and providential care attending humdrum domestic life, poets whose mission was to glorify God—such a vision was dreadful. And women could hardly be encouraged by the disciplines studying human behavior, which used the natural sciences as a model in the manner of Comte and defined women in terms of reproductive functions and analogies with childlike or "primitive" stages of life. Arguments from animal behavior, from other cultures, or from physiology, like examples from history, were adduced to reinforce old stereotypes of women's inferiority and their necessary subordination. Women gravitated, therefore, to the fringes of science, where they were most likely to find allies. Phrenology, for instance, which argued that will and behavior could modify the physical facts that determined character, encouraged the radical development of women's capacities.[4] Like spiritualism, mesmerism, and clairvoyance, which pleased many women by baffling the materialistic explanations of authoritative men, phrenology existed on the margins of culture where rigid gender difference got muddled and social hierarchy blurred.

Among the voices speaking for science only one woman's is distinctly audible. Mary Somerville worked primarily in mathematics and physical science, areas in which ideas about gender were not obviously woven into the fabric of the subject matter itself. To women like Martineau and Cobbe, Somerville was an inspiring proof that the female mind was capable of scientific thought and that the highest intellectual development was compatible with womanliness. To us she may seem an awe-inspiring example of intellectual force triumphing over apparently insuperable obstacles. The fifth of seven children in a Scottish family of famous military men, she was taught reading, writing, drawing, music, modern languages, and domestic and social accomplishments, but beyond that she had to study on her own, often secretly and against the expressed wishes of her parents. In her early teens she was fascinated but baffled by some algebra that she happened to see in a friend's magazine, and later she overheard her drawing master mentioning Euclid, but until a tutor arrived to teach her youngest brother she could learn nothing whatever about mathematics or geometry. The tutor procured her a copy of Euclid, which she studied at night until her father forbade it (" 'we must put a stop to this,' he declared, 'or we shall have Mary in a strait-jacket' "), and then she worked from memory. "I was often very sad and forlorn," she recalls in her autobiography, "not a hand held out to help me."[5] But she persevered, through a brief marriage to a man who despised the female intellect and then as a widow who could buy books and ignore familial disapproval. She solved problems in a mathematics journal and corresponded with the editor, and he told her what books to buy. And then she married a physician who moved with her in scientific circles in London, helped with her researches and publications, and cherished and delighted in her fame.

In 1826 she published her first experimental paper, based on studies of sunlight and magnetism done with simple apparatus at home, which established her reputation among scientists. It was the first paper, apart from astronomical observations by Caroline Herschel, to appear under a woman's name in the transactions of the Royal Society, and there was no other until she herself contributed again in 1845.[6] She became widely known for an exposition of Laplace's *Mechanique celeste* (regarded at the time as second only to Newton's *Principia* in importance, and of corresponding difficulty) entitled *The Mechanism of the Heavens*, published in 1831—a project she undertook with great diffidence at the suggestion and urging of others. She also published *On the Connection of the Physical Sciences* (1834), *Physical Geography* (1848), and *On Molecular and Microscopic Science* (1869)—authoritative and often original and pioneering expositions of a very wide range of material. She was welcomed as a friend and colleague by the greatest scientists in Britain and France and had drawers stuffed with certificates of honor. In 1840, however, she moved to Italy, out of the orbit of the scientific community, because of her husband's ill health.

Somerville's scientific activity, like other women's writing, was embedded in a thoroughly gendered context. After tending to her household and her children she worked in the drawing room, like Jane Austen, hiding her papers when visitors came. In her late teens she had been "intensely ambitious to excel in something" (60), most likely painting, but she was diffident in society and reluctant to speak. Reviewers almost universally praised her, but they took note of her gender too, usually with the familiar backhanded compliment that she demonstrated the highest mental powers achieved by her sex. "Her book," said the *Athenaeum*, "is at the same time a fit companion for the philosopher in her study and for the literary lady in her boudoir."[7] She was sometimes denigrated as a mere expositor of other people's work, and she herself doubted women's creative power.

In the climax of my great success, the approbation of some of the first scientific men of the age and of the public in general I was highly gratified, but much less elated than might have been expected, for although I had recorded in a clear point of view some of the most refined and difficult analytical processes and astronomical discoveries, I was conscious that I had made no discovery myself, that I had no originality. I have perseverance and intelligence but no genius, that spark from heaven is not granted to the sex, we are of the earth, earthy, whether higher powers may be allotted to us in another state of existence God knows, original genius in science at least is hopeless in this.[8]

One is reminded of Martineau disavowing the possession of imagination, and of Rossetti, hopeless of matching men in this world, looking for equality in the next. In science as in poetry and religion, woman is part of nature, and the "spark from heaven"—the phrase Matthew Arnold used in "The Scholar-Gipsy" for poetic inspiration—does not fall on them. The work in question, appropriately, is *The Mechanism of the Heavens*.

Somerville's autobiography is filled with fine descriptions of nature that juxtapose beauty and terror, especially storms and volcanic eruptions, and she makes the same gender associations poets do. Her mother, she says, was terrified of thunder and lightning and communicated her fears to her young daughter (16).

> My bedroom had a window to the south, and a small closet near had one to the north. At these I spent many hours, studying the stars by the aid of the celestial globe. Although I watched and admired the magnificent displays of the Aurora, which frequently occurred, they seemed to be so nearly allied to lightning that I was somewhat afraid of them. At an earlier period of my life there was a comet, which I dreaded exceedingly. (30)

Her father, on the other hand, was fearless and aggressive toward nature, a keen sportsman who captured a whale on the beach where she herself wondered at the strangeness and beauty of sea creatures and would not so much as kill a mussel to get a pearl. Like Ouida and Frances Power Cobbe, she became a passionate champion of animals, and her imaginative relation to nature is like that of Barrett Browning, who characterized her father as Jove the thunderer and said that submission to him spoiled her mother's sweetness, as thunder spoils milk.[9]

Still, the symbolic structure that allied woman with nature rather than with those who dominate and interpret it did allow some leeway. There had been many female amateurs of science in the preceding century, and in the nineteenth century the most advanced girls' schools were more likely than boys' to teach science, which conferred no social prestige and was useless for winning university fellowships. Early in the century Jane Marcet wrote introductions to natural philosophy, vegetable physiology, and political economy as well as *Conversations on Chemistry, Intended More Especially for the Female Sex* (1805), which introduced Michael Faraday to the study of chemistry; but she was not an original thinker or researcher. An eighteenth-century writer identified only as "Sophia" argued that the study of physics was "particularly suited to women, for all that is required by way of preparation is close observation, a keen eye for detail, patience and energy—precisely the skills that women who have been obliged to spend hours sewing and embroidering have to excess."[10] Science did not require the classical training that dominated the schools, and was often taught through public lectures, often for working-class audiences, which many women attended. Many scientists, like women, were self-educated in their fields, and many kinds of observations and experiments could be done at home; institutional laboratories had not yet become the only proprietors of research equipment. Science was an avocation for all classes: the poor working-man Job Legh in *Mary Barton* collects natural specimens as avidly as the highly cultivated Mr. Farebrother in *Middlemarch*, and a shared enthusiasm for botany was a link between the young Quaker Mary Howitt and the man she was to marry. What could be more appropriate for a young woman than gathering flowers?

Sara Coleridge, her daughter reported, enjoyed what was then called natural history:

> The beauty of nature . . . delighted her poetical imagination; while the signs of divine Wisdom and Goodness, revealed in all the works of creation, furnished a constant theme for the contemplation of a thoughtful piety. . . . The outdoor interests which they provided, the habits of careful observation which they rendered necessary, aided in the harmonious development of her faculties. . . . She could turn at any time from the most abstruse metaphysical speculations, to inspect the domestic architecture of a spider, or describe the corolla of a rose.[11]

As the century progressed, however, nature was less surely marked with the signs of divine benevolence, and science was increasingly defined as a matter of finding general laws rather than collecting specimens or observing floral beauty and arachnid domesticity. Observation itself tended to involve unlady-like activities: tomboyish excursions into the countryside that ended in muddy feet, torn clothes, a tanned complexion, and messes carried into the house. And even before scientific careers required university training they generally depended at their inception on pursuits that only men could follow: Darwin's observations as official naturalist on the voyage of the *Beagle*, Huxley's travels as a naval surgeon, the physicist John Tyndall's experience as a road surveyor, a civil engineer, and a teacher of mathematics studying physics in Germany.

In the early nineteenth century scientific men congregated in drawing rooms, and the tools and materials of science were privately owned and shared among friends when men and women gathered socially together. Dinner parties and scientific activities flowed pleasantly into each other. But scientists also met in clubs and associations where women rarely or never appeared. By mid-century science was becoming a profession, with the systematic training and barriers to entrance that professionalism implies. Somerville held honorary membership in scientific societies in many countries, but she did not participate in their activities. When women gained entrance to the universities, moreover, feminist strategy directed them toward the arena of highest prestige, the classics, while the opening of medical training to women in the 1870s provided an outlet for the scientifically ambitious more in tune with traditional feminine concerns.[12] Mary Somerville had no successors of comparable eminence in her century.

Victorian science repeated in a darker key the Romantic conception of women as part of the mysterious, maternal nature whose sons interpret her: in Somerville's terms, they are of the earth, earthy. At first such an alliance between science and poetry may seem odd. Wordsworth's "A Poet's Epitaph" speaks for much of Romanticism in its scorn for the unfilial "fingering slave" who "would peep and botanize / Upon his mother's grave." But when Victorian writers ceased to believe in the benignant maternity of nature they gave the familiar gender dichotomy a different spin. In *In Memoriam* (published almost a decade before *The Origin of Species* but expressing a similar vision) nature is a mother who is at best indifferent to her children, at worst "red in tooth and claw" with their blood. Carlyle, whose writings were powerful formative influences in the self-educations of Huxley and other scientists and also of poets, wrote in 1843, "Nature, like the Sphinx, is of womanly celestial loveliness and tenderness: the face and bosom of a goddess, but ending in claws and the body of a lioness." And Huxley, the preeminent spokesman for science, describes nature as the cold, harsh mother of an unloved child: "Nature's discipline is not even a word and a blow, and the blow first; but the blow without the word. It is left to you to find out why your ears are boxed."[13]

For Huxley as for Wordsworth, nature is maternal, mysterious, and silent, and while she is man's teacher, men—Wordsworth as poet, Huxley as scientist—are her interpreters: reading her riddle, turning her laws into language.

> That man, I think, has had a liberal education, who has been so trained in youth that his body is the ready servant of his will, and does with ease and pleasure all the work that, as a mechanism, it is capable of; whose intellect is a clear, cold, logic engine, with all its parts of equal strength, and in smooth working order . . . whose mind is stored with a knowledge of the great and fundamental truths of Nature and of the laws of her operations; one who, no stunted ascetic, is full of life and fire, but whose passions are trained to come to heel by a vigorous will, the servant of a tender conscience; who has learned to love all beauty, whether of Nature or of art, to hate all vileness, and to respect others as himself.
>
> Such an one and no other, I conceive, has had a liberal education; for he is, as completely as a man can be, in harmony with Nature. He will make the best of her, and she of him . . . she as his ever beneficent mother; he as her mouth-piece, her conscious self, her minister and interpreter.[14]

But what education does Nature, who trains her sons to such hard masculinity, give her daughters?

She was a harsh mother to women poets, reinforcing their isolation from the cultural mainstream. Tennyson, Browning, Hardy, and Meredith wrote poetry saturated with science and its implications, but women did not. So far as women's poems are concerned, the earth might still be no more than 6,000 years old, as Barrett Browning's "Earth and Her Praisers" explicitly states. Jean Ingelow's "Honours" evokes the godless universe revealed by geology and astronomy, Tennyson's "terrible Muses,"[15] with almost Tennysonian strength of visual and tactile imagery and a Tennysonian mixture of irony and horror; but she does so only to urge a return to pre-Victorian innocence. Science is a baby playing irresponsibly with geological and fossil evidence—shells and stones and bones—that

> Hints at a pedigree withdrawn and vast,
>   Terrible deeps, and old obscurities,
> Or soulless origin, and twilight passed
>   In the primeval seas. (p. 16)

Under this influence,

>   fain to learn we lean into the dark,
> And grope to feel the floor of the abyss,
> Or find the secret boundary lines which mark
>   Where soul and matter kiss. (p. 15)

To the distempered imagination earth looms like a sea monster among her young, while God vanishes. The antidote is retreat from intellection into humility, faith, love, work, prayer—anything to screen out the terrible emptiness. Ingelow's imagination resonates powerfully, like Tennyson's, to the image of nature as cruel mother; but unlike Tennyson she simply retreats into the poetic faith of the past. "You were to me the world's interpreter," the poet in "Honours" is told by his friend, "The man that taught me Nature's unknown tongue" (9). Ingelow wants a pious Romantic poet, not an irresponsible infant science, to interpret nature—even at the price of her own intellectual marginality and exclusion as a woman.

For female novelists, science had more to give, especially when, like Eliza Lynn Linton, they were in revolt against religion. Eliot's novels are saturated with scientific thought, and their omniscient narrators are just such authoritative observers, interpreters, and teachers as Huxley describes. Huxley defines education as "the instruction of the intellect in the laws of Nature, under which name I include not merely things and their forces, but men and their ways; and the fashioning of the affections and of the will into an earnest and loving desire to move in harmony with those laws"[16]—a definition that exactly describes Eliot's intentions in her novels. And conversely, she defines science in terms that describe her own activity as a novelist: science depends on "the imagination that reveals subtle actions inaccessible by any sort of lens, but tracked in that outer darkness through long pathways of necessary sequence by the inward light which is the last refinement of Energy, capable of bathing even the ethereal atoms in its ideally illuminated space" (*Middlemarch*, 194). The Higher Criticism suggested that the mythic universe could be remade; science conceived as an imaginative activity offered a model for doing so.

Science also gave Eliot a standing-point from which to challenge the literary canon. By assuming its authority she could become, in effect, what Elizabeth Barrett had aspired to be: the feminine of Homer—or as Eliot would probably have preferred to think of it, a Homer (or Milton) without distinction of gender. Like Elizabeth Barrett writing *The Seraphim* and *A Drama of Exile*, she knew something important that the great male precursors did not: the young poet had Christianity, Eliot had science. The narrator of Eliot's novels is an essentially genderless seer, occasionally specified as male but without the obtrusive masculinity of Huxley's lawgiving prophetic persona. Eliot's cast of mind was inclusive and synthetic—all knowledge was the province of her novels—and Victorian science promised a vision of the world that could incorporate all kinds of matter, all forms of life, in a complex, coherent moral and imaginative whole. In *Middlemarch*, where Eliot uses science most openly as a model and the act of observation is itself continually observed, both Farebrother, with his old-fashioned, unconceptualized collection of natural objects, and Lydgate, whose search for the "primitive tissue" underlying all forms of life is misdirected although right in spirit, are inferior to the narrator as scientific observers. But for the characters in her novels, science is a pursuit followed only by men.

In Gaskell's last and finest work, *Wives and Daughters*, science is also a male profession with significant resemblance to the novelist's craft. Gaskell carefully marks its connections with the feminine world. The hero, Roger Hamley, is a young naturalist modeled on Charles Darwin whose first significant encounter with Molly Gibson, the heroine, occurs when he is looking for rare plants and instead finds her sitting on the ground in a passion of weeping. A "lover of nature" (148), he is careful not to tread heavily on either the plants or her sorrow, and by the end of the book he is her lover as well as nature's.[17] Under his tutelage Molly becomes an amateur of science herself, although she is not intellectually ambitious and would "rather be a dunce than a blue-stocking" (308). Science is defined in simpler terms than Eliot's, primarily as observation, but Gaskell's scientists like Eliot's learn that they must observe people with the same care they give to nature. Roger, like Molly's physician father and Eliot's Lydgate, is beguiled by a beautiful, shallow woman, whereas Molly reads character as clearly as Roger reads nature, and her unobtrusive insight and finely discriminating judgment are like the novelist's own.

Roger shares with women a degree of social marginality and alienation from classical culture. Not adept in the classical studies valued at school, he has been slighted by his parents in favor of his pretentiously cultured older brother, Osborne, whose extravagance impoverishes the family estate while Roger like a daughter makes do with very little. But Roger turns out to be brilliantly successful at Cambridge, in his profession, and even in society—he goes off on a three-year voyage of research, like Darwin and Huxley, and returns home famous—while the elegant Osborne is weak and sentimental, disappoints his parents, and dies young. As the battle of science and culture plays itself out in the Hamley family, science wins on every count; and Molly, whose resistance to conventional notions of femininity and truthfulness of speech and observation make her a fit match for Roger, wins too.

Wives and Daughters is a poised, peaceful, self-confident book, ignoring the great public issues that Gaskell had engaged with in *Mary Barton*, *North and South*, and *Ruth*—the sort of book critics dismissively praise as being in the delightful vein of Jane Austen. And yet while Gaskell's vision has less intellectual intensity than Eliot's, its efficacy is of the same kind. For a brief period after mid-century, science gave women novelists an authoritative model of sympathetic, morally precise observation, and an ally against the culture of exclusion. Gaskell's narrator stands apart from high culture and observes society with loving impersonality, taking as a field of observation the inhabitants of a small provincial world—the families of doctor, lawyer, clergyman, and squire, the aristocracy, the lowest fringes of county-town gentility, cooks, maidservants, governesses, unscrupulous outsiders, and many more—and tracing their interactions like Darwin tracing the multifarious interactions of plants and animals in the English countryside. Like Roger, too, the narrator moves up and down the social scale at will.

For the scientist as for the novelist, nothing is too trivial to be important. Small domestic details, the rituals and mishaps of mating, the strange crisscrossing of social paths that women write about, are analogous to or identical with the stuff of science. In *Wives and Daughters*, "fate" is something small and charming that might be observed by a naturalist: "fate is a cunning hussy, and builds up her plans as imperceptibly as a bird builds her nest; and with the same kind of unconsidered trifles" (107). A maid's misconduct, a cook's resentment, a child in a distant town who contracts scarlet fever—these and other apparently irrelevant trifles are the materials fate works with. The meticulous mapping of such small causes is explicitly the novelist's work in *Wives and Daughters*, as in *Middlemarch*, and it is also Darwin's work in *The Origin of Species*, which had been published less than a decade before *Wives and Daughters*.

For example, Darwin describes the effect of enclosure on the growth of some Scotch firs:

> I was so much surprised at their numbers that I went to several points of view, whence I could examine hundreds of acres of the unenclosed heath, and literally I could not see a single Scotch fir, except the old planted clumps. But on looking closely between the stems of the heath, I found a multitude of seedlings and little trees which had been perpetually browsed down by the cattle. In one square yard, at a point some hundred yards distant from one of the old clumps, I counted thirty-two little trees; and one of them, with twenty-six rings of growth, had, during many years tried to raise its head above the stems of the heath, and had failed.[18]

The setting is a patch of open countryside, not a laboratory; the effective mode of observation is close inspection on the ground; and a general law is deduced from small objects that the observer "literally" sees. This scientist seems to require nothing but willingness to descend to the ground, knowledge of common plants and birds, and the ability to count. The muted notes of Romantic wonder ("I was so much surprised") and of anthropomorphic pathos (the single tree that tried to raise its head and failed) are further links to the novelist's art, not least in focusing on the difficulty of rising above the ordinary, a recurrent Victorian theme. (Darwin's next example, however, is from Paraguay, the kind of exotic place where Roger Hamley goes but the novel does not follow.) Similarly, in a lecture for workingmen called "On a Piece of Chalk" Huxley reaches wide-ranging conclusions about the history of the earth, the evolution of organic life, and the veracity of the Book of Genesis from considering a piece of chalk.

Gaskell is less eager than Eliot to deduce general laws, as Darwin and Huxley do, from the facts she observes, but like them she delights in painstakingly tracing the surprising workings of cause and effect in everyday affairs. She follows the history of fate's "imperceptibly" constructed bird's nest to show how small natural causes bring about large and apparently unrelated results. In this respect science, like religion, validates the work of women novelists who accept the restrictions imposed by convention and the limits of feminine experience on their subject matter. As the power of religion diminished, science stepped in to reinforce the value of the kind of novelistic analysis that women writers were thought to do best.

Still, male authority continually reasserts itself. *Wives and Daughters* appears at a transitional moment: someone remarks in regard to Roger Hamley that "science is not a remunerative profession, if profession it can be called" (676), but in the course of the novel he has earned both the remuneration and the prestige of the kind of professional success that allies men with the established powers. And the fact that Mr. Gibson, Molly's father, is both powerful and good (the first such father in Gaskell's novels), combining as a physician a woman's kindness, a scientist's power of observation, and a man's authority, means that Molly, unlike the heroines of *Mary Barton*, *Ruth*, and *North and South*, is protected from the need—and the opportunity—to act in the world on her own.

There is a recurrent fear in *Wives and Daughters* as in *The Origin of Species*, moreover, that looking too closely can be a source of pain. "We behold the face of nature," says Darwin in a famous purple passage,

> bright with gladness, we often see superabundance of food; we do not see or we forget, that the birds which are idly singing round us mostly live on insects or seeds, and are thus constantly destroying life; or we forget how largely these songsters, or their eggs, or their nestlings, are destroyed by birds and beasts of prey; we do not always bear in mind, that, though food may be now superabundant, it is not so at all seasons of each recurrent year.[19]

Vision similar to this one works in the novel to give negative value to feminine feeling and to suppress female speech. For a while Mr. Gibson is half-willfully oblivious, like Darwin's superficial observer, of his pretty new wife's faults of character, but when his eventual awareness makes him unhappy and disagreeable Molly "learnt to long after the vanished blindness in which her father had passed the first year of his marriage" (457) and "could not imagine how she had at one time wished for [his] eyes to be opened" (458). What close observation threatens to reveal, for Mr. Gibson as for Darwin, is the darkness behind a bright female face.

Similarly, most of Molly's perplexities concern how much she should reveal of what she sees—about her stepmother primarily, but also about her stepsister's blackmailing ex-lover or Osborne's secret marriage. "It was a wonder to Molly," keeping silent at home to spare her father pain, "whether this silence was right or wrong" (407). In fact, the narrator makes clear, it is right; but the self-suppression is very painful. And when Molly suffers from unrequited love, her father asks for a face (in Darwin's term) bright with gladness again.

> "I get quite enough of tears in the day, shed for real causes, not to want them at home, where, I hope, they are shed for no cause at all. There's nothing really the matter, is there, my dear?" he continued, holding her a little away from him that he might look in her face. She smiled at him through her tears; and he did not see [Darwin says, "we do not see, or we forget"] the look of sadness which returned to her face after he had left her. (445)

Whether as observer or as object of observation, Molly is enjoined to silence lest she cause pain.

In biology and in medical, psychological, and social science, woman was defined primarily in terms of the natural functions of attracting a mate and producing and nurturing children. Intellectual activity or anything else that might distract her from domesticity was seen as limited by and destructive to her reproductive function. The old assumption that woman's essential attribute is physical beauty, which discouraged female poets for centuries and against which much of Charlotte Brontë's fiction struggles, reappeared with new authority in Darwin's theory of sexual selection. John Stuart Mill's arguments for women's rights were dismissed as unscientific by Darwin and others, who were not interested in cultural explanations of what seemed biologically determined social facts. The idea that biology is destiny appears in Francis Galton's *Hereditary Genius* as the argument that every individual achieves whatever he (all Galton's examples are male) is capable of, giving "scientific" validation to the idea that woman's inferior social position and accomplishments mirror her inferior abilities. Galton also makes the discouraging observation that genius is rarely transmitted in the female line, perhaps (he speculates) because women of genius are unlikely to marry.[20]

In the biological and social sciences women were linked with children and what the Victorians called "savage" races. The savages who fascinated Victorians were not noble but bestial, survivals of primitive creatures from which civilized man had evolved. Anthropologists found in prehistory the equivalent of Carlyle's sphinx and Tennyson's nature red in tooth and claw, the bad mother whom masculine civilization must know and master. John F. McLennan's *Primitive Marriage*, which by tracing human society back to matrilineal, polyandrous beginnings might seem (as J. J. Bachofen's *Das Mutterrecht* has seemed to some feminists) empowering for women, in fact describes that primal world as one of promiscuity, infanticide, and "a precarious life of squalid misery." A patriarchal system of kinship, McLennan says, requires knowledge of an individual's paternity, made more difficult by the possibility that "the connection between father and child is less intimate than that between mother and child as regards the transmission of characteristics, mental or physical" — ignorance of the mechanisms of heredity giving additional justification for consigning woman to the sphere of reproduction. "The requisite degree of certainty can be had only when the mother is appropriated to a particular man as his wife, or to men of one blood as wife, and when women thus appropriated are usually found faithful to their lords."[21] Civilization, that is to say, is built on the subjugation of women. And the maternal icon that for writers like Jameson, Eliot, and Rossetti symbolized female spiritual force became a figure of nightmare: mere savage, primal instinct.

Perhaps the most instructive example of how social science turned its strength against women is that of Herbert Spencer, who was a towering presence in Victorian intellectual life although he has been almost totally forgotten since. Spencer was George Eliot's most important intellectual companion before G. H. Lewes. Like Comte he spent his formidable career evolving an evolutionary theory of everything: organic and inorganic nature, society and social institutions, woman and man. When Eliot first knew him he shared her feminist views. But he soon reversed himself, maintaining that in the light of evolutionary theory woman's most important quality was her ability to attract men, the one thing he had found Eliot lacking — he rejected her love because she did not attract him sexually.[22] When Eliot began writing, science seemed to be on her side, but later women would not find it so.

For Eliot, "science" meant a way of seeing that might be able to circumvent the inevitable egocentrism of the observer and expose, like Darwin's ecological analyses in *The Origin of Species*, the endlessly subtle and surprising interconnections among living things. Science gave Eliot themes and points of view for her novels and also, increasingly, a voice to speak in, a place to stand, and a source of impersonal authority. Whereas for women like Ingelow science was only a threat to religious faith, and others ignored it entirely, Eliot took it as a standing-point from which to remake a world already bereft of God — a radical revision for which gender opposed no bars. The Victorian inclination to think in terms of development and progress, to be fascinated by origins and both hopeful and afraid of what was yet to come, at first seemed to open limitless possibilities to women, who could expect to profit from almost any kind of change. But as Darwinian evolution became the dominant form of the developmental idea and science came to seem in every respect—ideological, social, professional—derogatory of women, such hopes were hard to sustain. It is not surprising that with the usual exceptions to such rules, Martineau and Eliot, all the nineteenth-century literary figures most associated with science are men.

Conclusion

❦ ❦ ❦

Limitations on imagination and desire imposed by religion, science, literary culture, social and economic conditions, and the ideology of domesticity set the framework for girls' experiences of literature, imposed constraints and restrictions, but also gave impetus, energy, and significant form to women's writing. In Charlotte Brontë's last novel, *Villette*, the ostensibly competing claims of imagination and what the book defines as real life are played out in open-ended reciprocity. Lucy Snowe regards the meagerness of her existence, from her occluded childhood up to but not including the glorious moment near the end of the book when M. Paul declares his love and promises to return in a few years from his voyage to the Indies and marry her, as the lot appointed to her by God and as typical of the human condition. "I see that a great many men, and more women, hold their span of life on conditions of denial and privation. I find no reason why I should be of the few favored. . . . I believe that this life is not all; neither the beginning nor the end" (451). For Lucy, religion gives drama and significance to privation: like girls who dreamed of martyrdom, she is prepared to testify and suffer—to risk the loss of M. Paul—for her Protestant faith. Imagination, in contrast, offers a way of evading both privation and heroic action.

At first imagination enforces passivity. "I seemed to hold two lives—the life of thought, and that of reality; and, provided the former was nourished with a sufficiency of the strange necromantic joys of fancy, the privileges of the latter might remain limited to daily bread, hourly work, and a roof of shelter" (140). Later, imagination appears as itself a kind of a female divinity, like the vision of Eve in *Shirley*.

> [I have] seen in the sky a head amidst circling stars, of which the midmost and the brightest lent a ray sympathetic and attent. A spirit . . . has descended with quiet flight to the waste—bringing all round her a sphere of air borrowed of eternal summer; bringing perfume of flowers which cannot fade—fragrance of trees whose fruit is life, bringing breezes pure from a world whose day needs no sun to lighten it. My hunger has this good angel appeased with food, sweet and strange. . . . Divine, compassionate, succourable influence! When I bend the knee to other than God, it shall be at thy white and winged feet, beautiful on mountain or on plain. . . . To thee neither hands build, nor lips consecrate; but hearts, through ages, are faithful to thy worship. A dwelling thou hast, too wide for walls, too

> high for dome—a temple whose floors are space—rites whose mysteries transpire
> in presence, to the kindling, the harmony of worlds! (308)

But even in this transfiguration imagination gives only dreams, although gilded ones, and so Lucy returns to reason, faith, reality. As she sinks deeper into solitude and loss, however, the dreams become malign: forms of madness and despair fill the vacancy of her existence, and her faith in providential care is intertwined with its reciprocal opposite, paranoia.

At the end of the book, when Paul is almost home, happy and prosperous, a storm comes up at sea.

> Here pause: pause at once. There is enough said. Trouble no quiet, kind heart;
> leave sunny imaginations hope. Let it be theirs to conceive the delight of joy born
> again fresh out of great terror, the rapture of rescue from peril, the wondrous re-
> prieve from dread, the fruition of return. Let them picture union and a happy suc-
> ceeding life! (596)

To us, who know that Brontë attributed this gesture toward open-endedness to her father's desire for a happy ending,[1] it is evident that the hope of sunny imaginations goes against everything the book says and feels. But some of Brontë's contemporaries, for whom the entrenched expectations of novel reading were as strong as the contrary signals, wanted to know what "really happened." And in a way they were right to be uncertain. For in this most powerfully imagined of Brontë's novels, imagination may not bring the plot around to felicity; it may be renounced as a source of somnolence and delusion; but it transfigures deprivation and restriction, brings a phantasmagoric world into apparently "real" existence, and presses beyond the boundaries of Victorian realism to show how the most potent imagination and the most strictly construed "reality"—like the phantom nun who is both the projection of Lucy's repressed desire and a commonplace young man in disguise—are two faces of one experience, two sides of the same art.

George Eliot's *Daniel Deronda* also presses against the conventional boundaries of women's fiction. Published in 1876, it is the last major work, except for Oliphant's *Autobiography*, by a Victorian woman writer. The Brontë sisters had been dead for decades: Emily in 1848, Anne in 1849, Charlotte in 1855, two years after the publication of *Villette*. Barrett Browning died in 1861, Gaskell in 1865, Somerville in 1872, Martineau in 1876, the year of *Deronda*. Rossetti, Ingelow, Yonge, and Oliphant survived into the 1890s, Cobbe, Ouida, and Braddon into the next century, but after 1880 they had almost without exception finished their best and best-known work. Only Augusta Webster was still in the prime of her career. Eliot herself died in 1880, having married a man much younger than herself soon after Lewes's death and thereby acquired a new legal name and become respectable enough for her brother to acknowledge her. And in 1882 Virginia Woolf, daughter of the quintessential late-Victorian man of letters, Leslie Stephen, was born.

Rising to the historical occasion, *Daniel Deronda* brings the main threads of women's writing together in a richly woven, untidily integrated composition that attempts to go beyond gender, rationality, and Europe for its resolutions. Its juxtaposition of two stories with very different tonalities—what have come to be known as the English plot and the Jewish plot—formalizes the perceived split between imagination and reality, art and life, aspiration and the limits of gender, that formed women's sense of themselves and their work. Through the main female characters it explores the situation of the woman artist as performer, and its eponymous hero awaits and confronts his destiny in both masculine and feminine terms. The book is saturated, moreover, with the language and concepts of science,[2] and problems of identity and vocation are resolved in terms both of race—a concept central to Victorian social science—and religion.

As at the beginning of the Victorian period, women's art is conceived as public performance and as such is morally very dubious. Mirah, the woman Daniel marries, is a singer whose wicked father forced her to appear on the stage to earn money for him to squander, but she hates performing in public—"she would strongly object to being exhibited" (516) even in a painting—and is glad that her voice is too weak for anything but concerts in private houses. Once she marries, of course, she will no longer have to perform at all. For the heroine of the so-called English plot, Gwendolyn Harleth, marriage and performance are also opposing choices. Gwendolyn conceives of art as self-display for money, and so when she is faced with the intolerable prospect of becoming a governess she wants to support herself and her family as a singer or actress. But since she has no talent, only beauty and vanity, and is incapable of the self-discipline and sacrifice of social position that would be necessary for any chance of success, she sells herself in marriage instead.[3]

Daniel's mother, a famous singer known as Al Charisi, is a great and genuine artist. Rather than being impelled by circumstances, altruism, or masculine authority, she had defied her dead father's prohibition and bent her husband to her will, moving from patriarchal Judaism into the wide world and fulfilling Maggie's childish ambitions. "For nine years I was a queen" (702). But like Mary Barton, Hetty, or Lucy Snowe on trial, she could not in the end keep her body from betraying her. She began to sing out of tune and in a moment of consequent desperation married for a second time, and when she recovered control of her voice it was too late to return to the stage. At last, pricked by a painful disease, the approach of death, and ancestral voices she would like to defy but cannot, she reveals herself and his ancestry to Daniel, whom she had hoped to free from the bonds of Jewishness by having him raised by a kindly English aristocrat. She seems compelled by a "strange coercion," like a heroine on trial, "to lay her mind bare" (695) to her son. But even so, duplicity, "double consciousness" (691), is the condition of her being; she presents herself to him with "what may be called sincere acting: this woman's nature was one in which all feeling—and all the more when it was tragic as well as real—immediately became matter of conscious representation: experience immediately passed into drama, and she acted her own emotions" (691). The virtuous Mirah, in pointed contrast, failed as an actress (and was happy to do so) because she could never be other than herself.

Daniel yearns for a mother he had imagined as the heroine of a seduction-and-betrayal story, a tender, bruised being to whom his filial love would make amends. But Al Charisi has ruled her own life, and she entirely lacks the maternal feelings by which women writers, including Eliot herself, defined essential womanhood. She gave up her child willingly. "I did not want affection. I had been stifled with it. I wanted to live out the life that was in me, and not to be hampered with other lives" (688). She rejects his love and his proffered understanding. "You are not a woman. You may try—but you can never imagine what it is to have a man's force of genius in you, and yet to suffer the slavery of being a girl" (694). But when she is dying, the paternal force that had enslaved her as a girl compels her to reveal his ancestry to Daniel, who eagerly embraces the creed of his fathers. To him, she is "a mysterious Fate" (688), the source of his identity. Filial and maternal functions define her, after all, great artist though she is; biology is destiny.

For Daniel himself, biology in the racial sense is destiny, but in terms of gender it has a certain fluidity. He has many of the social characteristics of a woman. Aware of a mystery about his birth, he assumes that he is illegitimate and therefore, like a woman, marginal. Although he goes to Oxford he is unambitious, sacrificing his chance of distinction to help his friend Hans, and he is not interested in any available career. At the beginning of the story he is a young man with nothing in particular to do except be attentive, like a good daughter, to the adoptive parents whose estate, like a daughter, he cannot inherit. He waits for duty to declare itself, for an unknown destiny to find him out, like a girl waiting to be chosen in marriage. He is sensitive, sympathetic, gentle, overflowing with nurturing tenderness. Like Dinah in *Adam Bede*, he goes about doing good by influencing others. His anomalous situation and his sympathy for his unknown mother fire his sympathetic identification, as that of so many ambitious girls was fired, with everyone he perceives as oppressed. And his career is an enactment of girls' prepubertal daydreams. To Hans's sisters, he is a knight-errant, a prince of romance; he saves not only Hans but Mirah, who has tried to drown herself like a fallen woman in Victorian iconography. "Persons attracted him . . . in proportion to the possibility of his defending them, rescuing them, telling upon their lives with some sort of redeeming influence" (369)—defending like a man, influencing like a woman. And he does all this on a very grand scale. At the end of the book he has taken on the role of savior of the Jews—Moses, Jesus—and is heading for Jerusalem, like Beth to Greece or Maggie to the Gypsies. Palestine will be his Angria.

Daniel's political destiny is the product not of his own imagination, however, but of allowing himself to be transformed, like a woman in a poem, by the imaginations of others. The Jewish enthusiast Mordecai—ecstatic, alien, dying—says that Daniel must lead the Jews and be one himself, and Daniel, enthralled by this vision, discovers that he is indeed Jewish and that his grand-father had bequeathed him the same mission. Messianic leadership is forced on him by loyalty to his origins, his paternal ancestors, and his race. Ambition is redefined, that is, as duty to an enlarged family. Daniel's Judaism has no dog-matic content; it is religion in Feuerbach's sense, love for the human species conceived in familial terms. "To Daniel the words Father and Mother had the altar-fire in them" (526); but no actual parents claim authority over him. He has the virtues of a woman without the inconveniences of being one, while the bad qualities associated with female imagination and ambition are dispersed between Gwendolyn and his mother.

Daniel is modeled on the Jesus authorized by the Higher Critics, who com-bined masculine and feminine virtues. As in *Romola* and *Shirley*, however, the attempt to remake religion leads outside the realms in which Victorian fiction could comfortably operate. Mordecai's ecstatic prose, Mirah's humble sweet-ness, Daniel's moral near-perfection, and other aspects of the "Jewish plot" have repelled readers. Eliot herself explained that plot in pedagogical terms: she wanted to "widen the English vision a little" in regard to Jews, as she had already tried to do for Italy and Spain.[4] But the Jewish theme was more than an exercise of authorial altruism. Loyalty to race or country was an acceptable excuse for fame, as with Joan of Arc or in Procter's "Legend of Bregenz." Fed-alma, the heroine of Eliot's long dramatic poem, *The Spanish Gipsy*, prefigures Daniel: discovering that she is a Gypsy, she renounces her noble lover and joins her father in leading their people to an ancestral homeland in Africa. When her father dies, she becomes the leader in his stead. At the beginning of the poem Fedalma is a performer, too, arousing both her lover's and her father's disap-proval by dancing in the public square. Like *Romola*, *The Spanish Gipsy* takes place long ago and far away, the plot is melodramatic and highly unrealistic, and the language is not prose. *Daniel Deronda* brings the story into modern England, but only by splitting the heroine into a man who leads his people and women who perform.

Gwendolyn's story is wonderfully told, the novel is firmly grounded in con-temporary scientific and religious thought, and Daniel's implausible Zionist project has been vindicated by history. But the Jewish plot often falls into the high-flown unreality and false diction that mar *Romola* and the mythic sec-tions of *Shirley*. Jewish life is as foreign to Eliot as Renaissance Florence, and Mirah's idealized singleness and purity ring false against the finely imagined duplicities of Gwendolyn and Al Charisi. Eliot demonstrated in her own person that the life of a woman artist could successfully be lived, but she could not tell it in fiction except as a story of transgression and failure. No other plots or conventions of character were available: women could not be Byron and By-ron's beloved, the rescuing knight and the virtuous damsel, subject and object of transfiguring vision.

Lady Godiva presented herself to be seen only on condition that no one look, and while she made her husband ameliorate his oppressive behavior she did not act directly herself: as in *Daniel Deronda*, the woman exposes her body while the man acts (another meaning of "performance") in the political arena. In poems—*The Spanish Gipsy*, *Aurora Leigh*—women could lead national movements or write epics to reform their country. In real life women writers not only could defend Italian nationalism or the English working class or American slaves but also could be loved and happy without having to eradicate ambition and renounce fame. But in Victorian prose fiction such things were beyond the realm of available plots, especially in contemporary settings. And yet the situation of the woman artist was still, for Eliot as for Barrett Browning, the Brontës, Gaskell, and Rossetti, the central and essential story. *Daniel Deronda* tries to resolve this story not in a heroine but in a hero: a man who is not an artist but a charismatic leader, whose mission is both chosen and bestowed by a racial destiny that alienates him from English society and seeks fulfillment far from England. In this novel Eliot brings the cultural and intellectual resources of the age to bear on the central concerns of women's writing; but she is least successful where she tries hardest for resolution.

Eliot's perceived failure to integrate the novel's two plots into a satisfying artistic whole was one more justification for defining women writers out of the new mainstream of high literary culture.[5] What was beyond Eliot's power, one could assume, was beyond any woman's. By 1880 the high moral seriousness and social plenitude of Victorian fiction was being challenged by a new valorization of formal artistry, and women novelists, who had been ambiguously praised all along for moral worth or artless sincerity, were now denigrated for being deficient in art. The lack of tonal cohesion in *Daniel Deronda* is not the same as the helpless fragmentation fictionalized in Jameson's *Diary of an Ennuyée*, but it is not entirely different either. The increasing professionalization of literature, as of other intellectual arenas, meant that prose fiction joined poetry and nonfictional prose in the domain of high culture,[6] where it could be defined in terms of skills that women were assumed not to possess. And at the same time the impulse that set women's writing going with such force and power earlier in the century had worn itself out. The excitement and danger of pioneering—of Godiva's ride—were over. Women, like men, could now feel the enervating pressure of belatedness: Barrett Browning and Rossetti had shown that women could be poets, the Brontës that they could write passionate prose, and George Eliot was as formidable a precursor as Milton. The overreaching magnificence of *Daniel Deronda* concludes the first great age of women's writing in English.

Notes

Introduction

1. [Anna Jameson], *Diary of an Ennuyée* (Boston: Lilly, Wait, Colman, & Holden, 1833), p. 1.

2. On links between writing and prostitution see Catherine Gallagher, "George Eliot and *Daniel Deronda*: The Prostitute and the Jewish Question," in *Sex, Politics, and Science in the Nineteenth-Century Novel*, Selected Papers from the English Institute, 1983-84, ed. Ruth Bernard Yeazell (Baltimore: Johns Hopkins Univ. Press, 1986), pp. 39-62. Barbara Leah Harmon discusses issues of public and private in "In Promiscuous Company: Female Public Appearance in Elizabeth Gaskell's *North and South*," *Victorian Studies* 31 (1988): 351-74. See also Robyn R. Warhol, *Gendered Interventions: Narrative Discourse in the Victorian Novel* (New Brunswick: Rutgers Univ. Press, 1989), pp. 159-91. Warhol suggests that writing, for women, is a safe version of public speaking: "Both preacher and novelist want to 'touch' the audience. The Victorian male preacher does so by using his voice as an extension of his body; the Victorian female novelist shields her body by placing her voice in a text" (p. 191).

3. *A Commonplace Book of Thoughts, Memories, and Fancies, Original and Selected* (London: Longman, Brown, Green, & Longmans, 1854), p. 358. Her daydreams are recorded on p. 135. In 1857 Victoria gave Albert "a gilded silver statuette of a nude Lady Godiva, side saddle on her horse"; Stanley Weintraub, *Victoria: An Intimate Biography* (New York: E. P. Dutton, 1987), p. 239. The point of the gift, Weintraub implies, was erotic, not political.

Lady Godiva was a frequent subject of Victorian visual art. She was the wife of an eleventh-century earl of Coventry who, according to legend, agreed to lower the taxes he exacted if she would ride naked through the marketplace. She did so, her body covered by her long hair, and the only person who looked at her—"Peeping Tom"—was struck blind. The history of the legend and its variants are given by Joan C. Lancaster and H. R. Ellis Davidson in *Godiva of Coventry* (Coventry: Coventry Corporation, 1967). There are obvious parallels to the myth of Diana and Actaeon and to that of Medusa. On Tennyson's association of poetic power with the forbidden gaze on female nakedness see Carol Christ, "The Feminine Subject in Victorian Poetry," *ELH* 54 (1987), 385-401.

4. Quoted by Elizabeth Chambers Patterson, *Mary Somerville and the Cultivation of Science, 1815-1840* (Boston: Martinus Nijhoff, 1983), p. 89.

5. Major studies include those by Moers, Showalter, Gilbert and Gubar, Homans, Poovey, Armstrong, Davidoff and Hall, Helsinger et al., Sanders, and David, listed in the bibliography. Angela Leighton's *Victorian Women Poets: Writing against the Heart* (Charlottesville: Univ. Press of Virginia, 1992) appeared too late to be used in this study.

1. Beginning to Write

1. *The Letters of Robert Browning and Elizabeth Barrett Barrett, 1845-1846*, ed. Elvan Kintner, 2 vols. (Cambridge: Belknap Press of Harvard Univ., 1969), 2: 1012.

2. Elizabeth Gaskell, *The Life of Charlotte Bronte*, (Harmondsworth: Penguin Books [1857], 1975), p. 508.

3. Brontë read Austen for the first time after publishing *Jane Eyre*, and like Barrett Browning found her lacking in passion and intensity. Barrett mentions Mme. de Staël in a list of famous women in a poem written when she was in her teens; printed by Kay Moser in "Elizabeth Barrett's Youthful Feminism: Fragment of 'An Essay on Women,' " *Studies in Browning and His Circle* 12 (Spring-Fall 1984): 13-26, in which the only other writer is Hannah More; the point of the poem is how few eminent women there are. Ellen Moers traces the influence of *Corinne* in *Literary Women* (New York: Oxford Univ. Press [1963], 1985), pp. 173-210. Moers finds Corinne reincarnate in Brontë's Angrian heroine Zenobia Percy, "the prima donna of the Angrian Court, the most learned woman of her age, the modern Cleopatra, the Verdopolitan de Staël," who was added to the ongoing Angrian saga when Brontë was eighteen (p. 178).

4. Women writers and readers did and do, of course, identify with male as well as female heroes. See Carolyn G. Heilbrun, *Toward a Recognition of Androgyny* (New York: Alfred A. Knopf, 1973), p. 58. Elaine Showalter says, "When women wrote, they identified with the power and privilege of the male world, and their heroes enabled them to think out their own unrealized ambitions"; *A Literature of Their Own: British Women Novelists from Brontë to Lessing* (Princeton: Princeton Univ. Press, 1977), p. 137. This may be true, but such identification runs into problems when amatory elements intrude or gender becomes an issue within the narrative.

5. *The Love Letters of Thomas Carlyle and Jane Welsh*, ed. Alexander Carlyle, 2 vols (London: John Lane, 1909), 1: 366-67. Hallam Tennyson, *Alfred Lord Tennyson: A Memoir* (New York: Macmillan, 1898), p. 4.

6. See Winifred Gérin, "Byron's Influence on the Brontës," *Keats-Shelley Memorial Bulletin* 17 (1966): 1.

7. Frances Ann Kemble, *Records of a Girlhood*, (New York: Henry Holt, 1879), p. 57.

8. Pauline Marie Armande Aglaé Craven, *Life of Lady Georgiana Fullerton*, from the French of Mrs. Augustus Craven. By Henry James Coleridge of the Society of Jesus (London: Richard Bentley & Son, 1888), pp. 34-35. Her mother having read passages from *Childe Harold's Pilgrimage* and *The Corsair* aloud to her daughters, the young Georgiana reread those passages ("I had a scruple about reading much else" [p. 34]) over and over by herself.

9. As Helene Moglen says, "Because [Charlotte Brontë] was female, her identification with their [Charlotte and Branwell's] beloved, Byronic Zamorna was equivocal. She could not, after all, *be* the fantasized hero. . . . [T]he dream by which she was fascinated could not contain her." *Charlotte Brontë: The Self Conceived* (New York: Norton, 1976), p. 33. Emily and Anne's kingdom of Gondal, unlike Angria, apparently had female heroes; since the prose narratives of Gondal have not survived, however, we know little about them.

10. Jameson, *Commonplace Book*, p. 135.

11. *The Brownings' Correspondence*, ed. Philip Kelley and Ronald Hudson, 9 vols. to date (Winfield, Kansas: Wedgestone Press, 1984-   ), 1: 361-62.

12. Jameson, *Commonplace Book*, p. 135.

13. Gilbert and Gubar point out the centrality in nineteenth-century women's writings of images of imprisonment, enclosure, and escape in *The Madwoman in the Attic: The Woman Writer and the Nineteenth-Century Literary Imagination* (New Haven: Yale Univ. Press, 1979), pp. 85-88, as well as the importance of travel for Jane Austen's heroines (pp. 122-24). Sally Mitchell notes that in the fiction of the 1860s women who ride get into trouble. "Before a riding heroine can reach a happy ending, she must suffer enough weakness, illness and humiliation to melt her down into

chastened femininity." *The Fallen Angel: Chastity, Class and Women's Reading, 1835-1880* (Bowling Green: Bowling Green Univ. Popular Press, 1981), p. 75.

14. Christine Alexander, *The Early Writings of Charlotte Brontë* (Buffalo, NY: Prometheus Books, 1983), p. 140.

15. Another time, alone in the school dining room on a bleak and cheerless evening, Brontë thinks of her desolation and her visions and recalls: "last night I did indeed lean upon the thunder-wakening wings of such a stormy blast ... , and it whirled me away ... for five seconds of ecstasy; and as I sat by myself in the dining-room ... verily this foot trod the war shaken shores ... and these eyes saw ... Adrianopolis its lights on the river." She walked through the terraced garden of a splendid palace, ascended marble stairs, and eventually entered a splendid room which evokes not one but a succession of solitary figures: she sees the portrait of a handsome young man, "a solitary prisoner"; she remembers the young lady whose boudoir it is, and who usually sits there alone, "a book in her hand her head bent"; and finally—a more novelistic note—she sees a drunken man on the couch ("Well here I am at Roe Head," The Pierpont Morgan Library, New York. MA 2696). Another journal entry concludes a description of the scenery on a journey through Africa by focusing on a solitary deer ("Now as I have a little bit of time," Roe Head journal, Feb. 4, 1836, The Pierpont Morgan Library, New York. MA 2696.) Passages quoted by permission of The Pierpont Morgan Library.

16. Kemble, pp. 165-67.

17. As Inga-Stina Ewbank points out, Heathcliff is the Byronic hero as seen by his victims. *Their Proper Sphere: A Study of the Brontë Sisters as Early-Victorian Female Novelists* (Cambridge, Mass.: Harvard Univ. Press, 1966), p. 99. Ewbank discusses various transformations and repudiations of Byron in the works of all three Brontë sisters.

18. Eliot's widower and biographer, John Cross, uses *The Mill on the Floss* to flesh out his account of her childhood, remarking that "No doubt the early part of Maggie's portraiture is the best autobiographical representation we can have of George Eliot's own feelings in her childhood"; *George Eliot's Life as Related in Her Letters and Journals*, 3 vols., ed. J. W. Cross (New York: Harper & Brothers, 1885), 1: 22.

19. *The George Eliot Letters*, ed. Gordon S. Haight, 9 vols. (New Haven: Yale Univ. Press, 1954-78), 1: 284. Her mother died when Eliot was sixteen. Her dearest childhood companion was a brother three years older than herself but inferior to her intellectually, whose early defection into masculine concerns deeply wounded her. Elizabeth Gaskell was brought up by a widowed aunt; her mother had died when Gaskell was an infant, and she had little to do with her father and his second wife, whom she disliked. Her much-loved older brother joined the navy and (like Elizabeth Barrett's dearest brother) died at sea. Rossetti's mother was the mainstay of the family and her brother Dante Gabriel had not only superior advantages but also—so she and everyone else believed—superior talents. Gaskell and Rossetti have not, unfortunately, left much record of their early imaginative lives.

20. *Letters*, 1: 22, 1: 24. Ruby V. Redinger is the first critic of Eliot to take adequate account of these passages and of Eliot's fear of imagination and performance. *George Eliot: The Emergent Self* (New York: Alfred A. Knopf, 1975), pp. 81-93. "To her at this time imagination implied an admission of dissatisfaction ... , a turning away from reality, ... and exhibitionism" (p. 86). See also Rosemarie Bodenheimer, "Ambition and Its Audiences: George Eliot's Performing Figures," *Victorian Studies* 34 (1990), 7-31. Scott's biographer comments on Scott's desire to inhabit the world he imagined; J. G. Lockhart, *The Life of Sir Walter Scott*, 10 vols. (Edinburgh: Adam & Charles Black, 1862), 10: 227-31.

21. *Harriet Martineau's Autobiography*, ed. Maria Weston Chapman, 3 vols. (Boston: James R. Osgood, 1877), 1: 45.

22. Margaret Mare and Alicia C. Percival, *Victorian Best-Seller: The World of Charlotte M. Yonge* (London: George G. Harrap, 1948), p. 24.

23. Anthony Trollope, *An Autobiography* [1883], ed. Michael Sadleir and Frederick Page (London: Oxford Univ. Press, 1950), p. 43. "I learned in this way to maintain an interest in a fictitious story, to dwell on a work created by my own imagination, and to live in a world altogether outside the world of my own material life" (p. 43).

24. ["Farewell to Angria"], Fannie Elizabeth Ratchford, *The Brontës' Web of Childhood* (New York: Russell & Russell, 1964), p. 149.

25. *Personal Recollections*, in *The Works of Charlotte Elizabeth* [Tonna], with an introduction by Mrs. H. B. Stowe, 3 vols. (New York: M. W. Dodd, 1844-45), 1: 3, 13.

26. *The Life and Correspondence of Robert Southey*, 6 vols, ed. Charles Cuthbert Southey (London: Longman, Brown, Green, & Longmans, 1850), 6: 328-29. Similarly, Southey said Sara Coleridge should stop writing books once she became engaged, since it would disqualify her "for those duties which she will have to perform whenever she changes from the single to the married state." Quoted by Bradford Keyes Mudge, *Sara Coleridge, A Victorian Daughter, Her Life and Essays* (New Haven: Yale Univ. Press, 1989), p. 38. Charlotte Elizabeth "imbibed" from reading Shakespeare "a thorough contempt for women, children, and household affairs, entrenching myself behind invisible barriers that few, very few, could pass." *Personal Recollections: Works* 1: 9.

27. *Letters*, 1: 9.

28. *Life of Charlotte Brontë*, pp. 295, 334.

29. Southey, *Life and Correspondence*, 6: 329.

30. Eliot, *Letters*, 1: 19; 1: 40. *The Mill on the Floss*, p. 117. *The Brownings' Correspondence* 1: 352.

31. Anna Jameson, *Visits and Sketches at Home and Abroad*, 3d ed. 2 vols (London: Saunders & Otley, 1839), 1: 154-55.

32. Geraldine Ensor Jewsbury, *The Half-Sisters: A Tale*, 2 vols. (London: Chapman & Hall, 1848), 2: 18-19. In the same novel, a high-minded noblewoman who befriends the heroine supports a talented girl's training as a singer, although "to me, there is something revolting in an unmarried girl singing in public" (2: 283). Ellen Moers's chapter "Performing Heroism: The Myth of *Corinne*" details the influence of Mme. de Staël's heroine, a creative artist whose art is performance, and of George Sand's Consuelo, a singer, as models for English women's women writers; *Literary Women* (New York: Oxford Univ. Press [1963], 1985), pp. 173-210. The terrors that attached to the idea of writing as self-display in England, however, were not present in any similar degrees in *Corinne* or *Consuelo*.

33. On the significances (all bad) attached to women's appearances in public in the Victorian period see Barbara Leah Harmon, "In Promiscuous Company: Female Public Appearance in Elizabeth Gaskell's *North and South*," *Victorian Studies* 31 (1988) : 351-74. I have discussed the consciousness and terror attached to the idea of writing as self-display by the three most successful earlier women poets, in "Women Becoming Poets: Katherine Philips, Aphra Behn, Anne Finch," *English Literary History* 57 (1990) : 335-55.

34. Cross, 1: 10, 1: 19. Life at school, where she excelled, fed her desire for preeminence.

35. *Letters* 1: 9. The statue Eliot imagined on the pedestal was no doubt a human figure, probably female and probably nude.

2. Travel, Trials, Fame

1. Patricia Thomson in *George Sand and the Victorians: Her Influence and Reputation in Nineteenth-Century England* (New York: Columbia Univ. Press, 1977) shows that Sand was a powerful influence on Barrett Browning, Charlotte and Emily Brontë, Eliot, and other women writers. Gaskell and Rossetti, however, seem not to have been touched by her at all—nor, so far as we can tell, by Byron, although Byron's physician, John Polidori, was Rossetti's uncle. Consuelo is an opera singer, heroine of *Consuelo* and *The Countess of Rudolstadt*.

2. *The Letters of Elizabeth Barrett Browning to Mary Russell Mitford, 1836-1854,* ed. Meredith B. Raymond and Mary Rose Sullivan, 3 vols. (Winfield, Kan.: Armstrong Browning Library of Baylor University, Browning Institute, Wedgestone Press, and Wellesley College, 1983), 3: 31, 33, 36. *The Brownings' Correspondence* 4: 326. "The Contagious Diseases Acts I," *Daily News*, December 28, 1869, p. 4; reprinted in *Harriet Martineau on Women*, ed. Gayle Graham Yates (New Brunswick: Rutgers Univ. Press, 1985), p. 256. *Harriet Martineau's Autobiography*, 2: 506.

3. Tennyson imagines the artist's experience in terms of the same plot, but without the element of sexual shame which women attach to the moment of self-exposure. In "The Kraken" he describes a strange creature that lies silent and somnolent in the depths of the sea until the end of the world, when "once by man and angels to be seen, / In roaring he shall rise and on the surface die." In a poem of similar import, his Lady of Shalott is lured from her island solitude by the sexy figure of Lancelot, proclaims her identity on the boat that carries her to Camelot, and is dead when people finally see her. In *Great Expectations* a night journey by water leads to a trial at which Pip expiates his vanity and ambition by sitting next to Magwitch, the cynosure of hostile eyes. As with Tennyson, Dickens uses a plot like the women's, but desexualized. The original of these trial scenes is probably that of Effie Deans (on trial for infanticide) in Scott's *The Heart of Midlothian*, which also contains in the story of Jeanie Deans the paradigmatic story of a young woman's journey to save another.

4. Roe Head journal, Ratchford, p. 108.

5. Gérin, *Charlotte Brontë*, p. 107.

6. Ratchford, p. 109.

7. Lewes, review of *Jane Eyre*, *Westminister Review* 48 (1848): 581; "Recent Novels: French and English," *Fraser's Magazine* 36 (1847): 691. Review of *Villette*, *Eclectic Review*, n. s. 5 (1853): 319. Review of *Jane Eyre*, *Living Age* 17 (1848): 481. [Elizabeth Rigby], Review of *Jane Eyre*, *Quarterly Review* 84 (1848): 176.

Other reviews of *Jane Eyre* were much the same. "[I]t is difficult to avoid believing that much of the characters and incidents are taken from life"; [Eagles, John], "A Few Words about Novels," *Blackwood's Magazine* 64 (October 1848): 473. The characters are "drawn from the life"; [H. V. Hobart, "Thoughts on Modern English Literature," *Fraser's Magazine* 60 (1859): 103. "There is too little attractiveness in the heroine to account for a violent passion in such a man"; "It would not be so with us"; [John Skelton], "Charlotte Brontë," *Fraser's Magazine* 55 (1857): 579. One reviewer found Jane unlovable (review of *Jane Eyre*, The *Spectator* 20 [1847]: 1074); but another thought she could "wind herself as firmly round the heart of the reader as around that of her adorer, Mr. Rochester" (review of *Jane Eyre*, *Howitt's Journal* 2 [1847]: 333), and Lewes found that "you admire, you love her" (*Fraser's* 36 [1847]: 692). More lovable than another heroine under review, she waits pouting for the *North British* reviewer's attention ("Noteworthy Novels," *North British Review* 11 [1849]: 476, 482).

8. "Lord Byron," *Blackwood's Edinburgh Magazine* 17 (1825): 136-37. According to Thomas Moore, "all that [Byron] had felt strongly through life was, in some shape or other, reproduced in his poetry"; *Letters and Journals of Lord Byron: With Notices of His Life*, 2 vols. (New York: J. & J. Harper, 1830), 1: 34.

9. *The Letters and Private Papers of W. M. Thackeray*, ed. Gordon N. Ray, 4 vols (London: Oxford Univ. Press, 1945-46), 3: 233.

10. Gaskell, *Life of Charlotte Brontë*, p. 448.

11. Roe Head journal, Gérin, Charlotte Brontë, p. 104.

12. *The Brontës: Their Lives, Friendships and Correspondence*, ed. Thomas James Wise and John Alexander Symington, The Shakespeare Head Brontë, vols. 12-15 (Oxford: Blackwell, 1932), 2: 153. (See also Gaskell, *Life of Charlotte Brontë*, p. 330.)

13. *Life of Charlotte Brontë*, p. 443.

14. Even so, G. H. Lewes found "actual experience" to be the root of *Mary Barton*'s success, as of *Jane Eyre*'s. In both books the authors "have not invented, but reproduced. . . . Whatever of weakness may be pointed out in their works, will, we are positive, be mostly in those parts where experience is deserted . . . ; whatever has really affected the public mind is, we are equally certain, the transcript of some actual incident, character, or emotion." "The Lady Novelists," *Westminster Review* n. s. 2 (1852): 138.

15. *The Letters of Mrs. Gaskell*, ed. J. A. V. Chapple and Arthur Pollard (Cambridge, Mass: Harvard Univ. Press, 1967), pp. 223, 221, 220-21, 255-56.

16. They also recall the belief of some Victorian medical men, as described by Mary Poovey, that women should not be anesthetized in childbirth lest they express sexual excitation. *Uneven Developments: The Ideological Work of Gender in Mid-Victorian England* (Chicago: Univ. of Chicago Press, 1988), pp. 30-32. Mary Poovey points out the innate contradiction of female modesty, which "simultaneously concealed and revealed" sexuality, in *The Proper Lady and the Woman Writer: Ideology as Style in the Works of Mary Wollstonecraft, Mary Shelley, and Jane Austen* (Chicago: Univ. of Chicago Press, 1984), p. 23.

17. *Letters*, p. 74.

18. Margaret Hale in *North and South* mediates between the middle-class and the industrial workers as Gaskell's novels do. Barbara Leah Harmon has shown how "in merging private with public matters—displaying the private body on a public stage . . . and internalizing the taint of a public shame . . . — Gaskell both challenges the conventional boundaries between private and public and legitimizes public action for women." "In Promiscuous Company," 361. Scenes of exposure to sexual shame recur in *North and South* and *Wives and Daughters* when heroines expose themselves to misconstruction to protect others. In desexualized *Cranford* exposure occurs only in class terms: the heroine opens a shop with her name (discreetly) outside.

19. To Helena Michie it suggests sexual fire; *The Flesh Made Word: Female Figures and Women's Bodies* (New York: Oxford Univ. Press, 1987), p. 62. Ellen Moers places Dinah as a "performing heroine" in the tradition of Madame de Staël's Corinne; *Literary Women*, pp. 192-93. On the significances of blushing, see Ruth Bernard Yeazell, *Fictions of Modesty: Women and Courtship in the English Novel* (Chicago: Univ. of Chicago Press, 1991), pp. 65-77.

20. *Letters* 1: 22.

21. Thomas Carlyle, "Characteristics," *The Works of Thomas Carlyle*, 30 vols. (New York: Charles Scribner's Sons, 1896-1901), 28: 1.

22. Preface to the First Edition of *Poems* (1853), in *The Poems of Matthew Arnold*, ed. Kenneth Allott, 2d edition ed. Miriam Allott (New York: Longman, 1979), p. 654.

23. Augusta Webster, "Husband-Hunting and Match-Making," *A Housewife's Opinions* (London: Macmillan, 1879), p. 234.

24. [Sarah Lewis], *Woman's Mission*, 2d ed. (London: John W. Parker, 1839), p. 104.

Eliot admired both this book and the French original of which it was a partial translation.

25. *Letters* 2: 502, 503.

26. *Letters* 1: 73, 40.

27. *Saturday Review*, 26 Feb. 1859, vii: 250-51.

28. *Letters* 2: 503.

29. The germinal scene of *Adam Bede* recurs throughout Eliot's fiction, suggesting its profound importance for her. In her next novel, *The Mill on the Floss*, the roles and moral values are overtly reversed. Pure and blameless Lucy visits disgraced and apparently fallen Maggie, who has taken an apparently shameful journey, not only to love and comfort her but to attest her moral superiority by "confession": " 'Maggie,' she said in a low voice, that had the solemnity of confession in it, 'you are better than I am' " (p. 643). In the later novels, however, the confrontation of two morally opposed women upholds the obvious moral distinctions: Esther and Mrs. Transome in *Felix Holt*, Romola and Tessa in *Romola*, Dorothea and Rosamond in *Middlemarch*, and Mirah and Gwendolyn in *Daniel Deronda*. The last of these is least like the others: errant Gwendolyn visits virtuous Mirah, and no love passes between them. Maggie, Savonarola, Bulstrode, and Lydgate undergo nightmarish scenes of public obloquy (the predominance of men significantly generalizing the situation beyond gender), while virtuous women sympathize. Lydgate publicly accompanies the disgraced Bulstrode as Dinah does Hetty, although much less wholeheartedly, and is then himself disgraced. In another variation, Dorothea's compassionate but clear-sighted vision of his secret life destroys Casaubon. *Felix Holt* also repeats on a small scale the trial scene in *Mary Barton*: Esther appears at the trial of her lower-class lover, a political radical (like Mary's father) who has actually killed someone. After the trial Esther persuades influential men to get him pardoned.

30. The slipperiness of images of vision in *Middlemarch* is subtly explored by Neil Hertz, "Imagining Casaubon," *The End of the Line: Essays on Psychoanalysis and the Sublime* (New York: Columbia Univ. Press, 1985), 75-96; and J. Hillis Miller, "Optic and Semiotic in *Middlemarch*," *The Worlds of Victorian Fiction*, ed. Jerome H. Buckley (Cambridge, Mass.: Harvard Univ. Press, 1975), 125-45.

31. Margaret Oliphant, "The Sisters Brontë," in *Women Novelists of Queen Victoria's Reign: A Book of Appreciations*, by Mrs. Oliphant et al. (London: Hurst & Blackett, 1897), pp. 3, 5, 6-7.

32. "Modern Novelists — Great and Small," *Blackwood's Edinburgh Magazine* 77 (1855): 557.

33. Wise and Symington 2: 211. (See also Gaskell, *The Life of Charlotte Brontë*, p. 343.)

34. *Letters*, 1: 276.

35. *Letters of Robert Browning and Elizabeth Barrett Barrett*, 1: 3.

36. Maureen Peters, *Jean Ingelow: Victorian Poetess* (Totowa, NJ: Rowman & Littlefield, 1972), p. 69.

3. Entering the Literary Market

1. John Sutherland, *The Stanford Companion to Victorian Fiction* (Stanford: Stanford Univ. Press, 1989), p. 2. Of Sutherland's 312 women, the 113 who were unmarried were responsible for twenty-four novels apiece. According to Elaine Showalter, half the women writers in the nineteenth century married; *A Literature of Their Own*, p. 65. On women's exclusion later in the century see Gaye Tuchman, with Nina E. Fortin, *Edging Women Out: Victorian Novelists, Publishers, and Social Change* (New Haven: Yale Univ. Press, 1989). The estimate that half the novels were by women is given by Ian

Watt, *The Rise of the Novel: Studies in Defoe, Richardson, and Fielding* (Berkeley: Univ. of California Press, 1957), p. 298. Jane Spencer points out that women's association with the novel was emphasized in the eighteenth century, when its prestige was low, and was ignored by later critics who took fiction more seriously; *The Rise of the Woman Novelist: From Aphra Behn to Jane Austen* (Oxford: Basil Blackwell, 1986), viii.

2. Richard D. Altick, "The Sociology of Authorship: The Social Origins, Education, and Occupations of 1,100 British Writers, 1800-1935" [1962], in *Writers, Readers, and Occasions: Selected Essays on Victorian Literature and Life* (Columbus: Ohio State Univ. Press, 1989), p. 97. Included in these figures are "all but the very lowest stratum of hacks" (p. 97).

3. Altick, "The Sociology of Authorship," p. 141. See also Altick's *The English Common Reader: A Social History of the Mass Reading Public, 1800-1900* (Chicago: Univ. of Chicago Press, 1957).

4. Valerie Pichanick, *Harriet Martineau: The Woman and Her Work, 1802-76.* (Ann Arbor: Univ. of Michigan Press, 1980), p. 50.

5. Augusta Webster, *A Housewife's Opinions*, pp. 188, 191-92.

6. Again, this was the continuation of a trend. "The moral utility of literature was an all-pervasive concern of eighteenth-century critics; modesty in the writer and his work was becoming an important term of praise; and simplicity and spontaneity in writing became greatly admired as the century progressed. What was happening, in fact, was that the properly 'feminine' and the properly 'literary' were both being re-defined along the same lines." Spencer, *Rise of the Woman Novelist*, p. 77. On the identification of interiority with the female, see Myra Jehlen, "Archimedes and the Paradox of Feminist Criticism," *Signs* 6 (1981) : 596.

7. Terry Lovell notes, however, that male readership seemed to be increasing. "By the 1840s and in 'serious' realist fiction, women were writing novels which addressed men as well as women, and the novel-reading public now included a higher proportion of men"; and this, Lovell suggests, may help account for women's increased success in entering the canon, canonization perhaps depending on the maleness less of the author than of the audience. *Consuming Fiction* (London: Verso, 1987), p. 83.

8. Elizabeth K. Helsinger, Robin Lauterbach Sheets, and William Veeder, *The Woman Question: Society and Literature in Britain and America, 1837-1883*, 3 vols. (New York: Garland, 1983), 3: 65. In America, as Showalter points out, women were more likely to use feminine pseudonyms with pastoral overtones (p. 59). Gaye Tuchman's researches show that in the 1860s and 1870s men who submitted manuscripts to publishers were more likely to use female pseudonyms than women were to use either male or neuter names. *Edging Women Out*, pp. 53-54.

9. *Edmund Yates: His Recollections and Experiences*, 4th ed. (London: Richard Bentley & Son, 1885), pp. 354-55.

10. Showalter lists many of these considerations in *A Literature of Their Own* (pp. 57-60) and suggests that male names reflect childhood fantasies of being male (p. 58). On Eliot and her names, see Alexander Welsh, *George Eliot and Blackmail* (Cambridge, Mass.: Harvard Univ. Press, 1985), pp. 123-28. At first, Welsh points out, she "took advantage of her incognito by drawing more closely on her memory of actual persons and places than prudence afterward allowed" (p. 132). Gillian Beer suggests that Eliot used the male name in order to "slough off the contextuality of her own name and enter a neutral space"; "The 'we' of her text moves," Beer says, "often with deliberate disturbance, askance gender, class, and time." *George Eliot* (Bloomington: Indiana Univ. Press, 1986), pp. 25, 28. In the course of her life Eliot took many names: Mary Ann, Marian, and Marianne Evans, Polly, Pollian (from Apollyon), Clematis (meaning mental beauty, adopted in a youthful correspondence with a friend), Mrs. Lewes, George Eliot, and when she finally married, Mrs. John Cross. Lewes sometimes called her "Ma-

donna" and she was "Mutter" to his sons. Eliot herself remarked that "a nom de plume secures all the advantages without the disagreeables of reputation" (*Letters* 2: 292).

11. "Pseudonymity . . . cannot be regarded as solely a defensive maneuver . . . since it immediately fuels speculation and publicity for a successful book" (Welsh, *George Eliot and Blackmail*, p. 123).

12. *Selections from the Letters of Geraldine Endsor Jewsbury to Jane Welsh Carlyle,* ed. Mrs. Alexander Ireland (London: Longman's, Green; New York, 1892), p. 89; see also pp. 337, 387. The most famous, and regretted, papers destroyed by surviving friends were Byron's.

13. R. H. Hutton, "Novels by the Authoress of 'John Halifax,' " *North British Review* 29 (1858): 467.

14. Trollope, *Autobiography*, pp. 4-19. Closest, perhaps, (besides, of course, the Brontë children's brief but fatal sojourn at "Lowood") is Eliza Lynn Linton's experience as the youngest member of a large motherless family, neglected by her father and tormented by her elder siblings.

15. Gordon S. Haight, *George Eliot: A Biography* (Oxford: Oxford Univ. Press, 1968), pp. 11, 25, 470.

16. The anecdote about reading Homer in childhood is from Alfred H. Miles, ed., *The Poets and the Poetry of the Century*, 10 vols., VII: *Joanna Baillie to Mathilde Blind* (London: Hutchinson, 1891-97), p. 155. The correspondence "in the language of Homer" is reported in "Modern English Poets," *American Whig Review* 14 (1851): 463.

17. *Womankind*, 2 vols. (Leipzig: Tauchnitz, 1878), 1: 1.

18. Mackenzie Bell, *Christina Rossetti: A Biographical and Critical Study*, 4th ed. (1898; New York: Haskell House, 1971), p. 112. *Seek and Find: A Double Series of Short Studies of the Benedicite* (1869; New York: Pott, Young, 1879), p. 32.

19. The argument for providing employment for women was strengthened by a numerical preponderance of women that made it impossible for all of them to marry; Helsinger et al., 2: 135-36. The poet Adelaide Procter, among many others, actively supported expanding employment opportunities for women.

20. *Autobiography*, 1: 302-303.

21. Clara Thomas, *Love and Work Enough: The Life of Anna Jameson* (Toronto: Univ. of Toronto Press, 1967), p. 209, from *Letters of Anna Jameson to Ottilie von Goethe*, ed. G. H. Needler (London: Oxford Univ. Press, 1939), p. 234.

22. Bell, *Christina Rossetti*, p. 112.

23. Eliot, "Woman in France: Madame de Sablé," *Westminster Review* 62 n.s. 6 (1854): 449.

24. Trollope, *Autobiography*, p. 146. [Henry Longueville Manse], "Sensation Novels," *Quarterly Review* 113 (April 1863): 482; quoted in Robert Lee Wolff, *Sensational Victorian: The Life and Fiction of Mary Elizabeth Braddon* (New York: Garland, 1979), p. 190.

4. Poetry

1. Augusta Webster, "Poets and Personal Pronouns," *A Housewife's Opinions*, p. 153. This is the kind of joke Thackeray makes about poets in *Pendennis*.

2. It has been suggested that women lacked the sense of self and self-assertiveness that poetry requires and were too repressed to write strong lyrics. For these and other suggestions see Gilbert and Gubar, *The Madwoman in the Attic*, pp. 545-49. On women's difficulty in locating themselves as subject rather than object in romantic poetry see Margaret Homans, *Women Writers and Poetic Identity: Dorothy Wordsworth, Emily Brontë, and Emily Dickinson* (Princeton: Princeton Univ. Press, 1980). Male ob-

jects of male desire are identified with nature in poetry by men, as in parts of Tennyson's *In Memoriam* and the poems of Gerard Manley Hopkins, with disorienting and transgressive effect, but the tradition of classical pastoral provided models, context, and justification; on such poetry, see Richard Dellamora, *Masculine Desire: The Sexual Politics of Victorian Aestheticism* (Chapel Hill: Univ. of North Carolina Press, 1990), pp. 36-39, 48-49.

3. Christina Rossetti, "The Dead City," *The Poetical Works of Christina Georgina Rossetti*, ed. William Michael Rossetti (London: 1911), pp. 273-74. "The Dead City" first appeared in *Verses*, printed by Rossetti's grandfather, G. Polidori (London, 1847). Further quotations of Rossetti's poems are from *The Complete Poems of Christina Rossetti: A Variorum Edition*, ed. R. W. Crump (Baton Rouge: Louisiana State Univ. Press, 1979-   ) unless otherwise specified. Dolores Rosenblum examines Rossetti's dual role as artist and artist's model, subject and object of vision, in "Christina Rossetti: The Inward Pose," in *Shakespeare's Sisters: Feminist Essays on Women Poets*, ed. Sandra M. Gilbert and Susan Gubar (Bloomington: Indiana Univ. Press, 1979), and *Christina Rossetti: The Poetry of Endurance* (Carbondale: Southern Illinois Univ. Press, 1986). I have discussed Barrett Browning's explorations of this dilemma at length in *Elizabeth Barrett Browning: The Origins of a New Poetry* (Chicago: Univ. of Chicago Press, 1989).

4. Fannie Elizabeth Ratchford, *The Brontës' Web of Childhood*, pp. 154, 167.

5. This can be read, of course, as a poem about the muse. The woman poet's counterpart for the male poet's figure of the muse is rather like a rapist. See Joanne Feit Diehl, " 'Come Slowly—Eden': An Exploration of Women Poets and Their Muse," *Signs* 3 (1978): 572-87.

6. Preface to the 1850 edition, *Wuthering Heights* (Harmondsworth: Penguin, 1965), p. 40.

7. *Dante Gabriel Rossetti: His Family-Letters with a Memoir*, ed. William Michael Rossetti, 2 vols. (London: Ellis, 1895), 1: 133.

8. Edmund Gosse, *The Life of Algernon Charles Swinburne* (New York: Macmillan, 1917), p. 137. *Letters of Dante Gabriel Rossetti*, ed. Oswald Doughty and John Robert Wahl (Oxford: Clarendon Press, 1965), 1: 45.

9. *Poetical Works*, ed. William Michael Rossetti, p. 417.

10. Dante Gabriel Rossetti, "Body's Beauty," "Introduction." Mackenzie Bell, *Christina Rossetti*, p. 180. *The Letters of Robert Browning and Elizabeth Barrett Barrett, 1845-1846*, 1: 3.

11. *Letters of Dante Gabriel Rossetti*, ed. Oswald Doughty and John Robert Wahl (Oxford, 1967), 3: 1380.

12. For analyses of *Goblin Market* in relation to Pre-Raphaelite art and sisterhood with a different emphasis see Gilbert and Gubar, *The Madwoman in the Attic*, pp. 564-75; William T. Going, " 'Goblin Market' and the Pre-Raphaelite Brotherhood," *PreRaphaelite Review* 3 (1979): 1-11; Jerome McGann, "Christina Rossetti's Poems: A New Edition and a Revaluation," *Victorian Studies* 23 (1980): 237-54; Dolores Rosenblum, *Christina Rossetti: The Poetry of Endurance*, pp. 63-108.

13. *Three Rossettis: Unpublished Letters to and from Dante Gabriel, Christina, William*, ed. Janet Camp Troxell (Cambridge, Mass.: Harvard Univ. Press, 1937), p. 143.

14. *The Works of Felicia Hemans: Edited by Her Sister, with an Essay on Her Genius by Mrs. Sigourney* (New York: C. S. Francis, 1845), 1: xii. My copy of these volumes was awarded as the first prize in English composition at Yale College in 1847 and has written on the flyleaf the recipient's verse tribute to the "Sweet Songstress." On women and fame, love, and other themes, see Kathleen Hickok, *Representations of Women: Nineteenth-Century British Women's Poetry* (Westport: Greenwood Press, 1984).

15. On Procter, see Margaret Maison, "Queen Victoria's Favorite Poet," *The Listener*

73 (29 April 1965): 636-37. For Ingelow's sales see *The Athenaeum* 3639 (24 July 1897): 129.

16. Charles Dickens, "An Introduction," *The Poems of Adelaide A. Procter* (New York: Hurst, 1858), pp. 3, 10, 11.

17. W. M. Rossetti, introduction, pp. liv, lv.

18. W. M. Rossetti, introduction, p. lxviii. *Some Recollections of Jean Ingelow and Her Early Friends* (1901; Port Washington: Kennikat Press, 1972), p. 125. Although first published in 1901, the book was written by someone who had known Ingelow and reflects the ethos of an earlier period.

19. *Letters by the Late Frances Ridley Havergal*, edited by her sister M[aria]. V. G. H[avergal] (London: James Nisbet, 1885), p. 59. M[aria] V. G. Havergal, *Memorials of Frances Ridley Havergal* (London: James Nisbet, n.d.), p. 173.

20. William Michael Rossetti, Introductory Note to Webster's *Mother and Daughter: An Uncompleted Sonnet-Sequence* (London: Macmillan, 1895), p. 13. *The Family Letters of Christina Georgina Rossetti*, p. 175.

21. Theodore Watts, "Mrs. Augusta Webster," *The Athenaeum* 3490 (15 Sept. 1894), 355. See also *DNB*.

22. These poems appear in *Blanche Lisle and Other Poems*, by Cecil Home (1860), and *Dramatic Studies* (1866).

23. "Circe" and "A Castaway" appear in *Portraits* (1870). Quotations are from "Circe," p. 19, and "A Castaway," pp. 37, 46, 36, 38-39.

5. The Range of Prose Fiction

1. *The Autobiography of Elizabeth M. Sewell*, ed. Eleanor L. Sewell (London: Longmans, Green, 1907), p. 145.

2. *Edmund Yates: His Recollections and Experiences*, 4th ed. (London: Richard Bentley & Son, 1885), p. 355. On the subversive thrust of *Lady Audley's Secret* see Showalter, *A Literature of Their Own*, pp. 163-68.

3. Max Beerbohm, *More* (1899; London: John Lane, The Bodley Head, 2 ed., 1907), pp. 109, 112. The book is dedicated to Ouida.

4. "Romance and Realism," in *Frescoes and Other Stories*, (Leipzig: Tauchnitz, 1885), pp. 282-83. "The Last Will and Testament of Florence Marian Wellesley, " dated 5 January 1834, tidily written out in tiny print and witnessed in script by various Angrians, in imitation of a legal document, is in The Pierpont Morgan Library, New York (MA 2696). Bequests to individuals include jewels, gold, books, vases, and other luxurious objects, very specifically described, adding up to a detailed inventory of the trappings of a rich and glamorous life.

5. A decade earlier in a very different kind of story, Margaret Hale, the heroine of Gaskell's *North and South*, had protected the man she doesn't yet know she loves from a stone-throwing crowd; Margaret is not seriously injured, but the incident is taken as evidence of love.

6. *The Autobiography of Margaret Oliphant: The Complete Text*, ed. Elisabeth Jay (Oxford: Oxford Univ. Press, 1990), p. 133. Further citations are given in the text.

7. *The Diary of Arthur Christopher Benson*, ed. Percy Lubbock (London: Hutchinson, 1926), p. 47. Quoted by Merryn Williams, *Margaret Oliphant: A Critical Biography* (New York: St. Martin's Press, 1986), p. 57.

8. Estelle C. Jelinek notes that women's autobiographies are likely to be "episodic and anecdotal, nonchronological and disjunctive"; *The Tradition of Women's Autobiography: From Antiquity to the Present* (Boston: Twayne, 1986), p. xiii. On Victorian women's autobiography see Valerie Sanders, *The Private Lives of Victorian Women:*

Autobiography in Nineteenth-Century England (New York: St. Martin's Press, 1989), and Deborah Epstein Nord, *The Apprenticeship of Beatrice Webb* (1985; Ithaca: Cornell Univ. Press, 1989).

9. Anthony Trollope, *An Autobiography* (1883; London: Oxford Univ. Press, 1950), p. 1.

6. The Female Sage

1. John Gross, *The Rise and Fall of the Man of Letters: A Study of the Idiosyncratic and the Humane in Modern Literature.* (New York: Macmillan, 1969), p. 98. The absence of women in this tradition is addressed in *Victorian Sages and Cultural Discourse: Renegotiating Gender and Power*, ed. Thais E. Morgan (New Brunswick: Rutgers Univ. Press, 1990); see in particular Carol Christ, " 'The Hero as Man of Letters': Masculinity and Victorian Nonfiction Prose," pp. 19-31. See also Deirdre David, *Intellectual Women and Victorian Patriarchy: Harriet Martineau, Elizabeth Barrett Browning, George Eliot* (Ithaca: Cornell Univ. Press, 1987), which stresses the issue of authority and how women in a male-dominated culture can attain it.

2. Important recent studies of homosexuality and homophobia in Victorian England include Eve Kosofsky Sedgwick, *Between Men: English Literature and Male Homosocial Desire* (New York: Columbia Univ. Press, 1985) and *Epistemology of the Closet* (Berkeley & Los Angeles: Univ. of California Press, 1990), and Richard Dellamora, *Masculine Desire: The Sexual Politics of Victorian Aestheticism* (Chapel Hill: Univ. of North Carolina Press, 1990).

3. Agnes Strickland, *Lives of the Queens of England from the Norman Conquest* 12 vols [1840-1848] (Philadelphia: George Barrie & Sons, 1902), 1: xxxiv. The author of the *DNB* essay on Strickland remarks, with typical denigration of her unfashionable interest in ordinary life (much in fashion, however, today): "Her literary style is weak, and the popularity of her books is in great measure due to their trivial gossip and domestic details." Another woman historian was Mary Anne Everett Green, who published, among other scholarly and antiquarian works, *Lives of the Princesses of England* (1849-55).

4. Anna Jameson, *Memoirs of the Loves of the Poets, Biographical Sketches of Women Celebrated in Ancient and Modern Poetry* [1829] (Boston: Houghton, Mifflin, 1894), pp. vii, 22.

5. *Praeterita*, in *The Works of John Ruskin*, ed. E. T. Cook and Alexander Wedderburn, Library Edition, 39 vols. (London: G. Allen, 1903-1912), 35: 373-74.

6. *Memoir and Letters of Sara Coleridge*, edited by her daughter, 2 vols., 3rd ed. (1873; London: Henry S. King, 1873), p. 26.

7. *The Letters of Elizabeth Barrett Browning*, ed. Frederic G. Kenyon, 2 vols., 4th ed. (London: Macmillan, 1897), 1: 196-97. Robert Browning found the combination less attractive.

8. *Harriet Martineau's Autobiography*, ed. Maria Weston Chapman, 2 vols. (Boston: James R. Osgood, 1877), 1: 441. Further references appear parenthetically in the text.

9. "Autobiographical Sketch of Harriet Martineau," in *Biographical Sketches, 1852-1875*, 4th ed. (London: Macmillan, 1885), p. xxxiii. This obituary was written in 1855, in expectation of imminent death, for the *Daily News*, which published it when she died twenty-one years later.

10. On the importance of Milton for women writers, see Gilbert and Gubar, *The Madwoman in the Attic*, pp. 187-212.

11. This is from Chapman's *Memoir* in the *Autobiography*, 2: 319. The entry appears to be from 1839, and is in immediate reference to a letter from Margaret Fuller criti-

cizing her book on America. The unlikely reason she gives for her pleasure in bad reviews is that her feelings in such a case are "engrossed in concern for the perpetrators, and an anxious desire to do them good."

12. *Quarterly Review* 49 (April 1833): 136, 151. The tale in question is "Weal and Woe in Garveloch."

13. *Life in the Sick-Room, Essays* (Boston: Leonard C. Bowles & William Crosby, 1844), p. 188.

14. *Biographical Sketches*, p. xix.

15. Chapman, "Memorials," *Autobiography*, 2: 209.

7. Religion

1. *A Literature of Their Own*, p. 144. For similar phenomena in the United States, see Ann Douglas, *The Feminization of American Culture* (New York: Knopf, 1977).

2. "Of Queens' Gardens," *Sesame and Lilies, Works of John Ruskin*, 18: 127. Ruskin is otherwise willing to let girls study whatever boys do, so long as they learn only enough to facilitate conversation with their husbands (p. 128).

3. On women and the Church of England see John S. Reed, " 'A Female Movement': The Feminization of Nineteenth-Century Anglo-Catholicism," *Anglican and Episcopal History* 57 (1988): 199-238, and Catherine M. Prelinger, "The Female Diaconate in the Anglican Church: What Kind of Ministry for Women?" in *Religion in the Lives of English Women, 1760-1930*, ed Gail Malmgreen (Bloomington: Indiana Univ. Press, 1986), pp. 161-92.

4. Elisabeth Jay comments (with some overstatement, perhaps) that "Evangelicism, as a philosophy, was . . . calculated to appeal to the novelist since it invited him to contemplate characters who recognized no compulsion to conform to the standards of contemporary society." *The Religion of the Heart: Anglican Evangelicism in the Nineteenth-Century Novel* (Oxford: Clarendon Press, 1979), p. 7.

5. *Personal Recollections*, p. 58. Further autobiographical statements by Charlotte Elizabeth are from this volume and are identified parenthetically in the text.

6. *Memoir and Letters of Sara Coleridge*, p. 53.

7. *The Autobiography of Elizabeth M. Sewell*, p. 2. Sewell's novel *The Experience of Life* (1853) inculcates the moral that the humdrum life of a single woman can be a significant and happy one.

8. *Cassandra, an Essay by Florence Nightingale* (Old Westbury: The Feminist Press, 1979), p. 37.

9. *Mary Howitt, an Autobiography*, ed. Margaret Howitt (London: W. Isbister, 1889), pp. 68, 141, 190. Leonore Davidoff and Catherine Hall give a thorough discussion of women's changing place in nineteenth-century religion in Part One of *Family Fortunes: Men and Women of the English Middle Class, 1780-1850* (Chicago: Univ. of Chicago Press, 1987). On Quakers and Methodists, see pp. 137-40.

10. Booth, "Female Ministry: Or, Woman's Right to Preach the Gospel," *Papers on Practical Religion* (1878; London: John Snow, 1890), p. 95.

11. See Reed, "A 'Female Movement,' " 216-25.

12. In 1826 Maria Jane Jewsbury, renouncing literary ambition for "home *duties*," quoted these lines to Dora Wordsworth. See Norma Clarke, *Ambitious Heights: Writing, Friendship, Love — The Jewsbury Sisters, Felicia Hemans, and Jane Welsh Carlyle* (London: Routledge, 1990), p. 69 (from an unpublished letter).

13. As Richard D. Altick points out, "Faced with the alternative of a volume of sermons or *Paradise Lost*, [children] chose the less dull." *The English Common Reader: A Social History of the Mass Reading Public, 1800-1900* (Chicago: Univ. of Chicago Press, 1957; 1983), p. 127.

14. Deborah Epstein Nord points out that "Self-sacrifice, renunciation and saintliness—behaviour that to the twentieth-century eye appears self-punishing and neurotic—seemed to the Victorian girl available routes to importance and achievement." *The Apprenticeship of Beatrice Webb*, p. 66.

15. Susan Budd argues that most deconversions were based on moral, rather than scientific, grounds. *Varieties of Unbelief: Atheists and Agnostics in English Society, 1850-1960* (London: Heinemann, 1977), pp. 104-23.

16. "Autobiographical Sketch of Harriet Martineau," xxxi. Harriet Martineau, *Eastern Life, Present and Past* [1848], new ed. (London: E. Moxon, Son, n.d.), pp. 430, 488.

17. *Eastern Life*, p. 430; Jameson, *Legends of the Madonna, as Represented in the Fine Arts* [1860], rev. ed. (Boston: James R. Osgood, 1876), pp. 23, 22.

18. *Legends of the Madonna*, pp. 22, 402, 49, 50.

19. *Letters*, 1: 128-29.

20. Ludwig Feuerbach, *The Essence of Christianity*, trans. George Eliot (1854; New York: Harper & Row, 1957), p. 92.

21. *Letters*, 2: 153.

22. *Letters*, 4: 104.

23. *Letters*, 4: 97.

24. [Eliza] Lynn Linton, *My Literary Life* (London: Hodder & Stoughton, 1899), pp. 98-99.

25. *Letters*, 4: 103-104

26. *Cassandra*, p. 53.

27. *Life of Frances Power Cobbe as Told by Herself* (1894; London: Swan Sonnenschein, 1904), p. 439. Page references for Cobbe's works given in the text, unless otherwise identified, are to the *Life*.

28. Quoted in Norma Clark, *Ambitious Heights*, p. 173; from Guinevere Griest, *Mudie's Circulating Library and the Victorian Novel* (Bloomington: Indiana Univ. Press, 1970), p. 124.

29. *The Duties of Women: A Course of Lectures* (1881; Boston: Geo. H. Ellis, 1881), p. 26.

30. *Life of Frances Power Cobbe*, p. 439.

31. *Autobiography* (Philadelphia: Henry Altmus, 1893), p. 18.

8. Science

1. *Princess Ida, The Complete Plays of Gilbert and Sullivan* (New York: W. W. Norton, 1976), p. 273.

2. "We think M. Comte as great as either of these philosophers, and hardly more extravagant"; John Stuart Mill, *Auguste Comte and Positivism* (Ann Arbor: Univ. of Michigan Press, 1961), p. 200. George Henry Lewes, *Comte's Philosophy of the Sciences: Being an Exposition of the Principles of the Cours de Philosophie Positive of August Comte* (1858; London, George Bell & Sons, 1887), p. 1.

3. *Comte's Philosophy*, pp. 5, 6.

4. Cynthia Eagle Russett, *Sexual Science: The Victorian Construction of Womanhood* (Cambridge, Mass.: Harvard Univ. Press, 1989), pp. 19-22. Comte included phrenology, rather than psychology, among the sciences.

5. *Personal Recollections, from Early Life to Old Age, of Mary Somerville*, with selections from her correspondence, by her daughter, Martha Somerville (Boston: Roberts Bros., 1874), pp. 47, 54. Page numbers for further citations appear parenthetically in the text. Additional details of Somerville's life with excellent analysis are given by Elizabeth Chambers Patterson in *Mary Somerville and the Cultivation of Science, 1815-1840* (Boston: Martinus Nijhoff, 1983).

6. Patterson, p. 48.

7. *Athenaeum* 333 (January 1834): 202-203.

8. Patterson, p. 89.

9. *Letters of Robert Browning and Elizabeth Barrett Barrett* 2: 1012.

10. On women's scientific education see Patricia Phillips, *The Scientific Lady: A Social History of Women's Scientific Interests, 1520-1918* (New York: St. Martin's Press, 1990). "Sophia" is quoted in Phillips, p. 72.

11. Coleridge, p. 32.

12. On the professionalization of science, see T. W. Heyck, *The Transformation of Intellectual Life in Victorian England* (New York: St. Martin's Press, 1982), and Patterson, especially pp. ix-x; on women's commitment to classical studies see Phillips, p. 251-52. In Heyck's terminology, scientists, because of their specialization and commitment to research and specialist audiences (among other reasons), are not "men of letters."

13. Tennyson, *In Memoriam*, lvi. Thomas Carlyle, *Past and Present* [1843], *The Works of Thomas Carlyle*, 10: 7. Thomas Henry Huxley, "A Liberal Education, and Where to Find It" (1868), in *Lay Sermons, Addresses, and Reviews* (New York: D. Appleton, 1888), p. 34. See James Eli Adams, "Woman Red in Tooth and Claw: Nature and the Feminine in Tennyson and Darwin" *Victorian Studies* 33 (1989): 7-27.

14. "A Liberal Education, and Where to Find It," p. 35. Against this image of masculine pride controlling all nature, including his own body, we may set Mary Howitt's memory of her father, a land surveyor who supported the family during her childhood by supervising the enclosure and deforestation of wild forest land. In a highly charged passage of her autobiography (written in 1868), she describes "a scene of the most melancholy spoliation" when a forest—"older than the existing institutions of the kingdom, older than English history"—was cut down on Christmas Day, 1802: "small creatures" and birds died or "fled bewildered," and "fires destroyed the luxuriant growth of plants and shrubs"—an image that accurately reflects her sense of her father as the enemy of natural spontaneity and joy. *Mary Howitt, an Autobiography*, p. 18.

15. Tennyson, "Parnassus," l. 16.

16. Huxley, "A Liberal Education, and Where to Find It," p. 32. Of the many writers on Eliot and science, see especially Gillian Beer, *Darwin's Plots: Evolutionary Narrative in Darwin, George Eliot and Nineteenth-Century Fiction* (London: Routledge & Kegan Paul, 1983); Sally Shuttleworth, *George Eliot and Nineteenth-Century Science: The Make-Believe of a Beginning* (New York: Cambridge Univ. Press, 1984); and Nancy L. Paxton, *George Eliot and Herbert Spencer: Feminism, Evolutionism, and the Reconstruction of Gender* (Princeton: Princeton Univ. Press, 1991). Beer notes that evolution gave "a new creation myth" (p. 115), Paxton that science offered a new kind of authority to match that of the epic poets of the past (p. 12).

17. Margaret Homans points out that when Roger turns his attention from Molly, the narrator quotes Wordsworth's "A Slumber Did My Spirit Seal" to indicate that she seems to become a part of nature, dead, like Wordsworth's Lucy. *Bearing the Word: Language and Female Experience in Nineteenth-Century Women's Writing* (Chicago: Univ. of Chicago Press, 1986), pp. 260-61. "Just as Lucy's very existence depends on the consciousness of the poet," Homans points out, "so too Molly's existence seems at this moment to depend on Roger's consciousness of her" (p. 261). Patsy Stoneman analyzes the significance of science in *Wives and Daughters* in *Elizabeth Gaskell* (Bloomington: Indiana Univ. Press, 1987), pp. 177-78, 183-84, seeing Roger as exemplifying "maternal thinking" which "rooted in care, . . . takes the form of constant and acute attention to detail" (p. 178).

18. Charles Darwin, *The Origin of Species* [1859], 6th ed. (London: Oxford Univ. Press [World's Classics], 1951), p. 73. Gillian Beer in *Darwin's Plots* discusses many of the parallels between Darwin's writings and Victorian fiction, as does George Levine in

Darwin and the Novelists: Patterns of Science in Victorian Fiction (Cambridge, Mass.: Harvard Univ. Press, 1988). (Except for Eliot, all the novelists in Levine's book are men.) Beer notes in particular themes of transformation and metamorphosis, kinship, change and development, and the ecological model (see pp. 6-10). Levine defines the Darwinian world in relation to the novelists' as characterized by commitment to ideas of uniformitarianism, change and history, blurring of boundaries, ecological and genealogical connections, abundance, denial of design and teleology, mystery and order, and chance (pp. 15-20).

19. *The Origin of Species*, p. 64.

20. Francis Galton, *Hereditary Genius: An Inquiry into Its Laws and Consequences* [1869], 2d ed. (London: Macmillan, 1892), pp. 34–35, 318. On gender in Victorian science, see Russett, *Sexual Science*, and Flavia Alaya, "Victorian Science and the 'Genius' of Woman," *Journal of the History of Ideas* 38 (1977): 261-80. On the "intense somatic bias" of the social sciences see Russett, p. 48 and passim; on responses to Mill, pp. 12-13. The biases of medicine have received particular attention; see, e.g., Poovey, *Uneven Developments*, and Elaine Showalter, *The Female Malady: Women, Madness, and English Culture, 1830-1980* (New York: Pantheon Books, 1985).

21. John F. McLennan, *Primitive Marriage: An Inquiry into the Origin of the Form of Capture in Marriage Ceremonies* [1865], ed. Peter Rivière (Chicago: Univ. of Chicago Press, 1970), pp. 67, 65. McLennan's was not the accepted view of woman's role in prehistory, but it was widely known, and the imaginative coloring he gives it is thoroughly representative.

22. The connection between Eliot and Spencer and the increasing antifeminism of Spencer's views are set forth by Paxton.

Conclusion

1. Gaskell, *The Life of Charlotte Brontë*, p. 484.

2. See Beer, *Darwin's Plots*, chapter 6.

3. Catherine Gallagher notes that Gwendolyn's and Mirah's stories, as well as Al Charisi's, "indicate that art and prostitution are *alternatives* in women's lives, but alternatives with such similar structures that their very alternativeness calls attention to their interchangeability"; "George Eliot and *Daniel Deronda*: The Prostitute and the Jewish Question," in *Sex, Politics, and Science in the Nineteenth-Century Novel: Selected Papers from the English Institute, 1983-84*, ed. Ruth Bernard Yeazell (Baltimore: John Hopkins Univ. Press, 1986), p. 54.

4. *Letters*, 6: 304.

5. See Henry James, "*Daniel Deronda*: A Conversation" [1876], in *Partial Portraits* (London: Macmillan, 1888). The participants in this conversation call the book "a very ponderous and ill-made story," with "little art" but "a vast amount of life" (p. 92); "too scientific," "artificial" rather than "spontaneous" (p. 82).

6. This is the central argument of Tuchman's *Edging Women Out*.

Bibliography

I. Primary Texts

Arnold, Matthew. *The Poems of Matthew Arnold*. Ed. Kenneth Allott. London: Longman, 1965. 2d ed., ed. Miriam Allott, 1979.

Austen, Jane. *Northanger Abbey*. 1818. Harmondsworth: Penguin, 1972.

Besant, Annie. *Autobiographical Sketches*. London: Freethought Publishing Company, 1885.

————. *An Autobiography*. Philadelphia: Henry Altemus, 1893.

Blanchard, Laman. *Life and Literary Remains of L. E. L.* 2 vols. Philadelphia: Lea & Blanchard, 1841.

Bodichon, Barbara Leigh Smith. *Women and Work*. New York: C. S. Francis, 1859.

Booth, Catherine. *Papers on Practical Religion*. 1878. London: John Snow, 1890.

Braddon, Mary E. *Aurora Floyd*. 1863. London: Virago, 1984.

————. *Lady Audley's Secret*. 1862. New York: Viking Penguin, 1987.

Brontë, Anne. *The Tenant of Wildfell Hall*. 1848. New York: Oxford Univ. Press, 1992.

Brontë, Charlotte. *Jane Eyre*. 1847. Harmondsworth: Penguin, 1966.

————. *The Professor*. 1857. New York: Viking Penguin, 1989.

————. *Shirley*. 1849. Harmondsworth: Penguin, 1974.

————. *Villette*. 1853. Harmondsworth: Penguin, 1979.

————, and Patrick Branwell. *The Miscellaneous and Unpublished Writings of Charlotte and Branwell Brontë*. The Shakespeare Head Brontë. 2 vols. Ed. Thomas James Wise and John Alexander Symington. Oxford: Basil Blackwell, 1934.

————, et al. *The Brontës: Their Lives, Friendships and Correspondence*. Ed. Thomas James Wise and John Alexander Symington. The Shakespeare Head Brontë. 4 vols. Oxford: Blackwell, 1932.

Brontë, Emily. *The Complete Poems of Emily Jane Brontë*. Ed. C. W. Hatfield. New York: Columbia Univ. Press, 1941.

————. *Wuthering Heights*. 1847. Harmondsworth: Penguin, 1985.

Broughton, Rhoda. *Not Wisely, But Too Well*. 2 vols. Leipzig: Tauchnitz, 1867.

Browning, Elizabeth Barrett. *The Complete Works of Elizabeth Barrett Browning*. Ed. Charlotte Porter and Helen A. Clarke. 6 vols. New York: Thomas Y. Crowell, 1900. Reprinted New York: AMS Press, 1973.

————. *The Letters of Elizabeth Barrett Browning*. Ed. Frederic G. Kenyon. 2 vols. London: Macmillan, 1897.

————. *The Letters of Elizabeth Barrett Browning to Mary Russell Mitford 1836-1854*. Ed. Meredith B. Raymond and Mary Rose Sullivan. 3 vols. Winfield, Kan.: Armstrong Browning Library of Baylor University, Browning Institute, Wedgestone Press, and Wellesley College, 1983.

Browning, Robert. *The Poetical Works of Robert Browning*. Ed. Ian Jack. 4 vols. to date. New York: Oxford, 1983- .

Browning, Robert, and Elizabeth Barrett. *The Brownings' Correspondence*. Ed. Philip Kelley and Ronald Hudson. 9 vols. to date. Winfield, Kan.: Wedgestone Press, 1984- .

————. *The Letters of Robert Browning and Elizabeth Barrett Barrett, 1845-1846*. Ed. Elvan Kintner. 2 vols. Cambridge, Mass.: Belknap Press of Harvard Univ., 1969.

Byron, George Gordon. *The Complete Poetical Works*. Ed. Jerome G. McGann. 5 vols. to date. New York: Oxford Univ. Press, 1980- .

Carlyle, Thomas. *The Love Letters of Thomas Carlyle and Jane Welsh*. Ed. Alexander Carlyle. 2 vols. London: John Lane, 1909.

_____. *The Works of Thomas Carlyle*. 30 vols. New York: Charles Scribner's Sons, 1897.

Cobbe, Frances Power. *The Duties of Women: A Course of Lectures*. Boston: Geo. H. Ellis, 1881.

_____. *Life of Frances Power Cobbe as Told by Herself*. 1894. London: Swan Sonnenschein, 1904.

Coleridge, Sara. *Memoir and Letters of Sara Coleridge, Edited by Her Daughter*. 2 vols. 3 ed. London: Henry S. King, 1873.

Comte, Auguste. *The Positive Philosophy of Auguste Comte, Freely Translated and Condensed by Harriet Martineau*. 2 vols. London: John Chapman, 1853.

Darwin, Charles. *The Origin of Species*. 1859. 6th ed. London: Oxford Univ. Press [World's Classics], 1951.

Eliot, George. *Adam Bede*. 1859. Harmondsworth: Penguin, 1980.

_____. *Daniel Deronda*. 1876. Harmondsworth: Penguin, 1986.

_____. *Essays*. Ed. Thomas Pinney. New York: Columbia Univ. Press, 1963.

_____. *Felix Holt, the Radical*. 1866. New York: Oxford Univ. Press, 1980.

_____. *The Lifted Veil*. 1878. New York: Penguin-Virago, 1985.

_____. *The George Eliot Letters*. Ed. Gordon S. Haight. 9 vols. New Haven: Yale Univ. Press, 1954-78.

_____. *Middlemarch*. 1871-72. Harmondsworth: Penguin, 1965.

_____. *The Mill on the Floss*. 1860. Harmondsworth: Penguin, 1979.

_____. *The Poems of George Eliot*. New York: T. Y. Crowell, 1884.

_____. *Romola*. 1863. Harmondsworth: Penguin, 1980.

_____. "Woman in France: Madame de Sablé." *Westminster Review* 62, n. s. 6 (1854): 448-73.

Ellis, Sarah Stickney. *The Daughters of England, Their Position in Society, Character, and Responsibilities*. London: Fisher, Son, 1842.

_____. *The Mothers of England, Their Influence and Responsibility*. London: Fisher, 1843.

_____. *The Wives of England, Their Relative Duties, Domestic Influence and Social Obligations*. London: Fisher, 1843.

_____. *The Women of England, Their Social Duties and Domestic Habits*. 19th ed. London: Fisher, 1839.

Feuerbach, Ludwig. *The Essence of Christianity*. Trans. by George Eliot. 1854. New York: Harper & Row, 1957.

Fullerton, Lady Georgiana. *Ellen Middleton: A Tale*. Leipzig: Tauchnitz, 1846.

Galton, Francis. *Hereditary Genius: An Inquiry into Its Laws and Consequences*. 1869. 2d ed. London: Macmillan, 1892.

Gaskell, Elizabeth. *Cranford; and Cousin Phyllis*. 1853, 1864. Harmondsworth: Penguin, 1976.

_____. *The Letters of Mrs. Gaskell*. Ed. J. A. V. Chapple and Arthur Pollard. Cambridge, Mass: Harvard Univ. Press, 1967.

_____. *The Life of Charlotte Brontë*. 1857. Harmondsworth: Penguin, 1975.

_____. *Mary Barton: A Tale of Manchester Life*. 1848. Harmondsworth: Penguin, 1970.

_____. *North and South*. 1854-55. Harmondsworth: Penguin, 1970.

_____. *Ruth*. 1848. New York: Oxford Univ. Press, 1985.

_____. *Wives and Daughters*. 1864-66. Harmondsworth: Penguin, 1969.

Gilbert, W. S. *The Complete Plays of Gilbert and Sullivan.* New York: W. W. Norton, 1976.

Green, Mary Anne Everett. *Lives of the Princesses of England, from the Norman Conquest.* 6 vols. London: H. Colburn, 1849-55.

Hardy, Thomas. *The Hand of Ethelberta, a Comedy in Chapters.* 1876. New York: Harper, 1905.

Havergal, Frances Ridley. *Letters by the Late Frances Ridley Havergal.* Ed. M[aria]. V. G. H[avergal]. London: James Nisbet, 1885.

———. *The Poetical Works of Frances Ridley Havergal.* 2 vols. London: James Nisbet, 1884.

H[avergal], M[aria] V. G. *Memorials of Francis Ridley Havergal.* London: James Nisbet, 1880.

Hemans, Felicia. *The Works of Felicia Hemans: Edited by Her Sister, with an Essay on Her Genius by Mrs. Sigourney.* 3 vols. New York: C. S. Francis, 1845.

Howitt, Mary. *Mary Howitt, an Autobiography: Edited by Her Daughter, Margaret Howitt.* 1889. London: Isbister, 1890.

Huxley, Thomas Henry. *Lay Sermons, Addresses, and Reviews.* 1870. New York: D. Appleton, 1888.

Ingelow, Jean. *Poems by Jean Ingelow.* London: Oxford Univ. Press, 1926.

Jameson, Anna. *Anna Jameson: Letters and Friendships (1812-1860).* Ed. Mrs. Steuart Erskine. New York: E. P. Dutton, 1915.

———. *A Commonplace Book of Thoughts, Memories, and Fancies, Original and Selected.* London: Longman, Brown, Green, & Longmans, 1854.

———. *Diary of an Ennuyée.* Boston: Lilly, Wait, Colman, & Holden, 1833.

———. *Legends of the Madonna, as Represented in the Fine Arts.* 1852. Rev. ed. Boston: James R. Osgood, 1876.

———. *Memoirs of Celebrated Female Sovereigns.* 2 vols. 1831. New York: J. & J. Harper, 1832.

———. *Memoirs of the Beauties of the Court of Charles the Second, with Their Portraits, after Sir Peter Lely and Other Eminent Painters: Illustrating the Diaries of Pepys, Evelyn, Clarendon, and Other Contemporary Writers.* 2 vols. 2 ed. London: Henry Colburn, 1838.

———. *Memoirs of the Loves of the Poets: Biographical Sketches of Women Celebrated in Ancient and Modern Poetry.* 1829. Boston: Houghton Mifflin, 1894.

———. *Shakespeare's Heroines: Characteristics of Women, Moral, Poetical and Historical.* 1832. New York: A. L. Burt, 1905.

———. *Sisters of Charity, Catholic and Protestant. And The Communion of Labour.* 1855. Boston: Ticknor & Fields, 1857. Reprint ed. Westport: Hyperion Press, 1976.

———. *Visits and Sketches at Home and Abroad.* 3d ed. 2 vols. London: Saunders & Otley, 1839.

Jewsbury, Geraldine. *The Half-Sisters: A Tale.* 2 vols. London: Chapman & Hall, 1848.

———. *Selections from the Letters of Geraldine Endsor Jewsbury to Jane Welsh Carlyle.* Ed. Mrs. Alexander Ireland. London: Longmans, Green; New York, 1892.

———. *Zoë: The History of Two Lives.* 3 vols. London: Chapman and Hall, 1845. Facsimile ed. New York: Garland, 1975.

Kemble, Frances Ann. *Records of a Girlhood.* New York: Henry Holt, 1879.

Landon, Letitia E. *The Poetical Works of L. E. Landon.* 2 vols. Philadelphia: Jasper Harding, 1850.

[Lewis, Sarah.] *Woman's Mission.* 2d ed. London: John W. Parker, 1839.

Linton, [Eliza] Lynn. *The Girl of the Period, and Other Social Essays*. London: R. Bentley & Son, 1883.

_____. *My Literary Life*. London: Hodder & Stoughton, 1899.

_____. *The True History of Joshua Davidson*. Leipzig: Tauchnitz, 1873.

McLennan, John F. *Primitive Marriage: An Inquiry into the Origin of the Form of Capture in Marriage Ceremonies*. 1865. Chicago: Univ. of Chicago Press, 1970.

Martineau, Harriet. *Harriet Martineau's Autobiography*. Ed. Maria Weston Chapman. *Memorials of Harriet Martineau*, by Maria Weston Chapman. 2 vols. Boston: James R. Osgood, 1877.

_____. *Biographical Sketches, 1852-1875*. 4th ed. London: Macmillan, 1885.

_____. *Eastern Life, Present and Past*. 1848. New ed. London: E. Moxon, Son, n.d.

_____. *Harriet Martineau on Women*. Ed. Gayle Graham Yates. New Brunswick: Rutgers Univ. Press, 1985.

_____. *Household Education*. Boston: James R. Osgood, 1877.

_____. *Life in the Sick-Room, Essays*. Boston: Leonard C. Bowles & William Crosby, 1844.

_____. *Society in America*. 2 vols. New York: Saunders & Otley, 1837.

Nightingale, Florence. *Cassandra*. Ed. Myra Stark. Old Westbury: The Feminist Press, 1979.

Norton, Caroline. *The Child of the Islands. A Poem*. London: Chapman & Hall, 1845.

_____. *The Dream, and Other Poems*. London: H. Colburn, 1840.

_____. *Poems*. Boston: Allen & Ticknor, 1833.

_____. *The Undying One, and Other Poems*. London: H. Colburn & R. Bentley, 1830.

_____. *The Sorrows of Rosalie, a Tale; with Other Poems*. London: J. Ebers, 1829.

Oliphant, Margaret. *The Autobiography of Margaret Oliphant. The Complete Text*. Ed. Elisabeth Jay. New York: Oxford Univ. Press, 1990.

_____. *The Autobiography and Letters of Mrs. Oliphant. Arranged and Edited by Mrs. Harry Coghill*. Edinburgh: Blackwood, 1899.

_____. *Miss Marjoribanks*. 1866. New York: Viking Penguin, 1989.

_____. *The Perpetual Curate*. 1864. New York: Viking-Penguin, 1987.

_____. *Phoebe, Junior*. 1876. London: Virago, 1989.

Procter, Adelaide. *The Poems of Adelaide A. Procter*. New York: Thomas Y. Crowell, 1858.

Ramée, Louise de la ("Ouida"). *Under Two Flags*. 2 vols. Leipzig: Tauchnitz, 1871.

_____. *Frescoes and Other Stories*. Leipzig: Tauchnitz, 1883.

Ritchie, Anne Thackeray. *The Story of Elizabeth*. Leipzig: Tauchnitz, 1863.

Rossetti, Christina. *The Complete Poems of Christina Rossetti: A Variorum Edition*. Ed. R. W. Crump. 3 vols. Baton Rouge: Louisiana State Univ. Press, 1979-90.

_____. *The Family Letters of Christina Georgina Rossetti*. Ed. William Michael Rossetti. 1908. New York: Haskell House, 1968.

_____. *The Poetical Works of Christina Georgina Rossetti*. Ed. William Michael Rossetti. London: Macmillan, 1904.

_____. *Seek and Find: A Double Series of Short Studies of the Benedicite*. 1869. New York: Pott, Young, 1879.

_____. *Verses*. London: G. Polidori, 1847.

Rossetti, Dante Gabriel. *Dante Gabriel Rossetti: His Family Letters with a Memoir*. Ed. William Michael Rossetti. 2 vols. London: Ellis, 1895.

_____. *Letters of Dante Gabriel Rossetti*. Ed. Oswald Doughty and John Robert Wahl. 4 vols. Oxford: Clarendon Press, 1965-67.

_____. *The Works of Dante Gabriel Rossetti*. Ed. William M. Rossetti. London: Ellis, 1911.

_____, Dante Gabriel, Christina, William. *Three Rossettis: Unpublished Letters to and from Dante Gabriel, Christina, William*. Ed. Janet Camp Troxell. Cambridge, Mass.: Harvard Univ. Press, 1937.

Ruskin, John. *The Works of John Ruskin*. Ed. E. T. Cook and Alexander Wedderburn. 39 vols. New York: Longmans, Green, 1903-12.

Scott, Sir Walter. *The Heart of Midlothian*. 1818. New York: Dutton, 1943.

Sewell, Elizabeth M. *The Autobiography of Elizabeth M. Sewell*. Ed. Eleanor L. Sewell. London: Longmans, Green, 1907.

_____. *The Experience of Life; or, Aunt Sarah*. 2 vols. 1853. Leipzig: Bernhard Tauchnitz, 1874.

_____. *Principles of Education, Drawn from Nature and Revelation, and Applied to Female Education in the Upper Classes*. 1865. New York: D. Appleton, 1866.

Shelley, Percy Bysshe. *The Complete Poetical Works*. Ed. Roger Neville. 4 vols. Oxford: Oxford Univ. Press, 1972.

Skene, Felicia. *Hidden Depths*. 2 vols. Edinburgh: Edmonston and Douglas, 1866. In *Use and Abuse* [and] *Hidden Depths*, New York: Garland, 1975.

Somerville, Mary. *Personal Recollections, from Early Life to Old Age, of Mary Somerville, with Selections from Her Correspondence, by Her Daughter, Martha Somerville*. Boston: Roberts Bros., 1874.

Southey, Charles Cuthbert. *The Life and Correspondence of Robert Southey*. Ed. Charles Cuthbert Southey. 6 vols. London: Longman, Brown, Green & Longmans, 1850.

de Staël, Mme [Anne Louise-Germaine]. *Corinne, or Italy*. 1807. New Brunswick: Rutgers Univ. Press, 1987.

Strauss, David Friedrich. *The Life of Jesus, Critically Examined*. Trans. by George Eliot. 1846. 2d ed. London: Swan Sonnenschein, 1892.

Strickland, Agnes. *Lives of the Queens of England from the Norman Conquest*. 12 vols. 1840-1848. Philadelphia: George Barrie & Sons, 1902.

Tennyson, Alfred. *The Poems of Tennyson*. Ed. Christopher Ricks. London: Longman, 1969.

Thackeray, William Makepeace. *The History of Pendennis*. 1850. Harmondsworth: Penguin, 1972.

_____. *The Letters and Private Papers of W. M. Thackeray*. Ed. Gordon N. Ray. 4 vols. Cambridge, Mass.: Harvard Univ. Press, 1945-46.

[Tonna, Charlotte Elizabeth.] *The Works of Charlotte Elizabeth, with an Introduction by Mrs. H. B. Stowe*. New York: M. W. Dodd, 1844.

Trollope, Anthony. *An Autobiography*. 1883. London: Oxford Univ. Press, 1950.

_____. *The Way We Live Now*. 1875. London: Oxford Univ. Press, 1971.

Webster, Augusta. *Blanche Lisle and Other Poems*. By Cecil Home. Cambridge: Macmillan, 1860.

_____. *Dramatic Studies*. London: Macmillan, 1866.

_____. *A Housewife's Opinions*. London: Macmillan, 1879.

_____. *A Woman Sold and Other Poems*. London: Macmillan, 1867.

_____. *Mother and Daughter: An Uncompleted Sonnet Sequence*. London: Macmillan, 1895.

_____. *Portraits*. London: Macmillan, 1870.

_____. *The Sentence: A Drama*. London: T. Fisher Unwin, 1887.

Wood, Mrs. Henry. *East Lynne*. 1861. New Brunswick: Rutgers Univ. Press, 1984.

Woolf, Virginia. *Orlando: A Biography*. New York: Harcourt, Brace, 1928.

Yates, Edmund. *Edmund Yates: His Recollections and Experiences.* 1884. 4th ed. London: Richard Bentley & Son, 1885.

Yonge, Charlotte M. *The Clever Woman of the Family.* 1865. London: Virago, 1985

———. *The Daisy Chain.* 1856. New York: Garland, 1977.

———. *Heartsease, or, the Brother's Wife.* 1854. 2 vols. Leipzig: Tauchnitz, 1855.

———. *Hopes and Fears, or, Scenes from the Life of a Spinster.* 1860. 2 vols. Leipzig: Tauchnitz, 1861.

———. *The Pillars of the House; or, under Wode, under Rode.* 5 vols. Leipzig: Tauchnitz, 1873.

———. *Womankind.* 2 vols. Leipzig: Tauchnitz, 1878.

II. Secondary Sources

Abel, Elizabeth, Marianne Hirsch, and Elizabeth Langland, eds. *The Voyage In: Fictions of Female Development.* Hanover: Univ. Press of New England for Dartmouth College, 1983.

Adams, James Eli. "Woman Red in Tooth and Claw: Nature and the Feminine in Tennyson and Darwin." *Victorian Studies* 33 (1989): 7-27.

Alaya, Flavia. "Victorian Science and the 'Genius' of Woman." *Journal of the History of Ideas* 38 (1977): 261-80.

Alexander, Christine. *The Early Writings of Charlotte Brontë.* Buffalo, NY: Prometheus Books, 1983.

Allott, Miriam, ed. *The Brontës: The Critical Heritage.* London: Routledge & Kegan Paul, 1974.

Altick, Richard D. *The English Common Reader: A Social History of the Mass Reading Public, 1800-1900.* Chicago: Univ. of Chicago Press, 1957.

———. *Writers, Readers, and Occasions: Selected Essays on Victorian Literature and Life.* Columbus: Ohio State Univ. Press, 1989.

Anderson, Nancy Fix. *Woman against Women in Victorian England: A Life of Eliza Lynn Linton.* Bloomington: Indiana Univ. Press, 1987.

Armstrong, Nancy. *Desire and Domestic Fiction: A Political History of the Novel.* New York: Oxford Univ. Press, 1987.

Beer, Gillian. *Darwin's Plots: Evolutionary Narrative in Darwin, George Eliot and Nineteenth-Century Fiction.* London: Routlege & Kegan Paul, 1983.

———. *George Eliot.* Bloomington: Indiana Univ. Press, 1986.

Beerbohm, Max. *More.* 1899. 2nd ed. London: John Lane, The Bodley Head, 1907.

Bell, Mackenzie. *Christina Rossetti: A Biographical and Critical Study.* 1898. 4th ed. New York: Haskell House, 1971.

Bodenheimer, Rosemarie. "Ambition and Its Audiences: George Eliot's Performing Figures." *Victorian Studies* 34 (1990): 7-31.

———. "Jane Eyre in Search of Her Story." *Papers on Language and Literature* 16 (1980): 387-402.

———. *The Politics of Story in Victorian Social Fiction.* Ithaca: Cornell Univ. Press, 1988.

Brownell, David. "The Two Worlds of Charlotte Yonge." *Worlds of Victorian Fiction.* Ed. Jerome H. Buckley. Harvard English Studies 6. Cambridge, Mass.: Harvard Univ. Press, 1975.

Budd, Susan. *Varieties of Unbelief: Atheists and Agnostics in English Society, 1850-1960.* London: Heinemann, 1977.

Carroll, David, ed. *George Eliot: The Critical Heritage.* New York: Barnes & Noble, 1971.

Christ, Carol. "The Feminine Subject in Victorian Poetry." *ELH* 54 (1987): 385-401.

Clarke, Norma. *Ambitious Heights: Writing, Friendship, Love—The Jewsbury Sisters, Felicia Hemans and Jane Welsh Carlyle.* London: Routledge, 1990.

Corbett, Mary Jean. *Representing Femininity: Middle-Class Subjectivity in Victorian and Edwardian Women's Autobiographies.* New York: Oxford Univ. Press, 1992.

Craven, Pauline Marie Armande Aglaé. *Life of Lady Georgiana Fullerton. From the French of Mrs. Augustus Craven. By Henry James Coleridge of the Society of Jesus.* London: Richard Bentley & Son, 1888.

Cross, J[ohn] W[alter]. *George Eliot's Life as Related in Her Letters and Journals.* 3 vols. New York: Harper & Brothers, 1885.

Dale, Peter Allan. *In Pursuit of a Scientific Culture: Science, Art and Society in the Victorian Age.* Madison: Univ. of Wisconsin Press, 1989.

David, Deirdre. *Intellectual Women and Victorian Patriarchy: Harriet Martineau, Elizabeth Barrett Browning, George Eliot.* Ithaca: Cornell Univ. Press, 1987.

Davidoff, Leonore, and Catherine Hall. *Family Fortunes: Men and Women of the English Middle Class, 1780-1850.* Chicago: Univ. of Chicago Press, 1987.

Dellamora, Richard. *Masculine Desire: The Sexual Politics of Victorian Aestheticism.* Chapel Hill: Univ. of North Carolina Press, 1990.

Diehl, Joanne Feit. "'Come Slowly—Eden': An Exploration of Women Poets and Their Muse." *Signs* 3 (1978): 572-87.

Douglas, Ann. *The Feminization of American Culture.* New York: Knopf, 1977.

[Eagles, John.] "A Few Words About Novels." *Blackwood's Magazine* 64 (October 1848): 473-74.

Ewbank, Inga-Stina. *Their Proper Sphere: A Study of the Brontë Sisters as Early-Victorian Female Novelists.* Cambridge, Mass.: Harvard Univ. Press, 1966.

Feuerbach, Ludwig. *The Essence of Christianity.* Translated by George Eliot. 1854. New York: Harper & Row, 1957.

Gallagher, Catherine. "George Eliot and *Daniel Deronda*: The Prostitute and the Jewish Question." In *Sex, Politics, and Science in the Nineteenth-Century Novel: Selected Papers from the English Institute, 1983-84.* Ed. Ruth Bernard Yeazell. Baltimore: Johns Hopkins Univ. Press, 1986.

_____. *The Industrial Reformation of English Fiction: Social Discourse and Narrative Form, 1832-1867.* Chicago: Univ. of Chicago Press, 1985.

Gérin, Winifred. *Anne Thackeray Ritchie: A Biography.* Oxford: Oxford Univ. Press, 1981.

_____. "Byron's Influence on the Brontës." *Keats-Shelley Memorial Bulletin*, 17 (1966): 1-19.

_____. *Branwell Brontë.* London: Thomas Nelson & Sons, 1961.

_____. *Charlotte Brontë: The Evolution of Genius.* London: Oxford Univ. Press, 1967.

_____. *Elizabeth Gaskell: A Biography.* Oxford: Clarendon Press, 1976.

_____. *Emily Brontë: A Biography.* Oxford: Clarendon Press, 1971.

Gilbert, Sandra M., and Susan Gubar. *The Madwoman in the Attic: The Woman Writer and the Nineteenth-Century Literary Imagination.* New Haven: Yale Univ. Press, 1979.

Going, William T. "'Goblin Market' and the Pre-Raphaelite Brotherhood," *PreRaphaelite Review* 3 (1979): 1-11.

Gosse, Edmund. *The Life of Algernon Charles Swinburne.* New York: Macmillan, 1917.

Griest, Guinevere. *Mudie's Circulating Library and the Victorian Novel.* Bloomington: Indiana Univ. Press, 1970.

Gross, John. *The Rise and Fall of the Man of Letters: A Study of the Idiosyncratic and the Humane in Modern Literature.* New York: Macmillan, 1969.

Haight, Gordon S. *George Eliot: A Biography*. Oxford: Oxford Univ. Press, 1968.

Harmon, Barbara Leah. "In Promiscuous Company: Female Public Appearance in Elizabeth Gaskell's *North and South*." *Victorian Studies* 31 (1988): 351-74.

Harris, Janice H. "Not Suffering and Not Still: Women Writers at the *Cornhill Magazine*, 1860-1900." *Modern Language Quarterly* 47 (1986): 382-92.

Heilbrun, Carolyn. *Towards a Recognition of Androgyny*. New York: Alfred A. Knopf, 1973.

———. *Reinventing Womanhood*. New York: Norton, 1979.

Helsinger, Elizabeth K., Robin Lauterbach Sheets, and William Veeder. *The Woman Question: Society and Literature in Britain and America, 1837-1883*. 3 vols. New York: Garland, 1983.

Hertz, Neil. *The End of the Line: Essays on Psychoanalysis and the Sublime*. New York: Columbia Univ. Press, 1985.

Heyck, T. W. *The Transformation of Intellectual Life in Victorian England*. New York: St. Martin's Press, 1982.

Hickok, Kathleen. *Representations of Women: Nineteenth-Century British Women's Poetry*. Westport: Greenwood Press, 1984.

[Hobart, V. H.] "Thoughts on Modern English Literature." *Fraser's Magazine* 60 (1859): 96-110.

Homans, Margaret. *Bearing the Word: Language and Female Experience in Nineteenth-Century Women's Writing*. Chicago: Univ. of Chicago Press, 1986.

———. *Women Writers and Poetic Identity: Dorothy Wordsworth, Emily Brontë, and Emily Dickinson*. Princeton: Princeton Univ. Press, 1980.

Hughes, Winifred. *The Maniac in the Cellar: Sensation Novels of the 1860s*. Princeton: Princeton Univ. Press, 1980.

Hutton, Richard Holt. "Novels by the Authoress of 'John Halifax.'" *North British Review* 29 (1858): 466-81.

Jacobus, Mary. *Reading Woman: Essays in Feminist Criticism*. New York: Columbia Univ. Press, 1986.

James, Henry. *Partial Portraits*. London: Macmillan, 1888.

———. Rev. of *Jane Eyre*. *Howitt's Journal* 2 (1847): 333-34.

———. *Living Age* 17 (1848): 481-87.

———. *Spectator* 20 (1847): 1074-75.

Jay, Elisabeth. *The Religion of the Heart: Anglican Evangelicism and the Nineteenth-Century Novel*. Oxford: Clarendon Press, 1979.

Jehlen, Myra. "Archimedes and the Paradox of Feminist Criticism." *Signs* 6 (1981): 575-601.

Jelinek, Estelle C., ed. *Women's Autobiography: Essays in Criticism*. Bloomington: Indiana Univ. Press, 1980.

———. *The Tradition of Women's Autobiography: From Antiquity to the Present*. Boston: Twayne, 1986.

Johnson, Dale A. *Women in English Religion, 1700-1925*. Studies in Women and Religion 10. New York: Edwin Mellen Press, 1983.

Lancaster, Joan C. *Godiva of Coventry*. The Coventry Papers, 1. Coventry: Coventry Corporation, 1967.

Leighton, Angela. *Elizabeth Barrett Browning*. Bloomington: Indiana Univ. Press, 1986.

———. *Victorian Women Poets: Writing against the Heart*. Charlottesville: Univ. Press of Virginia, 1992.

Levine, George. *Darwin and the Novelists: Patterns of Science in Victorian Fiction*. Cambridge, Mass.: Harvard Univ. Press, 1988.

Levine, Philippa. *Victorian Feminism, 1850-1900*. Tallahassee: Florida State Univ. Press, 1987.

Lewes, George Henry. *Comte's Philosophy of the Sciences: Being an Exposition of the Principles of the Cours de Philosophie Positive of August Comte.* 1858. London: George Bell & Sons, 1887.

———. "The Lady Novelists." *Westminster Review* n.s. 2 (1852): 129-41.

———. "Recent Novels: French and English." *Fraser's Magazine* 36 (1847): 686-95.

———. Rev. of *Jane Eyre. Westminster Review* 48 (1848): 581-84.

Lochhead, Marion. *Elizabeth Rigby, Lady Eastlake.* London: John Murray, 1961.

Lockhart, J. G. *Life of Sir Walter Scott.* 10 vols. Edinburgh: Adam & Charles Black, 1862.

"Lord Byron." *Blackwood's Edinburgh Magazine* 17 (1825): 131-51.

Lovell, Terry. *Consuming Fiction.* London: Verso, 1987.

Macpherson, Gerardine. *Memoirs of the Life of Anna Jameson.* Boston: Roberts Brothers, 1878.

Maison, Margaret. "Queen Victoria's Favorite Poet." *The Listener* 73 (29 April 1965): 636-37.

[Manse, Henry Longueville.] "Sensation Novels." *Quarterly Review* 113 (April 1863): 481-514.

Mare, Margaret, and Alicia C. Percival. *Victorian Best-seller: The World of Charlotte M. Yonge.* London: George G. Harrap & Co., 1947.

Mayberry, Katherine J. *Christina Rossetti and the Poetry of Discovery.* Baton Rouge: Louisiana State Univ. Press, 1989.

Mermin, Dorothy. *Elizabeth Barrett Browning: The Origins of a New Poetry.* Chicago: Univ. of Chicago Press, 1989.

———. "Women Becoming Poets: Katherine Philips, Aphra Behn, Anne Finch." *English Literary History* 57 (1990): 335-55.

Michie, Helena. *The Flesh Made Word: Female Figures and Women's Bodies.* New York: Oxford Univ. Press, 1987.

Miles, Alfred H., ed. *The Poets and the Poetry of the Century.* 10 vols. London: Hutchinson, 1891-97.

Mill, John Stuart. *Auguste Comte and Positivism.* Ann Arbor: Univ. of Michigan Press, 1961.

Miller, J. Hillis. "Optic and Semiotic in *Middlemarch.*" In *The Worlds of Victorian Fiction,* ed. Jerome H. Buckley. Cambridge, Mass.: Harvard Univ. Press, 1975.

Mitchell, Sally. *The Fallen Angel: Chastity, Class and Women's Reading, 1835-1880.* Bowling Green: Bowling Green Univ. Popular Press, 1981.

Moers, Ellen. *Literary Women.* Garden City: Doubleday, 1976.

Moglen, Helene. *Charlotte Brontë: The Self Conceived.* New York: Norton, 1976.

Moore, Thomas. *Letters and Journals of Lord Byron: With Notices of His Life.* 2 vols. New York: J. & J. Harper, 1830.

Morgan, Susan. *Sisters in Time: Imagining Gender in Nineteenth-Century British Fiction.* New York: Oxford Univ. Press, 1989.

Morgan, Thais E., ed. *Victorian Sages and Cultural Discourse: Renegotiating Gender and Power.* New Brunswick: Rutgers Univ. Press, 1990.

Moser, Kay. "Elizabeth Barrett's Youthful Feminism: Fragment of 'An Essay on Woman.'" *Studies in Browning and His Circle* 12 (Spring-Fall 1984): 13-26.

Mudge, Bradford Keyes. *Sara Coleridge, a Victorian Daughter: Her Life and Essays.* New Haven: Yale Univ. Press, 1989.

Nethercot, Arthur H. *The First Five Lives of Annie Besant.* Chicago: Univ. of Chicago Press, 1960.

———. *The Last Four Lives of Annie Besant.* Chicago: Univ. of Chicago Press, 1963.

Nord, Deborah Epstein. *The Apprenticeship of Beatrice Webb.* 1985. Ithaca: Cornell Univ. Press, 1989.

"Noteworthy Novels." *North British Review* 11 (1849): 475-93.

Oliphant, Margaret. "Modern Novelists—Great and Small." *Blackwood's Magazine* 77 (1855): 554-68.

———, et al. *Women Novelists of Queen Victoria's Reign: A Book of Appreciations.* By Mrs. Oliphant, Mrs. Lynn Linton, Mrs. Alexander, Mrs. Macquoid, Mrs. Parr, Mrs. Marshall, Charlotte M. Yonge, Adeline Sergeant, and Edna Lyall. London: Hurst & Blackett, 1897.

Rev. of *On the Connection of the Physical Sciences. Athenaeum* 333 (January 15, 1834): 202-203.

Packer, Lona Mosk. *Christina Rossetti.* Berkeley and Los Angeles: Univ. of California Press, 1963.

Patterson, Elizabeth Chambers. *Mary Somerville and the Cultivation of Science, 1815-1840.* Boston: Martinus Nijhoff, 1983.

Paxton, Nancy L. *George Eliot and Herbert Spencer: Feminism, Evolutionism, and the Reconstruction of Gender.* Princeton: Princeton Univ. Press, 1991.

Peters, Maureen. *Jean Ingelow: Victorian Poetess.* Totowa, NJ: Rowman and Littlefield, 1972.

Peterson, Linda H. *Victorian Autobiography: The Tradition of Self-Interpretation.* New Haven: Yale Univ. Press, 1986.

Phillips, Patricia. *The Scientific Lady: A Social History of Women's Scientific Interests, 1520-1918.* New York: St. Martin's Press, 1990.

Pichanick, Valerie Kossew. *Harriet Martineau: The Woman and Her Work, 1802-76.* Ann Arbor: Univ. of Michigan Press, 1980.

Poovey, Mary. *The Proper Lady and the Woman Writer: Ideology as Style in the Works of Mary Wollstonecraft, Mary Shelley, and Jane Austen.* Chicago: Univ. of Chicago Press, 1984.

———. *Uneven Developments: The Ideological Work of Gender in Mid-Victorian England.* Chicago: Univ. of Chicago Press, 1988.

Prelinger, Catherine M. "The Female Diaconate in the Anglican Church: What Kind of Ministry for Women?" In *Religion in the Lives of English Women, 1760-1930.* Ed. Gail Malmgreen. Bloomington: Indiana Univ. Press, 1986.

Prochaska, F. K. *Women and Philanthropy in Nineteenth-Century England.* Oxford: Clarendon Press, 1980.

Ratchford, Fannie Elizabeth. *The Brontës' Web of Childhood.* New York: Columbia Univ. Press, 1941.

Redinger, Ruby V. *George Eliot: The Emergent Self.* New York: Alfred A. Knopf, 1975.

Reed, John S. "'A Female Movement': The Feminization of Nineteenth-Century Anglo-Catholicism." *Anglican and Episcopal History* 57 (1988): 199-238.

Rich, Adrienne Cecile. *On Lies, Secrets, and Silence: Selected Prose, 1966-1978.* New York: Norton, 1979.

[Rigby, Elizabeth.] Rev. of *Jane Eyre. Quarterly Review* 84 (1848): 153-85.

Rosenblum, Dolores. *Christina Rossetti: The Poetry of Endurance.* Carbondale: Southern Illinois Univ. Press, 1986.

Ross, Marlon B. *The Contours of Masculine Desire: Romanticism and the Rise of Women's Poetry.* New York: Oxford University Press, 1989.

Russett, Cynthia Eagle. *Sexual Science: The Victorian Construction of Womanhood.* Cambridge, Mass.: Harvard Univ. Press, 1989.

Sanders, Valerie. *The Private Lives of Victorian Women: Autobiography in Nineteenth-Century England.* New York: St. Martin's Press, 1989.

Sedgwick, Eve Kosofsky. *Between Men: English Literature and Male Homosocial Desire.* New York: Columbia Univ. Press, 1985.

———. *Epistemology of the Closet.* Berkeley and Los Angeles: Univ. of California Press, 1990.

Showalter, Elaine. *A Literature of Their Own: British Women Novelists from Brontë to Lessing.* Princeton: Princeton Univ. Press, 1977.

Shuttleworth, Sally. *George Eliot and Nineteenth-Century Science: The Make-Believe of a Beginning.* New York: Cambridge Univ. Press, 1984.

[Skelton, John.] "Charlotte Brontë." *Fraser's Magazine* 55 (1857): 569-82.

_____. *Some Recollections of Jean Ingelow and Her Early Friends.* 1901. Port Washington: Kennikat Press, 1972.

Spacks, Patricia Meyer. *The Female Imagination.* New York: Alfred A. Knopf, 1972.

_____. *Imagining a Self: Autobiography and Novel in Eighteenth-Century England.* Cambridge, Mass.: Harvard Univ. Press, 1976.

Spencer, Jane. *The Rise of the Woman Novelist: From Aphra Behn to Jane Austen.* Oxford: Basil Blackwell, 1986.

Stanton, Domna C. *The Female Autograph: Theory and Practice of Autobiography from the Tenth to the Twentieth Century.* 1984. Chicago: Univ. of Chicago Press, 1987.

Stirling, Monica. *The Fine and the Wicked: The Life and Times of Ouida.* London: Victor Gollancz, 1957.

Stoneman, Patsy. *Elizabeth Gaskell.* Bloomington: Indiana Univ. Press, 1987.

Sutherland, John. *The Stanford Companion to Victorian Fiction.* Stanford: Stanford Univ. Press, 1989.

Swindells, Julia. *Victorian Writing and Working Women: The Other Side of Silence.* Minneapolis: Univ. of Minnesota Press, 1985.

Taylor, Anne. *Annie Besant: A Biography.* New York: Oxford Univ. Press, 1992.

Tennyson, Hallam. *Alfred Lord Tennyson. A Memoir.* New York: Macmilllan, 1897.

Thomas, Clara. *Love and Work Enough: The Life of Anna Jameson.* Toronto: Univ. of Toronto Press, 1967.

Thomson, Patricia. *George Sand and the Victorians: Her Influence and Reputation in Nineteenth-Century England.* New York: Columbia Univ. Press, 1977.

Tillotson, Kathleen. *Novels of the Eighteen-Forties.* Oxford: Clarendon Press, 1954.

Tuchman, Gaye, with Nina E. Fortin. *Edging Women Out: Victorian Novelists, Publishers, and Social Change.* New Haven: Yale Univ. Press, 1989.

Vicinus, Martha. *Independent Women: Work and Community for Single Women, 1850-1920.* Chicago: Univ. of Chicago Press, 1985.

_____, ed. *Suffer and Be Still: Women in the Victorian Age.* Bloomington: Indiana Univ. Press, 1972.

_____, ed. *A Widening Sphere: Changing Roles of Victorian Women.* Bloomington: Indiana Univ. Press, 1977.

Rev. of *Villette. Eclectic Review* n.s. 5 (1853): 305-20.

Warhol. Robyn R. *Gendered Interventions: Narrative Discourse in the Victorian Novel.* New Brunswick: Rutgers Univ. Press, 1989.

Watt, Ian. *The Rise of the Novel: Studies in Defoe, Richardson, and Fielding.* Berkeley and Los Angeles: Univ. of California Press, 1957.

Watts, Theodore. "Mrs. Augusta Webster." *The Athenaeum* 3490 (15 September 1894): 335.

Weintraub, Stanley. *Victoria: An Intimate Biography.* New York: E. P. Dutton, 1987.

Welsh, Alexander. *George Eliot and Blackmail.* Cambridge, Mass.: Harvard Univ. Press, 1985.

Williams, Merryn. *Margaret Oliphant: A Critical Biography.* New York: St. Martin's Press, 1986.

Wolff, Robert Lee. *Gains and Losses: Novels of Faith and Doubt in Victorian England.* New York: Garland, 1977.

_____. *Sensational Victorian: The Life and Fiction of Mary Elizabeth Braddon.* New York: Garland, 1979.

Yeazell, Ruth Bernard. "Why Political Novels Have Heroines: *Sybil*, *Mary Barton*, and *Felix Holt*." *Novel* 18 (1985): 126-44.

_____. *Fictions of Modesty: Women and Courtship in the English Novel.* Chicago: Univ. of Chicago Press, 1991.

_____, ed. *Sex, Politics, and Science in the Nineteenth-Century Novel: Selected Papers from the English Institute, 1983-84.* Baltimore: Johns Hopkins Univ. Press, 1986.

Index

Abolitionism, 11, 67, 104, 105, 107

Actress, 45, 82, 83; as figure for female artist, 17, 25-26, 143-44

Alaya, Flavia, 162n.20

Albert (Prince Consort), xvi

Altick, Richard D., 154n.2, 154n.3, 159n.13

Amatory poetry, 65, 66, 73, 75-76

Ambition: in *Adam Bede*, 33; and Barrett Browning, 8, 9, 16, 18; and Brontë, 16, 18, 37; in *Daniel Deronda*, 145; and Eliot, 16, 18, 34; and Gaskell, 18; and Jameson, xiv; justified by altruism, xvi; male, 16; and Martineau, 102, 103; in *Pendennis*, 47; and Rossetti, 18; Southey on, 16; as vice for women, 8, 13, 16-17, 73, 107-108; in *Villette*, 26; women writers' disavowals of, 18, 87; writing as outlet for, xv; and Yonge, 19. *See also* Fame

Androgyny, 8, 26, 67, 79, 100-101, 144, 145

Anglican sisterhoods. *See* Sisterhoods

Anglo-Catholicism, 107, 113

Animals: Somerville and, 131; in women's poetry, 74, 75. *See also* Anti-vivisectionism

Anonymity. *See* Pseudonyms

Anti-vivisectionism, 96, 114, 125, 126

Arnold, Matthew, 17-18, 31, 114, 115-16; "Dover Beach," 115-16; "The Scholar-Gipsy," 131; "Stanzas from the Grande Chartreuse," 17-18

Arnold, Thomas, 51

Art history, xv, 96, 97

Astronomy, 133-34

Audiences, reading, xv, 44, 46, 154n.7

Augustine, Saint, 109

Austen, Jane, 5, 49, 87-88, 100, 110, 130, 136; *Northanger Abbey*, 46

Autobiography: male tradition of, 90; women's, 109, 157n.8

Bachofen, J. J.: *Das Mutterrecht*, 139

Balzac, Honoré de, 47

Barrett, Elizabeth. *See* Browning, Elizabeth Barrett

Beauty, 138

Beer, Gillian, 154n.10, 161n.16, 161n.18, 162n.2

Beerbohm, Max, 83

Besant, Annie (1847-1933), xviii, 112, 125-26, 128

Bible: women's speech in, 107, 111, 118, 119

Bildungsroman, 101

Birth control, 104, 125-26

Blackwood, John, 49

Blake, William, 75

Blavatsky, Mme (1831-91), 126

Blushing, 29, 30, 31, 35. *See also* Self-consciousness

Bodichon, Barbara Leigh Smith (1827-91), 96

Bonaparte, Napoleon, 5

Booth, Catherine (1829-90), 112. *See also* Salvation Army

Braddon, Mary Elizabeth (1837-1915), xviii, 57, 60, 85, 86, 142; and "bigamy novels," 82; and fame, 39; and Henry James, 83; life and career of, 82, 83; on pseudonymity, 49; on sensation novels, 82; *Aurora Floyd*, 49, 54, 82, 83; *Lady Audley's Secret*, 82

Brontë, Anne (1820-49), 7, 37, 61, 108; *The Tenant of Wildfell Hall*, 108

Brontë, Branwell (1817-48), 5, 19, 37, 67, 86; and Angria, 7, 22, 61; Byronic life of, 12; education of, 4, 52

Brontë, Charlotte (1816-55), xviii, 4, 5, 7, 8, 20, 30, 67, 121; and Angria, 7, 10, 11, 12, 14, 15, 22, 25, 31, 35, 61, 84, 144; and Byron, 7, 9, 11, 12, 24, 37; depicted by Gaskell, 15, 27, 37; education of, 52; and fame, 24, 37-38; on imagination, 27; influence of, xv, 37, 82; life of, 3-5, 37; relation to her characters, 22, 23, 24, 25; and religion, 113, 117-19; and Roe Head School, 9-10, 22, 25; Southey's advice to, 59, 71, 98, 121; and Thackeray, 24; *Jane Eyre*, 3, 4, 11, 12, 21, 22-23, 24, 34, 37, 63, 64, 67, 83, 100, 118; *The Professor*, 22; *Shirley*, 25, 67, 113, 118-19, 122, 123, 141, 145; *Villette*, 21, 22, 24, 25-27, 28, 29, 31, 34, 102, 113, 119, 141-42

Brontë, Emily (1818-48), 37, 53, 60, 62, 63, 64, 167; Gondal, 7, 61-62, 63, 148n.9; "Ah! why, because the dazzling sun," 62-63; "Silent is the House—all are laid asleep," 63; *Wuthering Heights*, 12, 67

Brontë, Maria, 4

Broughton, Rhoda (1840-1920), 85-86; *Not Wisely But Too Well*, 57

Browning, Elizabeth Barrett (1806-61), xviii, 8, 20, 21, 39, 57, 67, 71, 76, 79; and amatory poetry, 65, 66; on ambition, 16; and Byron, 7, 8, 11, 12; childhood and family of, xvi, 3-5, 45, 131; and dramatic monologue, 79; on double standard, xix; education, 51, 52, 53; and Godiva, xvi, 21, 27; and Homer, 8, 135; illnesses of, 4, 10, 77; influence of, xv, 60, 66-67, 76; and justification for writing, 18; on Martineau, 100; and motherhood, 58; and politics, 7, 11, 12, 38, 43, 67; and Pope, 5; publication in journals, 44; and quest romance, 61, 63; and religion, 112, 113; representations of women poets, 79; respectability of, 67; and Robert Browning, 4, 5, 11, 38, 67, 70; *Aurora Leigh*, xix, 4, 11, 12, 56, 58, 66, 67, 74, 98, 146; "The Battle of Marathon," 5, 7; "Beth," 8-9, 101, 144; "The Cry of the Children," 74; "The Deserted Garden," 61; "The Development of Genius," 10; *A Drama of Exile*, 113, 123, 135; "Earth and Her Praisers," 133; "Flush, My Dog," 74; "Flush or Faunus," 74; "Isobel's Child," 75; "The Lost Bower," 61; "A Musical Instrument," 64-65; "My Doves," 74; *Prometheus Bound*, 11, 52; *The Seraphim*, 113, 135; *Sonnets from the Portuguese*, 11, 12, 60, 65-66, 70, 73; "A Vision of Fame," 16
Browning, Robert, 48, 60, 79; classical education of, 53; and Elizabeth Barrett, 5, 11, 38, 53; identification of woman with poem, 70; narratives of, 73; on private correspondence, 50; and science, 133; and self-consciousness, 31; "Abt Vogler," 77
Budd, Susan, 160n.15
Byron, George Gordon, xv, 8, 10, 20, 61, 62, 151n.1; and Brontë, 24, 37; fame and influence of, xvi, 6-12, passim; as model for female rebellion, xvi, 7, 8, 11; and romantic travelogue, 99; and self-exposure, 17-18; *Cain*, 11; *Don Juan*, 8; *Manfred*, 11

Carlyle, Jane Welsh (1801-66), 50
Carlyle, Thomas, 6, 95, 97, 98, 105, 133, 139; "Characteristics," 31
Chapman, John, 44
Children: in Ingelow, 79; in women's poetry, 74, 75
Christ, Carol, 147n.3, 158n.1
Classical learning, 50, 51, 53-54, 65, 96, 108, 121, 131. *See also* Education
Clergymen, 108, 118
Clough, Arthur Hugh, 31, 60, 73, 114
Cobbe, Frances Power (1822-1904), xviii, 96, 112, 123-25, 128, 129, 131, 142; *Essay on the Theory of Intuitive Morals*, 124
Coleridge, Hartley, 105

Coleridge, Samuel Taylor, 98, 99; "The Ancient Mariner," 71
Coleridge, Sara (1802-52), 98-99, 109, 132, 150n.26
Comte, Auguste, 128; *Positive Philosophy*, 100
Cook, Eliza (1818-89): *Eliza Cook's Journal*, 44
Cornwall, Barry, 76
Crashaw, Richard, 72
Cross, John, 142, 149n.18

Darwin, Charles, 132, 135; *The Origin of Species*, 127, 133, 136-37, 139
David, Deirdre, 158n.1
Davidoff, Leonore, 159n.9
Daydreams, 15, 16, 46; and Brontë, 14, 25; and Barrett Browning, xvi, 7; and Eliot, 13, 31; and Jameson, xvi, 8, 9; and Martineau, 13, 19, 102, 103; and Trollope, 14; and Yonge, 14. *See also* Imagination
Deconversions, 115. *See also* Doubt, religious
Dellamora, Richard, 156n.2, 158n.2
Dickens, Charles, 39, 44, 53, 76-77, 105, 125; *Great Expectations*, 151n.3
Dickinson, Emily (1830-86), 70
Diehl, Joanne Feit, 156n.5
Donne, John, 72
Drama, 43
Dramatic monologue, 79-80

Eastlake, Lady (Elizabeth Rigby) (1809-93), 23-24, 100
Education, xv, 38, 44, 50-54, 55, 96, 107; in science, 131, 132. *See also* Classical learning
Eliot, George (1819-80), xv, xviii, 14, 58, 60, 82, 92, 95, 124, 128; on ambition, 16, 119; and childhood, 12, 13; compared to her fictional characters, 34; and Comte, 128; education of, 51, 52, 54, 128; and fame, 38; on father's death, 13; on imagination, 13, 14, 84, 102; and G. H. Lewes, 18, 30, 139; life of, 30, 83, 142; on motherhood, 57, 87, 117; narratorial technique of, 35, 36, 134, 135; Oliphant on, 91; and performance, 15, 18; and the prophetic character, 122, 123; and pseudonyms, 35, 49; and religion, 13, 112, 119-23; revisions of religious myths, 120-23; and Sand, 20; and science, 129, 132, 134-35, 139, 140, 143; and sexuality, 34; and unself-consciousness, 77; and *Westminster Review*, 44; *Adam Bede*, 21, 25, 30-31, 32, 33-35, 36, 77, 84, 91, 112, 120, 121, 123, 144; "Brother and Sister," 79; *Daniel Deronda*, xviii, 142, 143-46, 153n.29; *The Essence of Christianity* (trans.), 120; *Felix Holt*, 153n.29; *Life of Jesus* (trans.), 30, 120; "The Lifted Veil," 35; *Middlemarch*, 35, 36, 38, 54, 57, 121, 123, 132, 134, 135,

153n.29; *The Mill on the Floss*, 12-13, 16, 32-33, 53, 120, 121, 128, 144, 153n.29; *Romola*, 53-54, 120-23, 129, 145, 153n.29; *The Spanish Gipsy*, 145, 146
Elizabeth, Charlotte. *See* Tonna, Charlotte Elizabeth
Ellis, Sarah (?-1872), 55
Epic, 5-6
Evangelicalism, 107, 115; and Eliot, 13, 119; and imagination, 14; and novelists, 159n.4; satirized, 111
Evans, Mary Ann [George Eliot], 35, 49. *See also* Eliot, George
Eve, myth of: in men's writing, 123; in *Romola*, 121; in *Shirley*, 118, 119, 122, 141; used to subject women, 107
Evolutionary theory, 127, 140. *See also* Darwin, Charles
Ewbank, Inga-Stina, 149n.17

Fairy tales, 8, 72-73; Sleeping Beauty, 61, 62, 63, 64
Fame: and Braddon, 82; Brontë's experience of, 23-25, 37; fear of corrupting power of, 81; justified by patriotism, 145; and male writers, 39; and Martineau, 104, 105; positive consequences of, 37, 38, 39, 43; and pseudonymity, 49; and Sand, 20; as sexualized self-exposure, 20. *See also* Ambition
Fantasy. *See* Daydreams
Faraday, Michael, 131
Feminism: and Jameson, 97; and Martineau, 101; in non-fictional prose, 96; Victorian women's attitudes toward, xvii, 55; and Webster, 79, 80. *See also* Suffrage, women's
Feminization of literature, xvi-xvii, 15, 45-48, 95
Feminization of religion, 108
Feuerbach, Ludwig, 145; *The Essence of Christianity*, 120
Field, Michael [pseud. of Katherine Bradley (1846-1914) and Edith Cooper (1862-1913)], 49
Fielding, Henry, 53
Free thought, 107, 108, 112, 125
Fullerton, Georgiana (1812-85), 5, 6, 57-58, 81, 112, 113; *Ellen Middleton*, 81, 113

Gallagher, Catherine, 147n.2, 162n.3
Galton, Francis: *Hereditary Genius*, 138
Gaskell, Elizabeth (1810-65), 39, 60, 82, 121, 142; and anonymity, 49; on Emily Brontë, 38, 67; and Byron, 151n.1; education of, 51; fame of, 38; family of, 149n.19; and justification for writing, 18; and motherhood, 57, 58; political and sexual themes in, 27, 28, 111; relation of, to her characters, 28; and religion, 111, 112; respectability of, 27-28; and science, 132, 135-36, 137; *Cranford*, 152n.18; *Mary Barton*, 21, 26, 27, 28-30, 31, 33, 34, 35, 49, 58, 84, 100-101, 111, 132, 136, 137, 153n.29; *The Life of Charlotte Brontë*, 15, 27, 37, 38; *North and South*, 57, 123, 136, 137, 152n.18, 157n.5; *Ruth*, 27, 28, 58, 136, 137; *Wives and Daughters*, 135-36, 137, 138, 152n.18
Geology, 127; and Ingelow, 133-34
The Germ, 68, 69
Gilbert, Sandra, 148n.13, 155n.2, 156n.12, 158n.10
Gilbert, W. S.: *Patience*, 46; *Princess Ida*, 127
Godiva, Lady, 74, 145-46; and Barrett Browning, xvi, 20; and Gaskell, 28; and Jameson, xvi; and Martineau, xvi, 20-21, 104; as model for women writers, xvi, 20-21, 27; and privacy, xvii; protected by virtue, 21; and Tennyson, 21; and Victoria, xvi, 147n.3
Going, William T., 156n.12
Green, Mary Anne Everett (1818-95), 158n.3
Gross, John, 95
Gubar, Susan, 148n.13, 155n.2, 156n.12, 158n.10

Hall, Catherine, 159n.9
Hardy, Thomas, 48, 60, 133; *The Hand of Ethelberta*, 48
Harmon, Barbara, 147n.2, 150n.33, 152n.18
Havergal, Frances Ridley (1836-79), 78, 81
Heilbrun, Carolyn, 148n.4
Helsinger, Elizabeth K., 154n.8, 155n.19
Hemans, Felicia (1793-1835), 60, 75, 76; "Woman on the Field of Battle," 76
Herbert, George, 114
Heroinism: difficulty in portraying, 123; Jameson and, 97; the Stricklands and, 96-97
Herschel, Caroline, 130
Hertz, Neil, 153n.30
Heyck, T. W., 161n.12
Hickok, Kathleen, 156n.14
Higher Criticism, 107, 115, 116, 134, 145; and Eliot, 120; in *Shirley*, 118, 119; in *Zoë*, 117
History, 96
Homans, Margaret, 155n.2, 161n.17
Home, Cecil [Augusta Webster], 48-49. *See also* Webster, Augusta
Homer, 8, 135
Homoeroticism: in men's poetry, 155n.2; and Pater, 95-96
Hopkins, Gerard Manley, 60, 113, 114
Howitt, Mary (1799-1888), 87, 112, 132, 161n.14; *Autobiography*, 161n.14; *Howitt's Journal*, 44, 112
Hutton, Richard Holt, 60
Huxley, Thomas Henry, 132, 133, 134, 135; "Lay Sermons," 128; "On a Piece of Chalk," 137

Illness: and Martineau, 101-102; and women poets, 77

Imagination: in *Adam Bede*, 31; and Charlotte Brontë, 10, 26; and Emily Brontë, 63; and Barrett Browning, 9; and Sara Coleridge, 99; in *Daniel Deronda*, 144-45; vs. experience as source of women's writing, 27; figured as travel, 9, 21, 25; Hutton on, 50; negative effects of, 13, 14, 71, 102; and Ouida, 84; vs. realism in fiction, 84; and Tonna, 111; in *Villette*, 119, 141-42. *See also* Daydreams

Industrialism, 119; literature as antidote to, xvi, 15, 58; and Romantic nature, 61

Ingelow, Jean (1820-97), xviii, 38, 60, 76, 77, 78, 79, 81, 133-34, 139, 142; "Gladys and Her Island," 79; "Honors," 115, 133-34; "The Mariner's Cave," 75; "The Star's Monument," 78-79

Irony: absence of in Barrett Browning, 65; unsuitability for women, 65, 73-74

James, Henry, 83, 87

Jameson, Anna (1794-1860), xv, xvi, xviii, 24, 98, 101, 121, 122; and art history, xv, 96, 97; artlessness of, 46; daydreams of, xvi, 8, 9; on desire for fame, 16-17; on motherhood, 56, 87; and Ruskin, 98; and women, 55, 97, 113; *Diary of an Ennuyée*, xiii-xiv, xvi, 46, 88, 99, 146; *Legends of the Madonna*, 97, 116-17; *The Loves of the Poets*, 97; *Sacred and Legendary Art*, 100

Jay, Elisabeth, 159n.4

Jehlen, Myra, 154n.6

Jelinek, Estelle, 157n.8

Jewsbury, Geraldine (1812-80), 44, 45, 50; *The Half Sisters*, 17; *Zoë*, 117, 118, 119, 124

Jewsbury, Maria Jane (1800-1833), 150n.12

Joan of Arc, xiv, 145

Johnson, Samuel, 37

Journalism, 44-45, 124

Journeys (in women's writing). *See* Travel

Kant, Immanuel, 124

Keats, John, xv, 14, 53; "La Belle Dame Sans Merci," 71

Keble, John, 19, 109

Kemble, Fanny (1809-93), 6, 11, 100

Landon, Letitia (1802-38), 8, 12, 39, 60, 75, 76

Laplace, Pierre S. de: *Mechanique Celeste*, 130

Levine, George, 161n.18

Lewes, G. H.: 122, 142; on Comte, 128; and Eliot, 18, 30, 139; injunction to women writers, 27; on *Jane Eyre*, 23, 152n.14; on *Mary Barton*, 152n.14; and science, 127, 128

Lewis, Sarah: *Women's Mission*, 32, 152n.24

Linton, Eliza Lynn (1822-98), 111-12, 122, 134, 155n.14; "Girl of the Period," 55, 85; *Joshua Davidson*, 85, 111-12

Longfellow, Henry Wadsworth, 38

Lovell, Terry, 154n.7

Macaulay, Thomas Babington, 98

Marcet, Jane (1769-1858): *Conversations on Chemistry*, 131

Martineau, Harriet (1802-76): xviii, 125, 128, 142; and the body, 101-102, 115; childhood of, 103; and Comte, 100, 128; correspondence with Barrett Browning, 20-21; education of, 51, 103; and fame, 104, 105; and Godiva, xvi, 20-21, 27; and imagination, 102, 103, 131; and martyrdom, 13, 19, 111; on mothers, 101-103; political commitment of, 104, 105; and political economy, 105; and population control, 126; on private correspondence, 50; and prostitution, 21; range of works of, 100; rationalism of, 105; and religion, 112, 115, 116; and science, 129, 140; style of, 105; and travel, 100; and women, 55, 56; *Autobiography*, 101-102, 103-104, 105, 106, 109, 128; *Eastern Life*, 100, 116; *Household Education*, 102-103; *Illustrations of Political Economy*, 44, 96, 100, 101, 104

Martyrdom, xiv, 102, 103, 104, 111, 126

McGann, Jerome, 156n.12

McLennan, John F.: *Primitive Marriage*, 139

McLeod, Fiona [William Sharp], 49

Meredith, George, 60, 133

Mesmerism, 20, 100, 104, 125, 129

Methodism, 112

Michie, Helena, 152n.19

Middle-class women: and writing, xv, 45

Mill, John Stuart, 95, 96, 128, 129; *Autobiography*, 90

Miller, J. Hillis, 153n.30

Milton, John, 135; "Lycidas," 16; *Paradise Lost*, 103, 113, 115

Mitchell, Sally, 148n.13

Moers, Ellen, 148n.3, 152n.19

Moglen, Helene, 148n.9

Morris, William, 60

Motherhood: and Barrett Browning, 67; in *Daniel Deronda*, 144; as figured in science, 139; and the Madonna, 117; and Martineau, 102-103; as womanly ideal, xvii, 56-57, 58; and women's writing, 87, 92

Mudie's Circulating Library, 44

Nature: Christina Rossetti's identification with, 69; Romantic idea of, 60, 61, 118; in *Romola*, 121; in *Shirley*, 118, 119; in Victorian science, 131, 132, 133, 134; women writers' relation to, 133, 134; women's identification with, 61, 79, 131

Newman, John Henry, 95; *Apologia Pro Vita Sua*, 90

Nightingale, Florence (1820-1910), 36, 45, 57, 113; on "domestic duties," 110; on female Christ, 123; and *Romola*, 121; and women's suffrage, 56

Nord, Deborah Epstein, 158n.8, 160n.14

Norton, Caroline (1808-77), 8, 12, 56

Novels. *See* Prose Fiction

Oliphant, Margaret (1828-97), xviii, 51, 60, 87-88, 91, 101, 125, 142; ambition, 87; on Brontë's fame, 36-37; on clergymen, 108; conflict between love and literature in, 87, 92; on Eliot and Sand, 91; fictional characters of, 86, 87; life and career of, 86; as mother, 57, 87, 88; narrative style of, 89; and religion, 110-11; on women's education, 54; *Autobiography*, 87, 88-92, 142; *Chronicles of Carlingford*, 89-90; *Miss Marjoribanks*, 57, 110-11; *The Perpetual Curate*, 86, 108; *Phoebe, Jr.*, 54

Ouida [Louise de la Ramée] (1839-1908), xviii, 83-84, 85, 86, 131, 142, 157n.3; *Under Two Flags*, 84-85

Oxford Movement, 109

Pater, Walter, 95-96

Patterson, Elizabeth Chambers, 160n.5

Paxton, Nancy L., 161n.16, 162n.22

Performance: as figure for women's art, 17, 18, 143, 150n.32. *See also* Actress

Philanthropy: in *Aurora Leigh*, 66; and the Church, 108-109; and Martineau, 105; and prostitution, 71; and sisterhoods, 108; and Skene, 85; and women writers, 57-59, 60

Phillips, Patricia, 161n.10, 161n.12

Phrenology, 129

Physics, 131

Poetry, 60-80; alienating effects of, 14; education necessary for, 53, 54; male tradition in, 46; narrative used in, 73-74; and religion, 107, 113-14, 115; similarity to women's work, 45-46; status of, 38, 43, 45; women's, 43, 113; women's perceived unsuitability for, 50

Politics: in Barrett Browning, 43, 67; in *Mary Barton*, 28; in women's writing, 28, 85, 111

Positivism, 128. *See also* Comte, Auguste

Poovey, Mary, 152n.16, 162n.20

Prelinger, Catherine M., 159n.3

Pre-Raphaelite Brotherhood, 67-68

Private sphere: Strickland's valorization of, 97; women's relegation to, xiv, xv

Procter, Adelaide (1825-64), xviii, 60, 67, 76-77, 81, 112, 155n.19; "A Legend of Bregenz," 73, 145; "A Lost Chord," 77;

"The Requital," 74-75; "A Woman's Answer," 67

Prose Fiction: no exclusive male tradition in, xv, xvi, 46; status of, 43, 45; suited to women, xv, 50, 53

Prostitution, xiv, 21, 45, 57-58, 71, 85; writing likened to, 91

Pseudonyms, 24, 26, 35, 48-50, 76

Publication: consequences for women of, 38; and Gaskell, 30; increased opportunities for, xv, 44-45; in *Mary Barton*, 29; as sexual self-exposure, xiii, 29, 38, 49, 50. *See also* Pseudonyms; Self-exposure

Quest romance, 61, 63, 64

Ramée, Louise de la [Ouida]. *See* Ouida

Reading: dangers of, 52

Redinger, Ruby V., 149n.20

Reed, John S., 159n.3, 159n.11

Religion, 107-26; in *Adam Bede*, 30; challenged by science, 126, 127-28; in *Daniel Deronda*, 143; as inspiration, 77, 78; as justification for writing, xvi, 81, 109-13, 115; reinforcing separate spheres, 108; and restrictions on women, xvii, 55, 107-108; and revisionism, 116-19, 120-23, 145; and women's poetry, 76, 77

Reviews: of Gaskell, 27; of Braddon, 83; of George Sand, 20; of *Jane Eyre*, 23-24; of *Shirley*, 25; of Somerville, 130; of women writers, xv, xvii

Rigby, Elizabeth (Lady Eastlake), 23-24, 100

Ritchie, Anne Thackeray (1837-1919), 86; *The Story of Elizabeth*, 85

Ritualist movement, 107, 108

Roman Catholicism, 107, 108

Romanticism: and Byron, 6, 10; and Sara Coleridge, 99; and imagination, 102; and nature, 118, 133; and poetic speakers, 43; and science, 133; and unself-consciousness, 33; woman poet's subject position in, 60; and women, 98. *See also* Byron, George Gordon

Rosenblum, Dolores, 156n.3, 156n.12

Rossetti, Christina (1830-94), 38, 45, 77, 142, 146, 149n.19, 151n.1; artlessness of, 77; devotional poems of, 113, 114; education of, 51, 53; and fallen women, 18, 57-58, 71-72; femininity of, 67; identification with nature, 69; illness of, 77; on Ingelow, 70; and motherhood, 56-57, 87, 117; poetic speakers of, 61, 68, 69, 70, 71, 79; and Pre-Raphaelitism, 68, 71, 72, 73; and quest romance, 61, 63, 64; and religion, 76, 77, 112, 113; reputation of, 60, 76; and Dante Gabriel Rossetti, 67, 68, 69, 71; on the status of women, 55, 131; on Webster, 79; "Cousin Kate," 75; "The Dead City," 61, 156n.3; "Dream

Land," 69; *Goblin Market*, 18, 68, 71-73, 74, 113, 114; *Maude*, 68; *Monna Innominata*, 70, 73, 92; "My Dream," 74; *The Prince's Progress*, 63-64, 66, 72; "A Royal Princess," 71; "A Sketch," 74; "Sleeping at last," 69-70; "Up-Hill," 114; "When I am dead, my dearest," 69; "A Wish," 70

Rossetti, Dante Gabriel, 14, 60, 67, 68, 70, 71, 72; *The Girlhood of Mary Virgin*, 68; The House of Life, 70, 156n.10 "Jenny," 71; "My Sister's Sleep," 69

Rossetti, William Michael, 67-68, 77, 79

Ruskin, John, 95, 98, 108

Russett, Cynthia Eagle, 160n.4, 162n.19

Salvation Army, 107, 112

Sand, George (1804-76), 5, 20, 47, 53, 91; *Consuelo*, 20, 150n.32, 151n.1; *The Countess of Rudolstat*, 151n.1

Sanders, Valerie, 157n.8

Sappho, 23

Science, 127-40; literary men and, 95; misogyny of, xvii, 132; professionalization of, 132; religious authority undermined by, xvii, 126, 127; and Romantic nature, 61; and women writers, 133-38

Scott, Sir Walter, xv, xvi, 5, 49, 84

Sedgwick, Eve, 158n.2

Self-consciousness: in *Adam Bede*, 35; and Braddon, 82; Carlyle on, 31; of gender, in women's writing, xix, 33; male writers on, 31; and Martineau, 106; in *Mary Barton*, 29; and Oliphant, 89, 91, 92; in *Romola*, 123; sexualized for women, 31-32, 82; and Webster, 80. *See also* Blushing; Unself-consciousness

Self-division: in *Adam Bede*, 33; in *Daniel Deronda*, 143-44, 145; in *The Mill on the Floss*, 32; and Oliphant, 92; in *Romola*, 123; as theme of sensation novels, 82; in women's writing, 11

Self-exposure: in *Adam Bede*, 21-22, 30, 33, 35; autobiography as, 91; and Braddon, 82, 83; in Brontë's Angrian visions, 22; and Byron, 17, 18, 24; in *Diary of an Ennuyée*, xiii, xiv; discouraged by religion, 114; in *Daniel Deronda*, 146; and Eliot, 18, 30, 36; fame as sexualized, 20; and Gaskell, 28, 152n.18; inhibiting lyric poetry, 60, 61; in *Jane Eyre*, 21-23; and Jewsbury, 17; justified by religion, 109; and Martineau, 20-21; in *Mary Barton*, 21-22, 28, 29, 30; and power, xvi, 21; in *Villette*, 21-22, 25, 26, 27; and Webster, 80; writing as, 17-18, 49-50, 143

Selflessness, xvi, 18, 31, 37

Sensation fiction, 58, 81, 82, 83

Sewell, Elizabeth Missing (1815-1906), 51, 55, 81, 85, 109, 111; *The Experience of Life*, 159n.7; *Principles of Education*, 55

Sharp, William [Fiona McLeod]. *See* McLeod, Fiona

Sheets, Robin Lauterbach, 154n.8, 155n.19

Shelley, Percy B., xv; "To a Skylark," 33

Showalter, Elaine, 108, 148n.4, 153n.1, 154n.8, 154n.10, 157n.2, 162n.20

Sigourney, Lydia (1791-1865), 75

Sisterhoods, 108,113

Skene, Felicia (1821-99), 85, 86, 111; *Hidden Depths*, 85

Sociology, 128, 129, 138-39, 143

Somerville, Mary (1780-1872), xvii, xviii, 96, 129-30, 131, 132, 133, 142; *On the Connection of the Physical Sciences*, 130; *The Mechanism of the Heavens*, 130; *On Molecular and Microscopic Science*, 130; *Physical Geography*, 130

Southey, Robert: ballads of, 99; on women writers, 15, 16, 59, 71, 98, 99, 121

Spencer, Herbert, 139

Spencer, Jane, 154n.1, 154n.6

Spiritualism, 108, 112, 129

Staël, Germaine de (1766-1817), 53, 99, 148n.3, 150n.32; *Corinne*, 17, 20, 150n.32

Stephen, Leslie, 142

Stoneman, Patsy, 161n.17

Strauss, David Friedrich: *Life of Jesus*, 120

Strickland, Agnes [Agnes and Elizabeth Strickland] (1796-1874), 98; *Lives of the Queens of England*, 96-97

Subject position: and Charlotte Brontë, 10, 11, 22, and Emily Brontë, 62, 63, 64; and Barrett Browning, 8, 11; and Martineau, 101; and Augusta Webster, 80; of women in literature, 5, 6, 60, 61

Suffrage, women's, 56, 79, 124. *See also* Feminism

Sutherland, John, 43, 153n.1

Swedenborg, Emmanuel, 112

Swinburne, Algernon Charles, 14, 58, 60, 68

Taylor, Harriet (1807-1858), 96

Tennyson, Alfred, 15, 38, 60; and anonymity, 48; on Byron's death, 6; female figures in, 14; on nature, 133, 139; outsold by Procter, 76; and religion, 114; and science, 133, 134; "Godiva," 21; "The Holy Grail," 71; *Idylls of the King*, 123; *In Memoriam*, 74, 107, 114, 125, 133; "The Kraken," 151n.3; "The Lady of Shalott," 151n.3; "The Palace of Art," 14-15; "Parnassus," 134; "Tithonus," 71

Thackeray, 24, 44, 53; *Pendennis*, 46-48, 65-66, 77, 155n.1

Theresa, Saint, 111, 121

Thomson, Patricia, 151n.1

Tonna, Charlotte Elizabeth (1790-1846), 14, 81, 109, 111, 112; *Personal Recollections*, 111, 150n.26

Travel: in Charlotte Brontë, 8, 21, 22, 23, 25; in Barrett Browning, 8, 9; in *Diary of an Ennuyée*, 99; in Eliot, 12-13, 21, 34, 121; as figure for imaginative activity, 9, 10, 21; as incitement to writing, 99-100; in *Mary Barton*, 28; in *Under Two Flags*, 84

Trials, 34; in *Adam Bede*, 26, 33, 36; in *Felix Holt*, 153n.29; in *Mary Barton*, 26, 28, 29, 30, 35; in *Under Two Flags*, 84; in *Villette*, 22, 26-27

Trollope, Anthony, 14, 44, 48, 51, 53, 58; *An Autobiography*, 89-91; *The Way We Live Now*, 48, 97

Trollope, Frances (1780-1863), 85, 100

Tuchman, Gaye, 153n.1, 154n.8, 162n.6

Tyndall, John, 132

Unitarianism, 108, 112

University, 51, 79, 132. *See also* Education

Unself-consciousness: in *Adam Bede*, 30, 31, 33, 34-35; as artistic and womanly ideal, xiv, xvii, 28, 31, 32, 33, 77-78; in *Mary Barton*, 28, 29, 33; in Oliphant, 88, 89, 91-92

Veeder, William, 154n.8, 155n.19

Victoria (Queen) (1819-1901): fame of, 36; and Godiva, xvi, 147n.3; and motherhood, xvii, 57; misogyny of, xvii; and women's suffrage, 56

Warhol, Robin, 147n.2

Watt, Ian, 153n.1

Webster, Augusta (1837-94), 55, 57; compared to Brownings, 79; on dilemma of unself-consciousness, 32; and dramatic monologue, 79, 80; education of, 53, 79; poetry of, 60, 79-80; on poets, 60; political activism of, 56; and Pre-Raphaelitism, 80; and pseudonyms, 48-49; translations of Aeschylus and Euripides, 53, 79; on women writers, 45; "A Castaway," 80; "Circe," 80; "Mother and Daughter," 79; *The Sentence*, 79

Weintraub, Stanley, 147n.3

Welsh, Alexander, 154n.10, 155n.11

Wilde, Oscar, 14

Wood, Mrs. Henry (1814-87), 57, 82; *East Lynne*, 82

Woolf, Virginia (1882-1941), 142

Wordsworth, William, 75, 98, 99; "A Poet's Epitaph," 133

Working class: danger of fall into, 45; disconnection from Church, 107; and Hardy, 48; women, xviii

Yeazell, Ruth Bernard, 152n.19

Yonge, Charlotte M. (1823-1901), xviii, 60, 85, 142; and ambition, 18-19; daydreams of, 14; education of, 52; life and career of, 81; and Oxford Movement, 109; and religion, 110, 113; and religious journals, 109; on women's education, 54; *The Clever Woman of the Family*, 54; *The Daisy Chain*, 81; *Heartsease*, 110; *Hopes and Fears*, 115; *The Pillars of the House*, 19, 81, 102, 110; *Womankind*, 55

DOROTHY MERMIN, Professor of English at Cornell University, is the author of *Elizabeth Barrett Browning: The Origins of a New Poetry* and *The Audience in the Poem: Five Victorian Poets*.